HIGH PERFORMANCE

Long-Distance Running

This book should be returned to any branch of the Lancashire County Library on or before the date

Lancashire County Library
Bowran Street
Preston PR1 2UX

County Council

www.lancashire.gov.uk/libraries

HIGH PERFORMANCE
Long-Distance Running

David Sunderland

Foreword by Sebastian Coe KBE

THE CROWOOD PRESS

First published in 2011 by
The Crowood Press Ltd
Ramsbury, Marlborough
Wiltshire SN8 2HR

www.crowood.com

British Library Cataloguing-in-Publication Data
A catalogue record for this book is available from the British Library.

ISBN 978 1 84797 245 3

Disclaimer
Please note that the author and the publisher of this volume do not accept any responsibility
whatsoever for any error or omission, nor any loss, injury, damage, adverse outcome or liability
suffered as a result of the information contained in this book, or reliance upon it. Since long-
distance running can be dangerous and could involve physical activity that is too strenuous for
some individuals to engage in safely, it is essential that a doctor be consulted before undertaking
training.

Please note that throughout this book, 'he, him and his' have been used as neutral pronouns and
as such refer to both male and female.

Acknowledgements
Alison J. Smallman, for her help with illustrations, charts, graphs and diagrams.
Spencer G. Duval and Peter G. Brian for their help with photographs and editing.
Hayley Beard, Sonia Samuels and Sarah Waldron, for their help with photographs.

Typeset by The Manila Typesetting Company
Printed and bound in China by Everbest Printing Co. Ltd.

CONTENTS

FOREWORD

Rarely in life are there happy accidents, and I think few will argue with me that in top class sport they are even less frequent. The journey of the athlete from the moment they set foot in a club, are scooped up by their first coach and nurtured, is one of navigating obstacles, avoiding injury and attaining year-on-year improvements. None of this is the management of 'it'll be alright on the night'.

The only reason I have been asked, and was delighted to accept, the invitation to write this foreword is because I was the product of long-term, full-time, sensitive, world-class coaching. My father stewarded my career from my earliest teens to an Olympic Stadium and beyond. He was forensic in analysis and meticulous in every aspect of the art and science of coaching. Dave Sunderland is hewn from the same material. *High Performance Long-Distance Running* takes the athlete and the coach not only through the rudiments of all that is required of the endurance runner, but a good distance beyond. And Dave rightly attaches the need for integrity and honesty to sit at the heart of the relationship between athlete and coach.

I have known Dave for many years, enjoyed our conversations about a sport we are both passionate about and appreciated at all times his willingness to absorb knowledge, to inspire his charges and to challenge orthodoxy. This book is a significant contribution to those in my sport who choose the path of the endurance runner.

Sebastian Coe KBE

INTRODUCTION

Coaches and high performance athletes are constantly searching for new information to extend their knowledge so that they can gain that extra advantage or edge over their contemporaries and competitors. Fortunately, I have been given the opportunity to write a companion work to my book, *High Performance: Middle-Distance Running* (The Crowood Press, 2006), entitled *High Performance: Long-Distance Running*. Both books will contain similar generic elements, as they are both are about endurance running at the highest level. However, this book will focus upon the elements and requirements, no matter how large or small, that need to be encapsulated into a training programme in order to ensure success for the high performance long-distance runner.

I am pleased to share my thoughts and experiences of over forty years of coaching and hopefully these will go some way toward helping athletes to achieve future successes. I believe in helping other like-minded coaches and athletes with a thirst for knowledge and a passion for endurance running. Writing this book has also helped me to define and formalize my own views, ideas, beliefs and philosophy on how a high performance long-distance runner's season and career should be designed, developed and progressed.

My experiences encompass the whole spectrum of endurance running. I was a national standard athlete who gravitated toward coaching while at college. I was also a co-founding member of Cannock Chase Athletic Club in 1970. I have been the Midland's endurance staff coach as well as being in charge of coach education for the area. From here, I graduated to National Junior Coach, long distance and then to National Senior Coach, a position which I held for over fifteen years. At present, I am the England Athletics National Coach Mentor for Middle Distance, passing on my knowledge to and facilitating the needs and requirements of the next generation of outstanding coaches. I have constantly searched for ways of furthering my knowledge, for example, looking at training methods used in other endurance sports such as cycling, swimming, cross-country skiing, horse racing and rowing to see how these could be adapted to benefit my own athletes.

Because of my many roles at the highest level I have been fortunate in being able to witness at first hand high performance long-distance runners, in the cauldron of competition, at holding camps, at training camps and in their own training environments. I have been team coach at every major championship, including the Olympic Games, World Championships indoor and out, European Championships indoors and out, Commonwealth Games, World Junior Championships, European Junior Championships, World Cross-Country Championships and the European Cross-Country Championships.

On a personal coaching level, I have had eighteen medallists at these championships, including a world record holder, numerous national champions and medallists, on the track, the road, indoors and at cross-country, as well as well over sixty international athletes. I have also been heavily involved throughout the last thirty years in the development and delivery of the coach education system for United Kingdom Athletics (UKA). Similarly, for the last twenty-five years I have been a senior lecturer for the International Amateur Athletic Federation, lecturing in over a dozen countries on coach education. Throughout this time, not only with club athletics but also in my role as County Schools Secretary and team manager for Staffordshire schools, I have constantly been in touch with grass roots athletics. My range and breadth of experiences therefore are far reaching from both a personal coaching and also from a coach education perspective.

Coaching long-distance runners requires an understanding of the physiological requirements of the event and the type of training that will produce the desired effect. It requires good man-management skills, not only with athletes but also in building up and developing support teams for them. It also requires basic psychological skills to be able to motivate and lift athletes to get the best out of them. A good coaching eye is also essential to pick up any technical faults, overstraining or any prospective injuries or illness. The ability to plan and prepare, and also to develop and progress each individual athlete, not only through the season but throughout their athletic careers, is essential. Good time management is also of paramount importance to ensure that all these requirements are maximized. Using this knowledge and their experiences, each coach will evolve his own philosophy of coaching. Most coaches possess a knowledge and ability in most of these areas. The successful coach is the one who knows how to mix all these requirements together, then tailor them to each individual athlete's needs and requirements. This involves detailed planning, with the correct requirements being implemented at the correct time of year and in the correct proportions. To be successful, it means not just applying this knowledge in a yearly plan, but being able to implement it daily. The coach and athlete must have the confidence and ability to put their plan into practice in the training environment and determine how an athlete will progress. This is where coaching becomes an art. But this art can take years of experience to nurture, for example, knowing when and when not to include certain elements in the training programme. The coach must also have a thirst for knowledge and self-improvement, and be constantly reassessing and re-evaluating himself, his training programmes and his athletes.

This book, by drawing upon practical experience gained over many years in the field and at the highest level, will hopefully provide the knowledge and inspiration upon which a successful coaching programme and philosophy can be developed.

CHAPTER I

THE PHILOSOPHY OF COACHING AND TRAINING

Whatever one's coaching philosophy, the principal tenet should be that all athletes are individuals and must be treated as such in any coaching situation and through-out their careers. It is crucially important to make sure that athletes' individual training is progressed slowly through the correct stages and at the correct time of year. Particular attention and care must be made in the early stages of the athlete's career, both to their growth plates and to their physical development. It is quite possible with younger athletes that their biological development can outstrip their chronological age. Care must therefore be taken with loading, stress levels, the type of surfaces being used, the recoveries and the level of intensity of the sessions. This is particularly important with the developing young long-distance runner, who should build up a good mileage base progressively over a period of time, until he is mature enough to accept the workloads required to become a high performance long-distance runner.

Many coaches and athletes know the different types of training methods and the effects they can achieve, but the successful ones are those who can adopt these training methods into a proper progressive, planned structure and process, not just in the season but throughout an athlete's career. Planning a training programme is an art.

The training year should have certain objectives and goals, which will be reflected in the training plan. The training plan will then be implemented and the results recorded, evaluated and reviewed. To achieve the process, the plan will progress from a singular *training unit* (a particular exercise), such as a 10-mile run, which will take place during one training *session*, through to a group of training units called a *micro-cycle*. The latter is organized so that the athlete gains the optimum value from each unit. A micro-cycle may vary in length from a week up to a month. Each unit contained in a micro-cycle should have a specific objective, which should change from unit to unit. Similarly, the amount of the loading and the intensity of the units within the micro-cycle will vary from unit to unit. This process has clear objectives, is planned, implemented, evaluated and then refined. In practice, to get the optimum effect this means ensuring that a low-intensity training unit to aid recovery should always follow a high-intensity training unit. A unit of technique work or a co-ordination unit can precede an endurance-conditioning unit, but should never follow it. This process could take place on con-secutive days if the athlete is only training once per day, or in one day if the athlete is training two or three times per day. This is to ensure that the athlete is fresh when undertaking specific quality training such as technique and co-ordination work, or high intensity sessions.

While the micro-cycle results in varied training units, it is also systematic and ordered, leading to the correct and gradual progression required for proper development. The *macro-cycle* is the cumulative effect of repeating the progressive micro-cycles over a given period within the season, with a particular goal in mind. In the preparation phase of the athletic year this would be to lay a good aerobic endurance base in readiness for the more intense sessions, higher mileage volumes and specific work ses-sions that will follow later in the year. The macro-cycle is sometimes referred to as a block of training, or a *meso-cycle*. A macro-cycle should be continued for as long as it takes the athlete to achieve the training objectives, or for as long as he can maintain concentration and cope with the load and stresses of the repeated micro-cycles. With the pre-competition macro-cycle, the training intensity should either be slowly progressed or kept at the same level, with full recovery between units. The build-up to competition should be stress-free and psychologically stimulating, leading to the athlete performing at his peak in the competition.

The Process of Training

macro-cycle
↑
period
↑
phase
↑
meso-cycle
↑
micro-cycle
↑
session
↑
unit

The long-distance runner's training throughout the season is affected by three physiological laws: the *law of overload*, the *law of specificity* and the *law of reversibility*.

The Law of Overload

The law of overload means that any improvement in fitness requires a progressively increased training load in order to challenge the athlete's current fitness level. This acts as a stimulus to elicit a response and subsequent adaptation from the athlete's body (Fig. 1). The training loading or intensity causes fatigue, then when the training is concluded, recovery occurs. If the loading or intensity is correct, after recovery the fitness level will be improved through the body's adaptation. This overcompensation of the body, or training effect, is the objective that the training unit is designed to achieve. The training units and micro-cycles, if correctly planned and progressed, will result in an improved fitness level when the athlete has recovered from the training session. However, if the training load is too little, the overcompensation after recovery will be less than required and

there will be little adaptation. If the training load is too great, the athlete will be fortunate to return to the original fitness level and an overtraining situation could develop (Fig. 2a).

The Law of Specificity

The law of specificity means that the training load prescribed for each unit will determine the training effect. The training load must be specific to the individual athlete and his event. The training load becomes specific when it has the correct training ratio and loading structure. For example, in a track repetition session, the number of repetitions, the speed or intensity of the repetitions and the recovery between them is specific to the athlete's ability and to his event. This is so that he will be able to achieve the required training effect. The *intensity* of a training unit is the quality, or difficulty, of the training loads prescribed for that unit, and the speed of the required repetitions. The *extent* of the training load is the number of sets and repetitions, the time set to run the repetitions and the distance of the repetitions. The *recovery* is the prescribed time between the sets and repetitions. The *duration* of the training load is the combined total time it takes, including the distance of the repetitions and the set recovery times. *Specificity* in training means that it is specific to the athlete, the time of year and his event. Therefore, the specific training required for the long-distance runner will be different to that required for a thrower, hurdler, sprinter, jumper or middle-distance runner.

The Law of Reversibility

The law of reversibility means that fitness levels will fall if the loading is not constantly repeated and will revert to where it was prior to the start of training. If the training is not progressively challenging, the athlete's fitness will

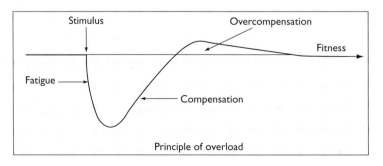

Fig. 1. This figure shows the principle of overload and depicts the correct training level. If loads are correct in their duration, intensity and frequency, overcompensation occurs. If the loads are increased progressively, repeated overcompensation and higher levels of fitness and adaptation occur.

Fig. 2a. This figure (adapted from Yakovlev) illustrates that if training loads, frequencies and intensities are the same or too far apart, there will be an increase in fitness levels. Similarly, if the training loads are too close or too great for the athlete's fitness level, overtraining and incomplete adaptation occurs. Adaptation is specific to the specific nature of the training.

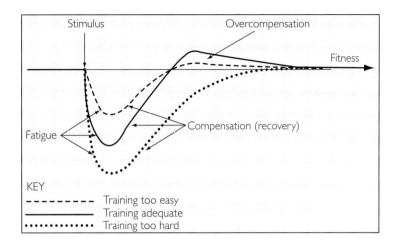

level off to a plateau. If the training ceases, the athlete's fitness level will gradually drop, because the body has no stimulus to which to adapt, until it reaches the level required for normal daily activities. Therefore, the training load must continue to increase if the athlete's general and specific fitness levels are to increase. The training load must increase regularly for the performance level to improve. This is known as progressive overload. After years of accumulative high volume training, interspersed with high intensity work, the high performance long-distance runner's fitness level, even during a short period of rest during the transition phase, will, when reversibility occurs, continually revert to a higher fitness base level. This is one of the key aspects of a training programme.

Rest, regeneration and recuperation are equally as important as the training load itself. If the correct recovery from the high training load is not achieved, the training effect will be diminished. It could also lead to overtraining (Fig. 2b). 'Active rest', particularly during the transition phase, is also beneficial. This light type of training includes jogging or participation in other sports such as cycling. It allows the athlete to recover both physically and mentally while maintaining a general fitness level.

Training Intensity

The athlete's training level or the intensity of a training unit is divided into three stages. The first stage is the *immediate training effect,* which for the long-distance athlete is an increase of his heart rate, a build up of lactate and fatigue. The second stage is known as the *residual effect;* this is what the immediate effect is turned into through time, till the next repetition or unit. This effect takes place in the post-training recovery phase and is the regenerative process. The third and final stage is known as the *cumulative effect.* This is brought about by the repeated residual effects of the training units in a micro-cycle combined with the correctly timed and progressive training loads.

To know how best to utilize these principles in the athlete's training programme, the coach needs to have a good knowledge of the training systems available that will produce these effects. Over the years, certain systems and training ideas have been introduced, developed and refined. Knowing his athlete's strengths and weaknesses, the judicious long-distance coach will select and blend into the training programme many of the following methods.

Fartlek

Fartlek is a Swedish word meaning speed play. It was introduced by Gösta Holmér, coach to Gunder Hägg and Arne Anderson, in the 1940s, but is just as beneficial today. This type of training is done on forest paths over undulating terrain. During a set period of time, the athlete runs as he pleases. He will alternate running hard with running easily; sometimes he will run on the flat, other times uphill. *Fartlek* aims to encourage the athlete to fulfil and challenge himself in a natural training

Fig 2b. Chart showing overtraining.

environment. In this way, he covers many miles and improves both his aerobic base and his cardiovascular system. In the track season, the *fartlek* sessions are integrated with track work. *Fartlek* is especially useful to the long-distance runner because he can maintain his high volume of mileage, while also covering the three energy pathways of alactate (speed), anaerobic (speed-endurance) and aerobic (endurance) in one training unit. Though invaluable, this type of training is currently much underused.

Interval Training

In the early 1920s and 1930s the Finnish runner Paavo Nurmi (twenty-two world records and twelve Olympic medals) and his coach Lauri Pikkala used shorter dura-tion training periods with adequate recovery in place of longer, slower endurance running. Without the scientific knowledge now available, they were unwittingly provid-ing a training intensity that stimulated a more intense response, which, coupled with the correct recovery, equipped Nurmi much better to meet the demands of his events. This was interval training in its infancy.

Waldemar Gerschler from Germany, coach to Rudolf Harbig and Josy Barthel and in conjunction with Dr H. Reindell, introduced interval training in the 1930s to a wider audience. In a training unit Gerschler would have a set number of repetitions. These were known as intervals and were run over distances of either 100m or 200m. The set recovery time allowed the athletes to run these repetitions very quickly. Interval training would require a large number of repetitions for the high performance long-distance runner.

This type of training was popularized and developed further in Britain in the 1950s by an Austrian, Franz Stampfl, coach to Roger Bannister and Ralph Doubell. Stampfl developed interval training by making the repeti-tion distances much longer, ranging from 400m to 1½ miles. Recovery times in his method were equal to the time of the repetition or longer, and the repetitions were run at faster than race pace. This type of interval work is highly suited to the high performance long-distance runner.

Mihály Iglói, a Hungarian responsible for numerous long-distance world record holders and many sub-4min milers, refined interval running even more in the 1960s. With his system, the total of the repetitions run was one-and-a half to double that of the race distance. For a 5,000m runner, this would mean running 7,500–10,000m using interval training in a training session. He also halved the recovery times and was the first coach to introduce sets into his athletes' training programmes,

for example: 2 × 5 × 600m, with 200m jog between the repetitions, and a 600m jog between the sets. This equates to a total − including jogged recoveries − of 8,200m.

Emil Zatopek, the great Czechoslovakian athlete of the 1950s, took interval training even further, introduc-ing a large quantity of repetitions and short recoveries between each repetition. This type of training is still undertaken by high performance long-distance runners today and shows what the human body is capable of undertaking if the training is progressive and systematic.

Yuri Suslov, the USSR coach responsible for the country's successful female middle-distance runners, took interval training to its extreme. With his method, the total of the intervals run was equivalent to the race distance, this allowing the repetitions to be run at faster than the required race pace. This type of training is quite applicable to the long-distance runner, for example, a high performance 30min female athlete would run 10 × 1,000m, all under the required 3min per kilometre of the race situation.

The success of these methods of interval training is that they are precise, easily measured and the progres-sions in training can be seen from micro-cycle to micro-cycle and from phase to phase. The coach can also control the variables involved, for example, the number of repetitions and sets, the speed of the repetitions, their distance and the recovery between them. The recovery phase can either be a jogged distance, a set time or a pulse recovery.

Block Training

Other coaches added a different perspective to distance training. One of these was the New Zealander, Arthur Lydiard, coach to Peter Snell and Murray Halberg in the 1950s. Lydiard introduced the system of block train-ing. With this method he would have a ten-week block of marathon training, which systematically progressed to well over 100 miles per week, including a 20-mile Sunday runner. However, the fourth week in each cycle dropped in volume to aid recovery, before moving to a higher volume phase during the next month. This was followed by a six-week block with the emphasis on uphill running, bounding and downhill running work. The final block of training had a greater emphasis on repeti-tion work, interval training and time trials. As well as being responsible for the introduction of block training, Lydiard introduced the concept of having an easy day of training after an intense training session and also the idea of athletes tapering their training to be able to peak for an important competition (see Chapter 6).

Total Conditioning

Percy Cerutty, the Australian coach to Herb Elliot in the 1950s, was yet another innovative coach who broadened the horizons of both coaches and athletes. He believed in running close to nature, so set up a training camp in the sand dunes near to the sea at Portsea, Australia. He used the sand dunes for resistance work and conditioning training. He also developed conditioning even further by introducing weight training into his athletes' training programmes. He also made athletes and coaches aware of the importance of diet, but above all how powerful a tool the mind is in both the training environment and in competition.

Oregon System

Bill Bowerman, coach to 5,000m runner Steve Prefontaine in Oregon, USA, developed a system referred to as either the 'Oregon system', or the 'complex system' in the 1960s. This system worked on a monthly cycle and each schedule was specific to the individual athlete. Bowerman believed in the optimum amount of work, incorporated with the optimum blend of different work. This meant that he would throughout the monthly cycle include each week a long run, a *fartlek* session, steady runs, plus two track sessions, both of which had goal times set for each month. The goal times were achieved by varying the number of sets, repetitions and recoveries so that the maximum number of repetitions, with the shortest possible recovery time, could be run at the set goal pace by the end of the month. Hence, it was named the complex system (see Chapter 6). Once this goal pace was achieved, for the next month it was reduced.

Long, Steady Distance

Ernst Van Aaken, from Germany, pioneered long, steady distance running, sometimes referred to as LSD, in the early 1960s. He believed that most athletes could run reasonably quickly, but did not have the endurance base to continue to run for any length of time. To achieve a large endurance base, he advocated lots of steady-state running with heart rates in the 130 region, interspersed with speed runs. His training ratio was 35 miles of steady running to 1 mile of speed running. He also believed that the key to achieving this high steady-state running mileage was to reduce the athlete's body weight to below the norm. The most successful exponent of his system was Harald Norpoth. The danger with this type

of training is that it can lead to anorexia, particularly in young female athletes. If done correctly, however, with the added use of vitamin supplements, the incidence of injury is very low.

Five-Pace System

In Britain certain coaches tend to favour the five-pace system of training. With this method, the repetition sessions for long-distance runners are done at marathon pace, 10,000m pace, 5,000m pace, 3,000m pace and 1,500m pace. The concept is to give the athlete over-distance endurance through the marathon and 10,000m pace repetitions, and under-distance speed through the 3,000m and 1,500m pace repetitions, while still training for his event-specific race distance, the 10,000m. The long-distance runner's adaptation of this type of training is from the original 5,000m, 3,000m, 1,500m, 800m and 400m used by the middle-distance runner. The five different paces are rotated so that over-distance work, event-specific work and under-distance work can all be covered. Then the process will commence again from over-distance training down to under-distance training. This method, favoured by, among others, Sebastian Coe is explained along with some of the other systems mentioned in greater detail later in the chapter on planning and preparation.

Summary

From these various training systems a coach will choose the ones that are best suited to the needs of an individual athlete. He will then blend them into a training programme. To do this successfully, he must understand when and where to use the methods and what are the effects of a particular type of training. These types of sessions for the high performance long-distance runner will be used judiciously on the back of a large volume of steady-state running.

In addition, the good coach also has to have expertise in many other areas. Possibly the key area is his interpersonal skills with his athletes and the relationship he builds up with each of them. He has to have integrity in case the athlete is undergoing personal or emotional problems. He should be fair and impartial so that each athlete receives individual attention. His role will undoubtedly differ from athlete to athlete. He will often become a surrogate father to his younger athletes and a confidant to his more mature athletes. He must get to know his athletes, not just in an athletic sense, but also their home backgrounds and personal situations.

This will serve to give him an insight into the ambition and determination of each athlete and an appreciation of what they are trying to achieve. The coach should be perceptive, picking up on the mood swings of his athletes. He should also be totally honest with them, so that they are capable of more than their abilities will allow. He should also be loyal to them and, through this and his honesty, should in return expect to earn their trust, loyalty and respect. The coach should also look and act the part. He should be well presented and punctual, the constant in the group who acts professionally at all times.

As a coach, he must have a great knowledge of each event and also have a good coaching eye, gained over years of experience, which will enable him to pick up on any problems with technique or stress and alter the training accordingly. Scientific testing should only confirm what he has observed over the previous weeks with his coaching eye. He must be able to see the potential of his athlete and develop that potential to the full. He is also the planner and controller, not just of the individual training units and the year's programme, but also of his athletes' whole careers. He therefore must be constantly appraising both himself and his athletes. He should be creative in his coaching, looking for different training environments and including different types of training when required, in order to give a fresh impetus and approach.

However, no coach is an island and when problems crop up he needs to know where to turn for advice. Therefore, he needs to build up over a period of time a variety of support systems, involving, for example, physiologists, physiotherapists and masseurs. A young, emerging coach may require an older, more experienced and successful coach as his mentor – someone he can turn to for advice and to bounce ideas off. These systems will be discussed in more detail later in the book.

With younger athletes, the coach needs to be constantly aware of their biological development as opposed to their assumed chronological development. This means that all their training should be progressed systematically. With older athletes, he should take into account how long they have been training and the physical demands of their event. The coach also needs to be a good motivator to get the best out of his athletes, using his knowledge to employ different motivational approaches for each of them.

But whatever motivational method the coach uses, he should, above all, be positive and inspire his athletes. Before a race, the coach should be there to encourage and reassure. If the training has been going well, the athlete will be confident. The coach needs to allow the athlete to learn to become self-sufficient before a race, as it is unlikely that he will have access to his athletes in the warm-up area of a major championship. If the race goes well, the athlete should be praised; if it does not, a candid assessment must be made to come up with the reason for the sub-standard performance. No athlete continually trains hard twice a day, day in, day out, to race deliberately badly . Therefore, once a period of time has elapsed to give time for reflection, an assessment of the possible reasons for the poor performance should be made, a solution arrived at and acted upon.

The coach must realize that for the high performance long-distance runner it is about more than just achieving good performances and results – it is also his career. The coach must therefore work closely with race promoters, agents and sports companies to ensure that the chosen race programmes will meet the financial needs of his athletes, while still giving them the flexibility to pursue their championship dreams. A marathon runner, for example in a big city marathon, will not only receive an appearance fee, but will also have built into his contract bonus payments for achieving certain times, achieving qualifying standards and setting either course, national or world records. Similarly, he will more than likely have a contract with a shoe or kit manufacturer, through which he will have a fixed annual contract fee with added bonus payments for championship performances, record and race times that he achieves.

Coaching experience comes from working with athletes at all levels. To give each athlete the individual attention they deserve and to ensure that they fulfil their potential, the coach should not dilute his energies and expertise by having a group of larger than six to ten athletes. The experience the coach gains in the field will show him that if an athlete is running and racing well, he does not need to train any harder. Similarly, if an athlete is training hard but the racing performances are not reflecting this effort, it could mean that the athlete is becoming stale. This could be caused by a number of reasons, such as a poor diet, insufficient sleep, too many races, iron deficiency, fatigue from daily occupation or emotional stresses and so on. The confidence and self-belief that the coach has gained through his field experience will help in overcoming these problems. Athletes will become a mirror image of their coach – a positive, confident coach will produce positive, confident athletes

The coach should leave no stone unturned in his quest for improvement. Through developing technique mobility and drills, he will make his athletes more economical. Through progressive training programmes, conditioning and the development of energy pathways, he will make his athletes more physiologically efficient. Through planning and preparation, tactics, motivation and the surrounding support systems, he will enable his athletes to execute this economy and efficiency through their performance in the competitive environment. In sum, *economy + efficiency + execution = excellence*.

Above all, the coach should be available. He will be the constant in the group and if he is not available and accessible, his athletes will either be poor attendees, or will go to a coach who is available. This extends beyond being there on race days, to being constantly accessible on the phone for any problems, help or advice. Any coach who feels he knows all there is to know is misguided. He should never stop learning, or fail to realize that there are other methods and ideas that may help his athletes. Any coach who is in the sport for his own personal advancement, and not the advancement of his athletes, will never be successful and fulfilled.

The successful coach is the one who takes a youngster from being a promising schoolboy through to international honours and major championships. The dialogue between the coach and athlete will move from being one way in the early days of their partnership to a far more open two-way dialogue as the athlete matures, with the athlete having far more input into his training programme, sessions and race selection. During this journey, the coach is working toward ultimate redundancy, so that by the time his athlete is competing at a major championship, he is additionally an adviser, confidant and friend.

CHAPTER 2

THE REQUIREMENTS FOR SUCCESS

The successful long-distance runner requires a large number of qualities, all of which have to be developed if he is to fulfil his potential. Therefore it is important that a holistic approach is taken, in which all of these qualities, where appropriate, are incorporated into the whole system. These qualities are all interlinked (see Fig. 3), but each has a different role and emphasis in the athlete's training programme, which may change slightly the longer he has been training. To understand each quality in more detail, we need to look at them separately to show what their physiological function is, to demonstrate what training will improve the function further and to illustrate the role of each quality in the race situation.

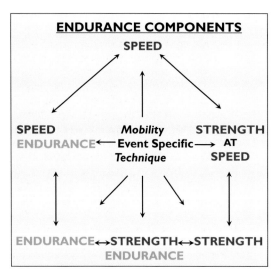

Fig. 3. This figure shows the interrelationship of the endurance components – how strength endurance, speed endurance and strength at speed (power) are interlinked and dependent on the main components of speed, endurance and strength. It also emphasizes the importance of the relationship of all of these components with technique, mobility and event-specific endurance.

The importance of each physiological function is shown in the percentage breakdown for each event (see Figs 4 and 4a) and the table shows their importance to each of the long-distance events (see Fig. 5). The more successful high performance long-distance runners develop each of the required qualities to their maximum extent. This will mean spending a great deal of time developing their aerobic base over a number of years, involving a high volume of miles/kilometres, sessions and training units, as well as developing running economy.

We will now look at the main qualities and extraneous requirements that are essential for success as a high performance long-distance runner. These will have been patiently developed over many years. All of them are important and have their part to play in an athlete's overall development, no matter how large or small their input may be in the overall picture. In subsequent chapters, the types of training, planning, preparation and tactics will be looked at in much greater detail, but here we will study the fundamentals.

SPEED

An athlete's genetic muscle fibre determines his basic speed. However, training to maximum speed should not be ignored. This is a common fault with long-distance athletes who lack speed. The tendency is to work on their stronger qualities, such as their endurance base, and to neglect their weaker ones. Pure speed, or absolute speed as it is sometimes referred to, unlike speed endurance consists of training using distances from 30m up to 120m. This type of training primarily uses the alactate or ATP (adenosine triphosphate – see Chapter 3) system. By training this system, which lasts for a maximum of 15sec, the athlete can improve both his basic speed and his ability to react quickly in the race situation. Pure speed cannot be maintained for the full duration of a long-distance race and will be mainly utilized at the beginning and end, or to counteract any sudden injections of pace within the race. Speed-

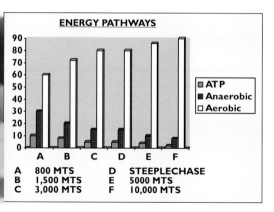

Fig. 4. The percentage breakdown of each of the three energy pathways – alactate (speed), lactate (speed endurance) and aerobic (oxygen) required for all the endurance events is here shown as a block graph. The requirements of these energy systems should be an integral part of the training programme.

orientated training is undertaken to improve the athlete's optimum speed during the race. It will also improve the athlete's reaction time and ability to accelerate and change pace. All high performance long-distance runners have the ability to 'kick' or sprint at the end of a major championship race.

Speed can be improved by downhill running, sprint drills, acceleration sprints and skills sprinting, up- and down-the-clock sessions, zigzag runs and dynamic stretching. An acceleration sprints session could be six repetitions over 150m, split into three segments of 50m, with each 50m segment getting progressively faster. The first 50m would be run at 80 per cent effort, the 50–100m segment at 90 per cent effort and the final 50m segment at 100 per cent effort. A down-the-clock session would involve six repetitions at maximum effort, starting at 100m, and each repetition would reduce by 10m, concluding with a final repetition of 50m. Both of these sessions – acceleration runs and a down-the-clock session – would require complete recoveries so that the athlete can operate at maximum speed where required. While this training is being carried out, relaxation procedures should also take place and attention should be paid to the athlete's technique. Technique is important with a long-distance runner, because the longer they are running, the greater the capacity for an incorrect technique to impair the outcome of the race.

Training for speed should take place throughout the season. During the preparation phases it will take the form of drills, up- and down-the-clock sessions and acceleration sprints. These sessions can take place after steady-state running sessions, or be incorporated into other training routines. The emphasis should be on technique, coordination and relaxation as well as the speed training. As the athlete moves into the pre-competitive and competitive periods, downhill running, sprint-skills running and flat-out sprints become not only the more important sessions, but also specific sessions. Once again, there should be a strong emphasis on technique and relaxation.

The ability to monitor, maintain and increase speed is clearly essential to all long-distance runners, particularly at the highest level. The long-distance athlete must be able to regulate and increase his speed during a race to cover any variations in pace and also at the end of a race, while also being able to follow a sustained pace. It is crucial for him to be able to react instantly in the race environment, which in the longer distance races may be when he is becoming fatigued and his concentration and focus level is at its lowest.

STRENGTH

Strength implies the use of maximum tension, or the greatest force that is possible with a single contraction. Strength training in this format is primarily static; it has little correlation to either speed or endurance. In long-distance training, the main focus of strength training is on the development of muscular strength. This ensures that a strong strength base is built, developed and maintained, from which all the other qualities can emanate.

As most of a long-distance runner's training will involve him being on his feet, putting in large amounts of miles/kilometres, it is essential that his legs are strong enough to withstand the constant pounding this entails. Therefore some form of strength or conditioning work should be part of the training programme.

Event	Alactate System	Lactate System	Anaerobic System	Aerobic System
5,000m	4%	10%	14%	86%
10,000m	2–3 %	8–12%	10–15%	85–90%
Marathon	0%	2–5%	2–5%	85–98%

Fig. 4a. This chart shows the specific breakdown for the long-distance running events.

REQUIREMENTS FOR EACH OF THE ENDURANCE EVENTS

EVENT	5/10K	S/Chase	MARATHON
MOBILITY	•	•	•
ENDURANCE (02)	•	•	•
SPEED (ALACTATE)	•	•	
SPEED ENDURANCE (LA02)	•	•	
STRENGTH	•	•	
STRENGTH ENDURANCE	•	•	•
POWER		(•)	
TECHNIQUE	•	•	•
TACTICS	•	•	•
RUNNING ECONOMY	•	•	•
CORE STABILITY	•	•	•

OVERVIEW

5k/10k	All aspects little power, strength and less lactate work
Steeplachase	All aspects + extra technique
Marathon	Certain key areas but predominantly 02 sysyem

Fig. 5. Using the endurance components from Fig. 3 and the percentages of each event from Fig. 4, an overview of the main requirements for each of the endurance events can be obtained. This is shown in diagrammatic form to provide an overview that will ensure that the correct requirements are incorporated into the training plan.

Many long-distance runners include weight training in their training programme. However, if weight training is used to build up strength, it is advisable to use loads of 85–100 per cent of the athlete's maximum lifting ability, with a low number of repetitions and a higher number of sets to get the most beneficial effect. The weight-training exercises must be practised the whole year round and be specific to long-distance running. The number of weight-training exercises used will be small and should be in the ratio of three leg exercises to two abdominal exercises to one arm exercise. The pre-dominance of leg-strengthening exercises reflects that these are the part of the body that are used the most and therefore need the most strengthening. It is also very important that if free weights, instead of a multi-gym, are used, that the correct technique is employed and that there are also spotters on either side of the lifter in case the lifter has a problem; the spotter's role is to step in and take the weight off the lifter if he is in trouble or requires support. If these technical and safety rules are not observed, it could lead to serious long-term injury.

As noted, it is important that strength training takes place throughout the training year. It should not be stopped when the pre-competitive period has been entered, otherwise all the strength that has been gained will be lost by the time the competitive climax is reached. The greatest amount of strength work should be done during the preparation period and the specific preparation period. As the pre-competitive and competitive periods are entered, the number of sessions, activities and repetitions should decrease.

Strength in the race situation is not as obvious or visible as the other qualities. However, it is one of the core elements, which allows for the development of the other, more essential, qualities that the long-distance runner requires. It is particularly important at the climax of a race, or in major championships, when the athlete has been running for a long period of time and when a number of races have to be undertaken to reach the final.

ENDURANCE

Endurance training primarily uses the oxygen transportation system. This means improving the efficiency of the heart, improving the blood circulation to increase the athlete's maximum volume uptake of oxygen and ensuring there is an efficient exchange and transportation of gases. Its purpose is to produce a more efficient energy production system, related to the demands of a high performance long-distance running. This type of training, therefore, is *aerobic* and involves a large volume of training.

This is type of aerobic training is the staple diet and key requirement for any high performance long-distance runner. It requires a great deal of steady-state running, punctuated by *fartlek* training, long steady-state runs, alternating-the-pace runs, threshold runs, extensive interval training and tempo runs. The emphasis is on steady output – the duration of the training run rather than the intensity. However, because of his ability level, the high performance long-distance runner will run his steady-state runs – the majority of his training – at a higher intensity and quicker pace than long-distance runners of lesser ability. The steady-state runs will be over distances of 6 miles/10km to 10 miles/16km, while the longer steady-state runs will be of at least an hour's duration and more in the case of marathon runners.

An accurate measure of aerobic training is the athlete's heart rate. This type of steady-state training should always fall into the area of 120 to 160 beats/min, although it will obviously go higher and fluctuate during certain aspects of the alternating pace training, *fartlek* sessions and tempo runs. It will be nearer to 175 beats/min with the threshold runs.

Endurance training takes place the whole year round, but the large endurance base is built in the preparation period, as well as during the previous number of years of training that serve to create a large endurance legacy. The largest amount of mileage/kilometres is reached during the general and specific preparation phases. As the pre-competitive and competitive periods are entered, the amount of sessions and the total mileage/kilometres decrease, although not dramatically. The endurance training during this period also helps to get rid of any waste products and stiffness that linger from the higher intensity sessions that now begin to be included in the training plan.

A high performance 5km track runner may be targeting a major track championship in August, whereas a high performance marathon runner may have a target of a major city marathon in April; their training periodized years will therefore be different. However, the principles of preparation and the progressions of endurance training remain the same for both athletes, even though the quantity of endurance training may be substantially different. Both are endurance athletes, albeit in different events, and therefore endurance training will provide the majority of their training.

Endurance training is the key element in all long-distance training. Without a good and large base upon which to draw, none of the other qualities, such as speed, speed endurance or power, can be as effectively utilized in the race situation. The ability to improve an athlete's maximum oxygen uptake ensures that he not only takes in enough oxygen to meet the demands of the race, but is also able to combat any changes in intensity required during the race. The greater the long-distance runner's endurance endowment or base, the more efficient will be his running economy. He will therefore be better able to utilize his intake of oxygen, maintain his technique and tire far less quickly.

SPEED ENDURANCE

The intensity of effort involved in speed-endurance training is much higher than that associated with endurance training, since the athlete is working to offset the build-up of lactic acid. This type of training is therefore *anaerobic*.

This type of training for the high performance long-distance track athlete will include flat-out, 100 per cent effort repetitions at either above or below the race distance, high intensity interval work, quality interval work and repetition work, over distances of between 200–3,000m. In all these sessions, the number of repetitions will be low, the recoveries long, more than one set could be involved and the intensity of effort will be high. In many cases, the athlete will not be able to take in enough oxygen to meet the demands of the training session and therefore the build up of lactic acid cannot be prevented. As a result, the quality of the training session will deteriorate or have to be stopped. This inability to take in the required amount of oxygen leaves a deficiency that is often referred to as 'oxygen debt'. The athlete's heart rate during speed-endurance repetition sessions will be well in excess of 170 beats/min and in some cases with the high performance athlete as high as 200 beats/min.

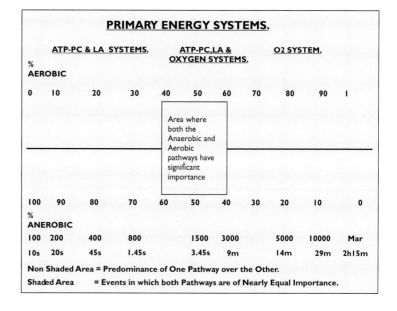

Fig. 6. The primary energy systems are shown with the aerobic (oxygen) continuum at the top, rising from 0 per cent (100m) to 100 per cent (marathon). At the foot of the diagram, the ATP-PC (alactate) and lactate systems (both anaerobic systems) continuum begins to diminish from 100 per cent (100m) down to 0 per cent (marathon).

PRIMARY ENERGY SYSTEMS.

| ATP-PC & LA SYSTEMS. | | | | ATP-PC,LA & OXYGEN SYSTEMS. | | | O2 SYSTEM. | | |

% AEROBIC

| 0 | 10 | 20 | 30 | 40 | 50 | 60 | 70 | 80 | 90 | 1 |

Area where both the Anaerobic and Aerobic pathways have significant importance

| 100 | 90 | 80 | 70 | 60 | 50 | 40 | 30 | 20 | 10 | 0 |

% ANAEROBIC

| 100 | 200 | 400 | 800 | | 1500 | 3000 | | 5000 | 10000 | Mar |
| 10s | 20s | 45s | 1.45s | | 3.45s | 9m | | 14m | 29m | 2h15m |

Non Shaded Area = Predominance of One Pathway over the Other.
Shaded Area = Events in which both Pathways are of Nearly Equal Importance.

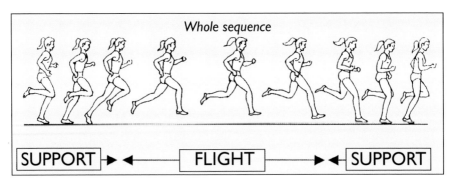

Fig. 7. The figure depicts the whole running sequence for the technical model, from the support phase thorough the flight phase back to the support phase. The velocity of the athlete will determine the foot placement, but with long-distance runners it will be a mid-foot placement. From the support phase the leg will swing forward with an open knee, with the lower leg nearly parallel to the ground. The thigh in the forward position at the maximum extension of the drive allows the hip, leg and foot to complete the cycle of movement. The free leg is now at its greatest flexion and swings through to replace the other leg. The knee-lift for a long-distance runner is lower and the arm movement not as dynamic as for the shorter events. The head and trunk are erect and the shoulders, neck and arms are relaxed to help aid posture and movement. The arms swing rhythmically forward in synchronization and slightly across the chest at an angle of approximately 90 degrees.

Although there will be a certain amount of speed-endurance work done throughout the athletic year, the main emphasis with this type of training will be during the pre-competitive and competitive periods. A variety of methods will be used to ensure that once the competitive climax approaches, the athlete is in peak condition.

High performance road or marathon runners will include these types of training in their programmes. However, they will be running for much longer distances than the 5,000m and 10,000m track runner, so the intensity will not be the same and their heart rates not as high. They will not give as much time in their training to these types of sessions as would the track runner, concentrating instead on constant running in a variety of forms and at different intensities.

These types of sessions are important to ensure that there is an efficient blood supply to the muscles; they result in a high tolerance to oxygen debt, lactate accumulation and the build-up of waste products. They also improve the ability to remove and reuse the waste products that accumulate in the body when working at this level of intensity. In a long-distance race this is important. The longer the athlete can maintain his oxygen intake, maintain his running economy and offset the build-up of lactic acid, not only will he be in a stronger situation at the climax of the race, he will also become a more efficient and successful runner.

continue to use his muscles while fatigue is setting in, while also trying to maintain the quality of his performance. The stronger the muscles become, the better their adaptation to the demands of the event.

This type of training is utilized as part of the long-distance runner's programme, with the most used methods being circuit training, stage training, long uphill running, repetition work, resistance work against the environment or against a force, the Oregon circuit and back-to-back repetitions. These types of training session help to make the long-distance athlete stronger and underpin the great amount of aerobic running that they undertake.

Like strength training, strength-endurance training should continue throughout the year. The main emphasis will be during the preparation phases, when a weekly session should be part of the training programme. Once the pre-competition and competition periods are entered the sessions should reduce in both number and extent.

Strength endurance is a fundamental part of conditioning and is a key ingredient in the race situation. This is particularly the case in the championship race situations, where there are could be a number of rounds to negotiate. The stronger the athlete, the better placed they will be to maintain their technique under pressure, offset the build up of lactic acid and utilize their speed to full effect.

STRENGTH ENDURANCE

This is sometimes referred to as local muscular endurance, or conditioning training. It is the athlete's ability to

POWER

Power is also referred to as strength at speed, elastic strength, or explosive strength. It is the ability of the athlete to utilize his strength at speed and to be able also to react explosively to any situation that may occur in a competition.

Although not a major ingredient in the longer running events, power is important in the training programme for steeplechasers and 5km and 10km runners. The following methods are the most often utilized in the improvement of power – hopping, plyometrics, bounding, weight training, resistance work, weighted belts and short hill work. Depth jumping – jumping from a height – can also be used, but only with the mature, experienced athlete and only in a safe environment. Power must always be developed alongside technique work.

Elements of power training will take place throughout the year. However, the main focus for power training will be during the pre-competitive and competitive periods, with the athlete becoming sharper, dynamic and more focused. The more powerful the athlete, the

Fig. 7a. The phase structure can be broken down into the rear support and swing phases, and the front support and swing phases. The rear support phase function is the production of force for the forward drive and the upward swing of the thigh of the leading leg. The foot is planted straight ahead and achieves this, allowing an extension in the foot, knee and hip. The trunk is upright with a controlled, slightly forward lean, with head upright, eyes looking ahead and facial muscles and shoulders relaxed. The elbow angle is at 90 degrees with arms swinging backward and then through slightly across the chest. The hands are relaxed and held as an open fist. The rear swinging phase function is a preparation for the knee lifting and should be relaxed. The rear relaxed leg swings backward and upward with an inactive heel lift to the buttock. This is the commencement of the rapid forward swing of the thigh to produce the forward stride. The front swinging phase function is to bring the foot through in preparation for landing and will also determine the length of his stride. The thigh swings forward and upward, the height of the thigh because of the speed of the long-distance runner will not be high. The backward lowering of the thigh initiates the landing into the front support phase, balanced by the arms and legs. The front support foot function absorbs the weight of the landing, while at the same time prepares to drive off into the next phase. The foot is placed on the ground, on the outer edge of the ball of the foot, in the mid-foot vertical position to allow for the absorption of the body weight on landing. The knee gives slightly so that the point of ground contact is not too far in front of the body's centre of gravity to ensure there is no braking effect.

better equipped he will be to react to any given race situation, reacting explosively if and when the situation warrants it.

It is important that any power activities are technically correct, safe and take place on a forgiving surface.

TECHNIQUE

Technique is of vital importance to the long-distance runner, with a good basic technical model being required from an early age. Incorrect movements of either the arms or head are both wasteful and energy consuming. Incorrect leg movements can be a hindrance in a sprint finish and can lead to either under- or over-striding. An incorrect foot plant can lead to pronation and injuries.

The ideal technique (see Figs 7, 7a and 8) is relaxed, economical and efficient. To aid technique development as well as the coach's eye, video analysis and digital sequential analysis can be used. In this way, each

Fig. 8b. Here the athlete has moved through the driving phase, with his head and upper body still erect, his eyes focused, arms and rear leg driving and the front thigh driving through to be parallel to the ground.

different segment of the technique – head, trunk, arms and legs – can be analysed in both isolation and in relation to the whole movement. Using these methods of feedback, the athlete can see any problems with his technique and work to rectify them during training sessions.

In the athlete's early years and during the transition phase, work should be done on technique so as to ensure that it can be maintained during race pressure. It is also advisable to include technique work in training sessions after a period of being out through injury, as this will stop overcompensation by the athlete, who may be subconsciously protecting his previous injury. Technique can be improved by sprint drills, dynamic stretching and core stability, and also during training sessions. Practice is permanent; correct practice is perfection.

The ability of an athlete to be as economical and effective as possible during the race is of paramount importance. This is especially the case for the long-

Fig. 8. With the long-distance runner the posture and centre of gravity are important, as is the foot placement, which should be a mid-foot placement. The whole aim is for the runner to be as economical and efficient as is possible, therefore conserving energy.

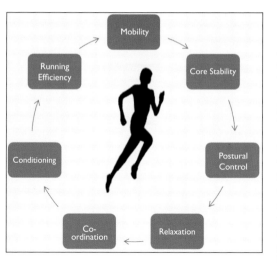

Fig. 9. The figure here shows that the technical model is supported, strengthened and improved by the utilization and development of the following areas: mobility to aid suppleness; stride length and range of movement. Core stability makes the core strong to hold the central running mechanical structure in place. Postural control ensures that the trunk, head and limbs remain in the correct position. Conditioning ensures that the required movements in a long-distance race can constantly be repeated effectively. Coordination ensures that all the limbs move in a synchronized sequence. Relaxation ensures that the whole of the technical model moves smoothly and easily. Finally, running efficiency ensures that all the components come together to make the technical model the most efficient it can be during the duration of the training programme or competition.

distance runner, who may be racing for for over two hours – incorrect technique will result in the expenditure of too much energy. Correct and efficient technique ensures that the athlete comes to the conclusion of the race in the best possible condition. In race situations, top athletes should be able to maintain their technique and keep relaxed while others are tensing up, fatiguing and losing form as the effects of the race and lactic acid take their toll. Video analysis through sophisticated systems such as Dartfish and Quintec can be valuable in aiding the development of the correct technical model, as can both normal and video cameras. However, these should simply serve as an added support system to the coach's eye and observations.

Also key to the technical model are the many support areas (see Fig. 9) that need to be worked on as well to ensure that the most efficient long-distance running model is produced.

MOBILITY

A full range of movement is essential to the long-distance runner. Mobility and suppleness begin to wane from the age of eight onward, therefore it is crucial that flexing and stretching exercises are part of the training programme (see Fig. 10). The muscles that cause the movement to take place in any joint action are called the protagonists. Opposing this movement and determining the mobility of the joint are the muscles and tissues being stretched, the antagonists. In any movement, these two groups of muscles work in harmony, one set of muscles causing the action, while the other opposes it. In mobility training the aim is to improve the range of movement by stretching the antagonist muscles slightly further. Many long-distance runners are stiff and have a poor range of movement, therefore PNF(Proprioceptive Neuromuscular Facilitation) exercises (Figs 11 and 12) and elasticized bands will assist them to develop their mobility and range of movement.

Mobility and flexibility training is best done when the body is warm, so it is advisable to do the exercises later in the day. The mobility exercises should preferably be done daily, throughout the year, and as an addition to any work done in a warm-up and cool-down session. A full range of exercises can be undertaken. They can be active, passive or kinetic exercises, or can be incorporated into a dynamic stretching routine.

Fig. 10. Sit in the hurdle position on the ground with the sole of the trail leg placed against the inside of the lead leg. Slowly move the hands as far as possible down the lead leg until the muscle can be felt to stretch. Then slowly stretch it a little further. Change the leg positions and repeat on each leg. This exercise is for the hips, lower back and hamstrings.

and particularly after a training session, and it is essential to stretch after a high intensity training session.

RUNNING ECONOMY

Running economy is linked with technique, mobility and a good technical model. It is usually defined as the oxygen cost of running at a certain speed, or running for a certain distance or length of time. Good running economy, for a given running speed, results in the utilization of a lower percentage of the athlete's VO_2 max (maximum oxygen uptake) while running at that speed. This results in a reduction in muscle glycogen utilization and potentially less reliance on the O_2-independent metabolism, or oxygen system, plus a lower lactate build-up rate. High performance long-distance runners

Fig. 11. In this exercise because of lack of flexibility, the athlete is unable to get her two hands to meet. This exercise is to stretch the arm muscles and the pectoral muscles as well as assisting with posture.

Active mobility exercises involve a slow stretch as far as it is possible for the athlete to reach, with the position being held for 10–12sec. The stretch position is then released, relaxed and the exercise repeated. Passive mobility exercises are performed with either a partner or a piece of equipment used to provide the force that stretches the muscles. Kinetic mobility exercises involve swinging, or rotating the limbs backward and forward, through their range of movement.

The more flexible and supple the athlete, the greater his range of movement. This means that in any race situation he will be more economical and cover more ground efficiently. If an athlete, for example, is losing a centimetre on every stride because poor flexibility is restricting his range of movement, he could lose up to a 150m during a 10,000m race, and more the further he races. Obviously this will have a profound effect on the athlete's performance in the race. Mobility will also aid his technique in the race situation and help him to react smoothly and efficiently to any explosive actions that may be required. It also helps the athlete to steer clear of injury, and, if injured, recover more quickly than the athlete who is less flexible.

It is advisable for the long-distance runner, because of the mileage covered in training, to stretch both before

Fig. 12. The same exercise is completed using the PNF method. The athlete's partner assists in easing her arms together, then holding them in position for the agreed time of the exercise. Most people have one side or arm that is more flexible than the other.

Fig. 14. This side view sees the athletes bringing their legs through the centre of the hurdle to be placed on the ground. This exercise stretches the gluteus and hamstring muscles and assists hip rotation.

Fig. 13. This exercise involves slow hurdling down the side of the hurdle. All the hurdle drills serve not only to improve flexibility, but also coordination, range of movement and stability. The athlete is bringing the outside leg over the outside of the hurdle. The body remains upright, the eyes focused ahead and the outside leg stable. This exercise routine strengthens and stretches the hip flexor, gluteus, abductor and adductor muscles.

tend to be more economical than middle-distance runners at submaximal running speeds.

Although a high VO_2 max is important for the high performance long-distance runner, this alone is not the determining factor; running economy is just as important in explaining individual differences in performance. Running economy is affected by several factors, including physiological demands, limb length and biomechanical factors connected to the running action, although the basic technical model is the most important. Good running economy can compensate in some instances for a relatively low VO_2 max value, particularly the further the distance being raced.

In tandem with mobility and good technique, the athlete should ensure that he has good *core stability*. This is not to be confused with *core strength*, which is developed by performing exercises specific to the muscles of the abdomen, buttock, back and hips. Most

of these exercises isolate a particular muscle group in order to develop specific strength (for example, back extensions). Core stability, on the other hand, is the integration of strength and coordinated movement. More specifically, it is the interaction of coordination and strength of the abdominal, back and buttock muscles during activity to ensure that the spine is stabilized. It provides a firm base to support both powerful and very basic everyday movements of the arms and legs.

POSTURE

Perfect posture is the basis of power and is interlinked with core stability. However, postural control is reduced through fatigue, which has significant implications for the high performance long-distance runner, who needs to be able to maintain this control throughout the duration of his event. Perfect posture should be a straight line through the whole of the body from the ear, through the shoulder, lumbar vertebrae three to five, down through the hip and knee to the foot.

The successful interlinking of mobility, core stability/strength and posture with the high performance long-distance runner's technical model is critical. Because of the requirement to perform for much longer than other disciplines, this technique must be correct and not break down during the course of the event through fatigue, pressure or stress. A good, relaxed technical model underpinned by perfect posture, core stability and

Fig. 15. The athlete moves down the centre of the hurdles as in the previous exercise. However, in this exercise the hurdles are closer together and instead of using the same leg over each hurdle, alternate legs have to be used. This has the effect of having to extend the lead leg. As in all the hurdle exercises, the athlete has to remain tall and have high knees. This exercise works hip mobility and the hip flexors.

mobility is much more likely to withstand competition stresses and training demands.

RELAXATION

An often neglected running technique is that of relaxation. The ability to relax in the race situation can be the difference between an average and a good performance, or a good performance and an outstanding one. It is particularly important for the high performance long-distance runner, who has to retain concentration and focus for long periods of time. There are three main areas in which the ability to relax has an important role to play. First, relaxing physically has a decided effect in both the training and competitive environments. Second, relaxing mentally avoids any undue stress, nerves or apprehension both prior to and during the racing situation. Finally, relaxing completely during rest and regeneration will aid and accelerate the recovery period.

It is therefore important that relaxation techniques don't become the neglected part of the training routine. This is not easy, particularly when there is so much else to include in a training programme. The following are

some of the methods that can be included in the three areas of physical, mental and relaxation training.

The physical side of relaxation training is a slow process that will evolve over a period of time. The first area to concentrate on is an efficient and economical technique, therefore drills and skills running must be included in the training programme. If the correct running technique or technical model is not in place it will be difficult for the runner to concentrate on relaxation. He must be constantly telling himself, and also being told by the coach if he has one, to relax, particularly during intense training sessions. In this way, it becomes automatic and the relaxed training model – even in high intensity sessions – can then be successfully transferred to the competitive situation.

The runner needs to bear in mind the following three key points when working hard or becoming fatigued. First, to keep the hands relaxed in the normal running position, not tensed or tight, so that there is no tension to spread to the shoulders and neck area. Second, to keep the head erect but relaxed, with no tension in the facial muscles and neck. Third, and possibly most importantly, the runner must concentrate on retaining his normal running stride length. The danger when working hard or feeling fatigued, is to let the normal running stride shorten, therefore losing distance on each subsequent stride. This is of particular importance in a long-distance race, where running economy needs to be maintained. If these three areas are constantly worked upon in training, they will become embedded in the running technique and therefore hold up much better in the stressful competition environment.

Some runners are naturally stronger mentally than others. When the training or race situation becomes tough, too many runners are likely to forget how to relax and succumb to a shortening of the stride, tensing and loss of technique, as mentioned above. However, the athlete who is stronger mentally will keep his focus and will be able to put these techniques into place even in the most stressful of conditions. Similarly, he is less likely to be affected by pre-competition nerves. Autogenic and mental rehearsal techniques can be useful in overcoming pre-competition nerves. In this situation, the runner sits down, composes himself, then goes through all the positive points that he needs to take into the competitive environment. These include such positives as how well training has been going, how he has improved over the last few months, how there is no one in the race to be worried about, how confident he is feeling and above all how much he is relishing the challenge of the race.

Once this positive frame of mind has been achieved, the runner needs to go through the areas of importance to focus on in the race. These will include the start,

Fig. 16. The support systems needed by the high performance long-distance runner.

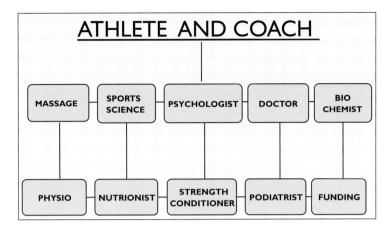

which needs to be a good, solid one but not too quick, pace judgment, relaxation, stride length and leaving enough energy for a strong finish. If the runner has a coach, he can assist in improving the athlete's self-belief by constantly reminding him of the positive points about his running. In this way, the runner will eventually overcome his nerves and put all the positive points into practice. Other mental relaxation techniques that can be used include meditation, progressive muscle relaxation (PMR), visualization techniques, autogenic training, breathing, flotation, restricted environment simulation therapy (REST) and music (see Chapter 5).

The third relaxation area to include is rest and regeneration. This can take many forms, but must be a complete break from running so that the athlete returns to training refreshed and reinvigorated both physically and mentally. One method is active rest, for example, cycling or playing a team activity. Another method is to have a massage, so that the tight, stiff muscles, particularly in the legs, are completely relaxed and regenerated ready for the next session. If this method is too costly or difficult to find, self-massage or water training is an ideal way of relaxing the muscles without any weight bearing taking place on them. The runner can employ normal aerobic training methods in the water, using a wet vest (buoyancy aid), or simply go through a swimming routine.

Therapies involving hot and cold techniques are another way to assist with rest, regeneration and relaxation. They can be carried out at a health centre using saunas and cold plunges, or they can simply involve alternating hot and cold showers for 30sec each. Taking a cold bath after a particularly intense training session or race can often help with getting rid of stiffness. It involves immersing either the whole body, or just the lower part, in a cold bath. The length of time will be dependent on how the runner reacts to this method. Initially, it should be for only a couple of minutes, until the body becomes used to the technique. Finally, the cheapest way to relax is to have a complete rest, so that there is no involvement with or thought about running.

SUPPORT SYSTEM

Because of the amount of time that a high performance long-distance runner spends training and the pressure he places on his body, the more likely he is to become injured. Having an effective support system in place will ensure that he is able to be proactive rather than reactive to any situation or development that may occur. A support system is necessary to ensure that training and racing take place without any problems (see Fig. 16), and could even be the difference between an athlete becoming a successful high performance long-distance runner, or just aspiring to be one. It could also be the difference between seriously injury, or diagnosing a problem quickly and preventing it being exacerbated further. The following should be included in an ideal support system: physiotherapist, nutritionist, masseur, psychologist, physiologist, bio-mechanic, doctor, podiatrist, financial support, facilities and, above all, rest and regeneration.

The concept of the support system is that it is athlete-centred, in order to ensure that the runner, during his intense training and heavy volume of mileage, remains injury-free. This then will ensure that he enters the race situation in the best shape possible, both physically and mentally. There can then be no excuses for a poor performance.

TACTICS

To ensure that all the hard work that has gone into the training programme reaches fruition, it is imperative that the athlete goes into a race with pre-arranged race tactics and that these tactics are successfully implemented. But they should also be flexible enough to cater for any eventualities that may occur in the course of the race.

A variety of methods can be included and adopted in training to simulate both tactical awareness and how to execute the tactics (see Chapter 7). These methods include the use of short sprints, long sprints, intermittent pace repetitions, increasing the pace repetitions, leading the pace throughout, acceleration sprints, reaction drills and an ability to increase pace in the middle of the repetitions. They should be practised throughout the year. They also help the body to adapt to the physiological demands of each tactic and aid the athlete's confidence and concentration levels.

The devised tactics, which will be one, or a combination, of the above, must be executed at the correct time and with the athlete being in the correct place to fulfil them. However, the plan should be flexible enough that the athlete can adapt it if anything goes wrong. This is particularly relevant to the longer distance races and the marathon, where the runner may not only have to react as instinctively and as explosively as in a middle-distance race, but there may also be other problems. Different tactics may need to be employed at different times and periods of the race and concentration and focus levels need to be maintained over a long period of time.

PSYCHOLOGICAL

Effective psychological preparation ensures that the athlete is both calm and confident, without being over-confident, about the forthcoming race. He needs to be in control of any emotions that could affect his performance and be totally committed to the forthcoming race.

The coach must ensure that his athlete is prepared both physically and mentally, and this is achieved during the training sessions. It is the coach's role to know his athlete and to be able to motivate him as required. This is only achieved after a great deal of interaction between the coach and athlete. The coach must appear calm at all times, as nervous coaches make nervous athletes. It is the role of the coach to give the athlete confidence, particularly in the way he is performing in training, so that the athlete can transfer this confidence to the race.

Many races are lost prior to the athlete stepping on to the track because of a lack of confidence, or by a failure of confidence during the race. The athlete has to be strong mentally as well as physically and have confidence in his own ability. He also has to have confidence in how his training has progressed and in his chosen tactical plan, otherwise all the hard training that

has gone before will not be maximized. In the longer distance races such as the marathon, where concentration levels, pain and fatigue are paramount, the high performance runner has to be very mentally resilient in order to succeed.

TIME MANAGEMENT

Time management is crucial, particularly for the high performance long-distance runner, as he has so much to fit into his hectic schedule. Because of the miles he needs to cover, time is at a premium. Without proper time management, planning and preparation, all the rest of the hard work, support,and training can flounder. Time management can only facilitate the specifics of a training programme – it is like the network of support systems that are required quality for a high performance long-distance runner to be successful. If correctly implemented, time management allows all the other qualities to be fully developed in the training sessions. It also allows the high performance long-distance runner time for rest and regeneration, a key component of the training programme.

As with the training session, time management is only a facilitator. However, it is of great importance on race days and particularly at major championships, when the athlete will be in a village situation and have his races spread over a number of days. The whole idea is to ensure that the athlete is correctly prepared and as fresh and rested as possible for the key race of the season.

NUTRITION

An athlete's body is like a Rolls-Royce car and therefore deserves to have the best fuel available put into it. This means having the correct carbohydrate loading, protein, vitamins, minerals, fats and fibre in the athlete's diet. The more miles/kilometres and sessions the high performance long-distance runner undertakes, the more of the correct food intake will be required. The marathon runner could also utilize a special carbohydrate-loading diet, which we will look at in more detail later. Special attention must also be paid to hydration, particularly as most major games take place in hot and/or humid environments.

Carbohydrates are the main source of energy. Bread, sugars, pasta, potatoes, rice and cakes are amongst the most common carbohydrate foods. Proteins are essential to growth and the repair of muscle and other body tissues, and can be found in such foods as vegetables, pulses, dairy products, meat, chicken, fish, milk and nuts.

Vitamins play an important role in many of the body's chemical processes. Different vitamins can be found in a variety of foodstuffs, but can be supplemented by multivitamin pills. It is of particular importance to take vitamin supplements for vitamin B, essential for energy production, and vitamin C, which is linked to oxygen transport and energy production. Both of these vitamins are water-soluble and therefore because of cooking and storage it cannot be assumed that the products that contain these two vitamins will have the required amounts when eaten. Both vitamins also become depleted during strenuous training and competition, so need to be replenished.

Minerals are crucial to the normal functioning of the body. Most diets contain sufficient quantities of minerals to meet the body's needs. However, because of the excessive training demands and loss through perspiration, it is advisable to take supplements in either tablet or liquid form. Fats are a source of energy and are important in relation to vitamins, but because of the length of time fatty foods take to digest and the fact that it takes more oxygen to release energy from fats than from carbohydrates, it is best to limit their intake. Fibre intake is very important to the health of the digestive system. Wholemeal bread and bran flakes are two examples of foods that supply essential roughage to help with the digestive system.

It is critical that the athlete, particularly after an intense training session, does not eat junk food or snacks. The food that he takes on board at this time should be applicable to his requirements, in order to help with the repair of body tissue. Fluid intake is also vital, particularly in hot weather and if leading up to a major games.

The race situation is similar to training, in that the body needs nourishing and invigorating. It is of particular importance that plenty of fluids are taken to help hydration, especially at major games, where there should be a constant intake of fluids and electrolyte drinks both before and during the games. The type of drink used should contain the same saltwater balance as the body and should be easily absorbed. The drink should also contain vitamin C, which is lost through perspiration, but should never be ice-cold, or have ice in them. It is also better for the athlete to sip the drinks, before, during and after competition, so as to replace water and salts lost from the body through perspiration. In a hot, humid climate the body requires more than double the normal fluid intake. Thirst is not a reliable guide to dehydration, although it is certainly an indicator. A strict check should be kept on bodyweight and the colour of the athlete's urine to ensure that he is not becoming dehydrated.

All of the above requirements – many of which are dealt with in greater detail in subsequent chapters – are part of the complicated jigsaw that comprises the complex make-up of the high performance long-distance runner. It is not only about running a high volume of miles. If attention is not given to all of the above requirements, in the correct proportions and ratios and with the correct balance, it could make the difference between being a winner, or a medallist, or just a finalist. Therefore great self-discipline and control are required by the high performance long-distance runner if he is to succeed.

CHAPTER 3

TRAINING METHODS AND EFFECTS

PHYSIOLOGICAL REQUIREMENTS

To understand what is required to be a successful long-distance runner, both the coach and athlete need to know what physiological elements and pathways are involved and, more importantly, how to train and develop them. This involves understanding how the body functions at rest and how these functions change when the body is working at maximum intensity, or, in long-distance running, how the body can maintain high performance levels for a sustained period of time. A clear understanding of which processes limit performance and how these limitations can be reduced through training is also necessary. However, all athletes are individuals and will respond differently to the different types of training. Similarly, because of their individual genetic composition, they will have different strengths and weaknesses. Therefore, using the scientific knowledge available, the training must be structured to meet each athlete's individual requirements.

FUNCTIONS AND SYSTEMS

The body is made up of many interdependent and interconnecting parts. The following are the most important in the long-distance runner's adaptation to training.

The smallest unit or building block in the body is the *cell*. The cell, whose processes are controlled internally by a nucleus, can adapt to what is required of it. Because of this, training levels can change fitness levels, as the body's cells adapt to what is required of them.

The human body comprises nine systems, which help the body to function. The *skeletal system* involves movement, protection, support, calcium storage and blood cell production.

The *muscular system* both supports and activates movement. There are three distinct types of muscle

tissue found in our bodies. Skeletal muscle is attached to bones and is the voluntary, contractile tissue that moves the skeleton about. Knowledge of the structure, function and response to training of this type of muscle is important. Smooth muscle is involuntary muscle and is found in the walls of the tubular organs such as the digestive, circulatory and respiratory systems. These muscles are concerned with the movement through these systems and their action is spontaneous. Cardiac muscle is an involuntary muscle found only in the heart. It contracts on its own, constantly and without becoming fatigued.

Muscle fibres fall into two categories. There are red, or slow twitch, fibres (categorized as Type I), which are characterized by a greater endurance capacity but relatively slow action. These muscles use predominantly aerobic sources and are very important to the long-distance runner. The opposite white, or fast twitch, muscle fibres (categorized as Type II), are characterized by a high speed of contraction but relatively low endurance capabilities. They use predominantly anaerobic and glycolytic pathways.

These two types of muscle fibre are the extreme opposite of each other and intermediary types of muscle fibres have now been identified. The fast twitch fibre group (Type II) can be subdivided into an intermediary group, between the slow and fast twitch fibres, known as Type IIa. The pure fast twitch fibre is known as Type IIb. The intermediary type of muscle fibres IIa shares features of both muscle Type I and muscle Type IIb and can be thought of as fast twitch, oxidative-glycolytic fibres. This fibre is able to obtain the energy it requires from both the oxidative pathways or from the anaerobic-glycolytic pathways. It is therefore of great importance to the endurance runner (see Fig. 17) and also the characteristics of the muscle types (see Fig. 17a).

Muscles are used or recruited in pairs and this accomplished by the:

- agonists, or prime movers, which are the muscles primarily responsible for movement

Type of Fibre	Type I Slow Twitch (ST) Oxidative	Type IIa Fast Twitch (FTa) Oxidative-Glycolytic	Type IIb Fast Twitch (FTb) Glycolytic
Aerobic or oxidative capacity	high	moderately high	low
Anaerobic or glycolytic capacity	low	high	highest
Number of mitochondria	high	intermediate	low
Contractile speed	slow	fast	fastest
Fatigue resistance	high	moderate	low

Fig. 17. Table of muscle fibres.

- antagonists, which are the muscles that oppose the agonists
- synergists, which are the muscles that assist the prime movers.

Similarly, muscle movement can be categorized into three types of action or movement:

- concentric action, which is when the muscle shortens – the actin and mysolin filaments slide across each other – to perform an action
- static action, which is when the muscle generates force without moving. This is often referred to as an isometric action. If enough motor units are recruited, it can become a dynamic action

- eccentric action, which is when the muscles exert force while lengthening. Because this involves a joint movement, it is also a dynamic action.

In high performance endurance runners, muscles are used in different ways. Muscular strength is the maximum amount of force generated by a muscle or group of muscles. Muscular power is the combination of strength and the speed of movement – strength at speed. Muscular endurance is the ability of the muscles to sustain repeated muscular actions without the onset of fatigue. Endurance-trained muscles store more glycogen and fat than untrained muscles; this is because with aerobic training the body becomes more efficient at using fat and as an energy source, allowing muscle and liver glycogen to be used at a slower rate.

Slow Twitch (ST) – Oxidative Fibres	Fast Twitch (FT) – Glycolytic Fibres
Red or tonic fibres, e.g. soleus	White or phasic fibres, e.g. triceps brachii
Longer muscle fibres – greater length change	Smaller muscle fibres – smaller length change
Maintenance of posture	More rapid voluntary movements
Quicker to recruit – smaller connecting neurons and lower threshold for recruitment	Slower to recruit – larger connecting neurons and needs higher stimulation
Longer time required to reach peak tension	Shorter time to reach peak tension
Fewer muscle cells per motor unit – less strength capability	More muscle cells per motor unit – greater strength capability
Good endurance – slow fatigability	Poor endurance – rapid fatigability
Oxidative enzymes predominant	Glycolytic enzymes predominant
More mitochondria	Fewer mitochondria
Greater surrounding capillarization	Lesser surrounding capillarization
No change in glycogen after repeated stimulation for 2hr	Stimulation at relatively low frequency reduces glycogen stores

Fig. 17a. Characteristics of slow and fast twitch muscle fibres.

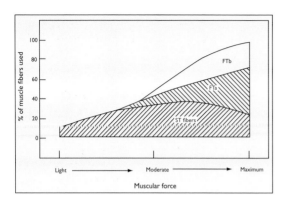

Fig. 18. A cross-section showing the different types of muscle fibres revealing the relationship between intensity and the utilization of fast and slow twitch fibres during exercise (after R. Uebel, 1987).

All of these movements and actions are planned, initiated and co-ordinated by the *nervous system*. The motor unit is the fundamental unit for muscle contraction and innervates muscle fibres of a single type. The integrated processes of recruitment, summation and synchronization achieve muscle control and regulation. Specific neuro-muscular training will contribute to a more efficient system.

The *circulatory system* ensures that the heart efficiently sends the oxygenated blood around the body. It carries oxygen from the lungs to the body cells, as well nutrients and hormones to them. It also takes away carbon dioxide and other waste products from the cells. It takes heat to the skin's surface to maintain the constant internal body temperature. It is a system that adapts well to training. Understanding how this system responds and adapts to training and its role in oxygen transportation is essential when designing a training programme.

The *respiratory system* is responsible for providing the body with oxygen and bringing it into close contact with the blood. It is also responsible for the exchange of gases with the environment, where note should be made of environmental pollution and risk of asthma. Improvement in an individual's VO_2 maximum is a reflection of an improvement of the function of the cardio-respiratory system and the total capacity for aerobic work.

The *immune system* provides a line of resistance and defence against invading bacteria, parasites and viruses. The system depends on the actions of specialized cells and antibodies, which eliminate or neutralize these foreign invaders that may cause illness. Unfortunately, one of the most serious consequences of heavy training is the negative effect it has on the body's immune system. Excessive or heavy training suppresses the normal immune function, increasing the athlete's susceptibility to infections. Short bouts of intense exercise can temporarily impair the immune response, with successive days of heavy training amplifying this suppression. Also, intense exercise during illness might decrease the ability to fight off infection and increase the risk of even greater complications. It is also judicious that after the blocks of high volume or intense training, the high performance long-distance runner has a less intense week to allow the body to adapt to the training levels and to recover. In this way, he will not be as susceptible to either illness or infection while his body is vulnerable.

The *digestive system* breaks down food and prepares it for absorption into the blood system. The *excretory system* deals with the elimination of the waste products from the body. The final system, the *endocrine, or hormonal, system*, is involved with the production of chemical messages that regulate the body's functions.

The systems also work together, for example, the skeletal and muscular systems work together and are referred to as the *musculo-skeletal system*. It is also worth noting that skeletal muscle mitochondria increase in both size and number with endurance training, providing the muscle with a more efficient oxidative metabolism. Skilled movement is the result of the co-ordinated activity of the nervous and muscular systems, referred to collectively as the *neuro-muscular system*. Any drill that assists the athlete in the development of his co-ordination can be referred to as a neuro-muscular exercise. The circulatory and respiratory systems work together. They transport oxygen to where it is needed and are known as the *cardio-respiratory system*. Training this system helps the body to sustain the prolonged exercise that is the basis of endurance running. Aerobic training also increases both the number of capillaries per muscle fibre and the cross-section of muscle, thus improving blood perfusion in the muscle. Because of this training, it stresses slow twitch fibres more than fast twitch fibres.

Homeostasis describes the maintenance of a stable internal environment within the body, which is essential for its effective operation. Homeostasis is achieved through the combined actions of the nervous and endocrine systems. The provision for this stable body environment, even when external conditions are making demands, is a whole-body function. It involves compensatory mechanisms, which influence all the cells to act as a whole and to adapt to changes, including the demands of training. Conditions that require control through homeostasis are body temperature, blood pressure, blood glucose levels, fluid and water balance and the oxygen and carbon dioxide concentration of the blood, all of which are important to the long-distance runner because of the duration of both his training and racing.

Hormones are the guardians of homeostasis, as they regulate organic functions through their individual and combined roles. An understanding of hormone function is essential to determine the athlete's fitness level, his health and ability to recover.

All of the above systems are important to the high performance long-distance runner, but the cardio-vascular, respiratory and the muscular systems are of particularly high importance. Using this knowledge, the coach and his athlete must ensure that their training has the correct effect, relative to the athlete, the event and the time of year.

A long-distance runner has to tailor his training to the physiological demands of his event. The three predominant energy pathways he uses are the *alactate system*, sometimes referred to as the *ATP-CP system*, the *anaerobic system*, sometimes referred to as the *lactic, or glycotic, system*, and the *aerobic system*, sometimes referred to as the O_2 *system*. The one the long-distance runner will train and utilize the most will be the aerobic, or O_2, system. Fig. 19 below highlights and emphasizes the role of this system in the requirements of the long-distance runner.

These three systems are inter-related. They also have different percentage involvement in the different long-distance events (see Figs 20–22). These systems are dependent on both the intensity and duration of the exercise. They all serve as different pathways to provide the energy for the resynthesis of ATP. Fig. 19 emphasizes the type and balance of training required by long-distance runners with regard to their particular events and how this should be incorporated into individual training programmes and long-term development.

None of these three systems can operate efficiently or be trained effectively without the support of the other highly complex systems of the body, which need to be functioning correctly.

Living cells are able to transform the potential chemical energy available within food into other forms of energy to maintain the normal functions of the body, such as mechanical energy, thermal energy for body heat and electrical energy to conduct nerve impulses. These processes are called metabolism. Exercise will affect the basal metabolic rate of an athlete, which is measured at rest. Metabolism is a remarkable process for providing the energy needed to power the body. Chemical energy is obtained from our nutrients in gradual stages and the most important substance in the body, which assists in the final release of energy, is *adenosine triphosphate* (ATP).

The *alactate*, or *ATP-CP*, *system* functions as follows: adenosine triphosphate (ATP) is broken down to adenosine diphosphate (ADP) to provide cells with energy for exercise and muscle contraction. The amount of ATP in cells, including muscle cells, is limited and is quickly depleted. However, ADP can be resynthesized back to ATP by the addition of another phosphate group. These two processes, one by which energy is utilized and the other, which produces energy, must be kept in balance; otherwise there could be a lowering of ATP levels. At maximum levels of effort, the ATP stored in the muscle will last for only 1–2sec of activity. The ATP-CP (creatine phosphate) is then activated as the main energy source to provide ATP, but at maximum effort will only provide it from between 5–7sec. Therefore using the ATP in the muscle, plus the resynthesized ATP using the ATP-CP system, maximum exercise can only be sustained from between 6–9sec. Therefore this system will be used predominantly in events such as the 100m. However, it still has an integral role to play within the long-distance runner's training programme. The formation of ATP provides the cells with a means of storing and conserving energy as a high energy compound.

Distance	ATP/CP (%)	Anaerobic-Lactate (%)	Total Anaerobic (%)	Aerobic (%)
100m	25	70	95	5
200m	15	60	75	25
400m	12	43	55	45
800m	10	30	40	60
1,500m	8	20	28	72
3,000m	5	15	20	80
5,000m	4	10	14	86
10,000m	2–3	8–12	10–15	85–90
Marathon	0	2–5	2–5	95–98

Fig. 19. Shares of energy supply mechanisms during different track events (according to Mader).

The *lactate system* – known also as the anaerobic or glycolytic system – will also make a contribution during these short maximum efforts of exercise. This system becomes the predominant supplier of ATP for longer, controlled, maximum efforts of up to 45sec in duration. The lactate system is dependent on glycogen and glucose as a fuel source in the muscle and involves the process of glycolysis, but in this case anaerobic glycolysis. Anaerobic glycolysis may work in the presence of oxygen, but does not require oxygen. It also produces quickly a small amount of ATP and also lactic acid. The lactate system is working all the time and not just when the body runs out of oxygen. Lactate is therefore being produced in the body at rest as well as during exercise. It is important to note that lactic acid and lactate are not the same compound. However, anaerobic glycolysis produces lactic acid, which quickly becomes lactate. Therefore, the terms are often interchangeable. The long-distance runner needs to ensure that his training programme evolves and develops so that he can build up a tolerance to lactic acidosis. Anaerobic training, unlike aerobic training, will help to improve muscle-buffering capacity, by increasing the ATP-CP and glycolytic enzymes.

This system can be sustained for up to 2min of intense exercise, but now the aerobic system (oxygen) begins to have a gradually increasing contribution. After 2min, the lactic system will no longer be the predominant energy source, but will switch to the aerobic system. This system is capable of fuelling relatively low-intensity exercise for a considerable period of time. The aerobic system is a complex system, which uses carbohydrate, fats and sometimes proteins in the provision of energy. Each of these fuels can eventually be combusted in the presence of oxygen to release energy to resynthesize ATP. This system produces more energy than the alactate or glycolytic systems. Therefore it is the system required

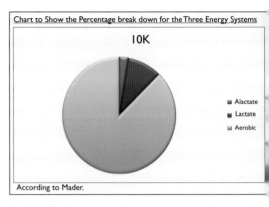

Fig. 21. *This chart shows the percentage breakdown of the energy pathway requirements for the 10,000m: alactate 2–3 per cent; anaerobic-lactate 8–12 per cent; aerobic 85–90 per cent.*

most by long-distance runners and should be a significant element their training programmes. It should be noted that within the total volume of the long-distance runner's training, through a variety of training methods, there will be a high percentage of aerobic running.

Using this knowledge of physiology and what the most effective training is for the high performance long-distance runner a training programme has to be devised. The training programme has not only to meet the demands of the event, but also maximize the athlete's strengths and weaknesses. With in the training programme the high performance athlete is also continually trying to develop four key areas that will enhance performance. These key areas described below are *maximum volume oxygen uptake* (VO_2 max), *running economy* (RE), *lactate threshold* (LT) and *lactate turning point* (LTP).

All of these key areas can be tested and monitored throughout the season by the use of treadmill tests.

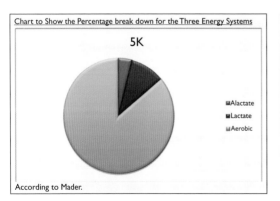

Fig. 20. *This chart shows the percentage breakdown of the energy pathway requirements for the 5,000m: alactate 4 per cent; anaerobic-lactate 10 per cent; aerobic 86 per cent.*

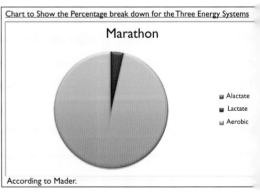

Fig. 22. *This chart shows the percentage breakdown of the energy pathway requirements for the marathon: alactate 0 per cent; anaerobic-lactate 2–5 per cent; aerobic 95–98 per cent.*

MAXIMUM VOLUME OXYGEN UPTAKE

One of the most common terminologies used in endurance running is maximum volume oxygen uptake, known as VO_2 max. What this actually means is the maximum rate at which ATP can be resynthesized through aerobic pathways, which is an important factor in endurance running performance. The test measures the percentages of the oxygen utilization against lactate levels (mL), the velocity (min-1) and bodyweight of the athlete (kg-1).

High performance male long-distance runners have VO_2 max values of 70–85 mL/ kg-1/min-1 (John Ngugi and Dave Bedford had values of 85 mL/kg-1/min-1), while their female counterparts have VO_2 max values of 60–75 mL/kg-1/min-1 (Grete Waitz was 73mL/kg-1/min-). These values are up to 45 per cent higher than non-athletic individuals of a similar age and gender.

In high performance long-distance runners, the highest VO_2 max values are found mainly in 5,000m specialists. This is because these athletes are required to run at 94–98 per cent VO_2 max to achieve their optimal performances. High performance 10,000m runners and marathon runners operate at approximately 90 per cent and 80 per cent respectively of their VO_2 max. Marathon runners run at lower intensities because other physiological factors become relatively more important to their success. High performance middle-distance athletes tend to have slightly lower VO_2 max values than high performance long-distance runners, reflecting the importance of the capacity to generate energy through oxygen-independent metabolism in these events, which are run at supramaximal intensities.

To highlight this further, the VO_2 uptake required to set world records for endurance events tends to rise incrementally from 800m (82.4 male/72.8 female) to a maximum at 5,000m and then begins to drop down the longer and more economical the distance being run. Maximal VO_2 is usually best assessed using an incremental treadmill test that brings the athlete to exhaustion in 7–10min, in which the treadmill gradient or speed is increased by 1 per cent, or 1km per hour, every minute (see Chapter 6).

RUNNING ECONOMY

Running economy (RE) is usually defined as the oxygen cost of running at a certain speed, or of running a certain distance. There is a great deal of individual variability in running economy, even with high performance long-distance runners. This is illustrated at a running speed of 16km (6min/mile pace). A running speed of 16km/h-1 is usually used in the assessment of RE because, in high performance distance runners, it is a submaximal speed that will be used as a staple part of their training. When RE is expressed in units of millimoles (mmol) of lactate, bodyweight and running speed, a value of around 200 is considered average, with values above and below this value representing poor and good economy, respectively. Good RE, for a given running speed, results in the utilization of a lower percentage of the athlete's VO_2 max while running at that speed, and therefore a reduction in muscle glycogen utilization and potentially less reliance on O_2-independent metabolism, resulting in a reduction in metabolic acidosis. High performance long-distance runners tend to be more economical than middle-distance runners at submaximal running speeds. This difference could be either genetic, or due to the larger training volumes that have to be undertaken by the high performance long-distance runner. Running economy is affected by various factors, such as physiological demands, limb length and biomechanical factors connected to the running action, with the basic technical model being the most important.

Running economy is usually measured over the range of submaximal running speeds at which the high performance long-distance runner performs in his endurance training programme. It is important that VO_2 is measured in the steady state, so stage durations in a treadmill test must be at least 3min long using incremental increases of 1 per cent. Although a high VO_2 max is important for the high performance long-distance runner, this alone is not the determining factor, particularly in groups of athletes with similarly high VO_2 max values. Here, factors such as RE are important in explaining individual differences in performance.

Good RE in some instances can compensate to a degree for a relatively low VO_2 max value in a high performance athlete. This emphasizes the importance of good running economy and efficiency. The difference between high performance long-distance runners who have the same maximum VO_2 is often determined by who has the most efficient RE at submaximal speeds, as the runner with the better RE will be able to run faster while utilizing less oxygen.

LACTATE THRESHOLD AND LACTATE TURNPOINT

Two terms that are similar, but in fact quite different, are lactate threshold (LT) and lactate turning point (LTP). The ability to exercise for long periods at percentages of

their maximum VO_2 is a characteristic of high performance long-distance runners and is also an important
factor of performance. The percentage utilization of
the maximum VO_2 during endurance competition is
linked to markers of blood lactate accumulation during
exercise, such as the lactate or ventilatory threshold,
lactate turnpoint, or onset of blood lactate accumulation (OBLA).

Lacate Threshold

The measurement of blood lactate concentration ([La-]
b) during exercise can provide useful information on
endurance performance potential and the extent of the
physiological adaptations to a sustained period of training.
An incremental treadmill test is used, involving between
seven to eight stages at progressively increasing speeds.
Initially, blood lactate levels remain close to the resting
value (that is, ~mM). However, at a particular running
speed, blood lactate begins to increase above this resting
value. The running speed at which this occurs is known as
the lactate threshold. The lactate threshold usually occurs
at 50–70 per cent of the maximum VO_2. However, it can
be as high as 80–85 per cent of maximum VO_2 in high
performance long-distance athletes.

The elevation of lactate in the blood at the lactate
threshold represents alterations to the metabolism and
does not necessarily indicate that the exercise has become
anaerobic. It should also be remembered that the blood
lactate reflects a balance between the rate of lactate production in the muscles, the rate of lactate flowing out of
the muscles to the blood and the clearance of lactate from
the blood. Exercise in high performance long-distance
runners near to the lactate threshold can be sustained for
up to 2hr, running at the same velocity, with blood lactate
being elevated but not accumulating over time. The lactate
threshold increases with consistent endurance training
at the correct levels. The lactate threshold is therefore a
good predictor for the performances of the high performance long-distance runner (see Fig. 23).

Lactate Turning Point

If the incremental treadmill test progresses on to higher
running speeds that exceed the lactate threshold, a
second sudden and sustained increase in blood lactate
(at around 2–4 mM) can be perceived. This second
threshold has become known as the lactate turning point
(LTP). During continuous longer term running between
20–60min, at running speeds between the lactate
threshold and the lactate turning point, blood lactate
will be raised above the original baseline values but will

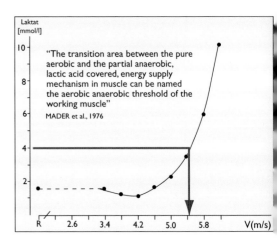

Fig. 23. Graph showing the lactate threshold level for a
long-distance runner. Here at a running speed of 5.6km
per hour with a lactate level of 4mmol, the athlete's
threshold level is reached. In many cases, these two
parameters are taken as the baseline.

remain relatively stable over a period of time. However,
during continuous exercise at running speeds above
the lactate turning point, blood lactate will continue to
increase with time until the exercise is terminated. The
lactate turning point therefore provides a good indicator
of the maximal lactate steady-state intensity. This is also
the point at which OBLA takes place and when the concentration of blood lactate reaches about 4mmol/L. The
maximal lactate steady state is when the running intensity
means that the maximal lactate clearance is equal to
the maximal lactate production. Fatigue in long-distance
endurance events has traditionally been linked to a
reduction in muscle cell efficiency, due indirectly to an
accumulation of blood lactate. Therefore, the ability to
delay and/or tolerate an increase in metabolic acidosis is
an important adaptation in endurance training.

An incremental treadmill test for the assessment of
lactate threshold (LT) and lactate turning point (LTP)
involves increasing running speed by 1km per hour, every
3min, and determining blood lactate from fingertip blood
samples taken during short breaks between stages.

The heart rate should also be monitored during the
last 30sec of each stage, enabling a number of heart rate
training zones for the athlete to be determined. This
is reflected in high performance long-distance runners
continuously running below the lactate threshold on
an easy run of between 20–40min, or longer, relaxed
runs of 60–120min. Continuous running between the
lactate threshold and lactate turning point is at the level
of good-quality steady-state aerobic running sessions of
between 30–60min. Continuous tempo or fast aerobic
running at just above the lactate turning point between

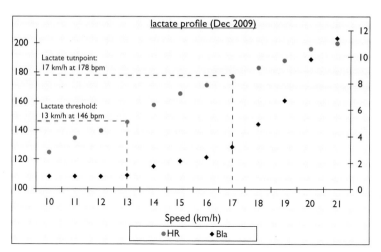

Fig. 24. Graph showing results of a scientific treadmill test. The heart rate is shown down the left-hand side of the graph, the running speed along the bottom and the lactate levels down the right-hand side. The lactate threshold was reached at a running speed of 13km per hour with a heart rate of 146 beats per minute and a lactate level of 5mmol. The lactate turning point was reached at a running speed of 17km per hour with a heart rate of 178 beats per minute and a lactate level of 8.5mmol. The circles on the graph depict the heart rate levels and the diamonds the blood lactate levels. This is part of a full assessment and should be used in conjunction with Fig. 131.

20–40min in total is equivalent to race preparation, also for raising the lactate turning point and for developing the athlete's lactate tolerance. Higher intensity training to stimulate the development of VO_2 max and the capacity to generate ATP through O_2-independent metabolism generally requires interval or repetition training at above the VO_2 max. These treadmill tests used throughout the season are a good indicator of how a training programme is progressing and developing, the adaptation and fitness levels of the athlete and any changes or modifications that may be required to the training programme.

Taking the above into account, a high performance long-distance runner needs to have:

- a high VO_2 max
- a high lactate threshold (or OBLA)

- a high lactate turning point
- a high running economy and utilization of effort
- a high percentage of slow twitch fibres.

Using this physiological knowledge, the devised training programme for the long-distance runner should ensure that the correct energy pathways, relevant to the athlete's event, are catered for in the correct percentages and developed at the correct rates. The following are the types of training effects that will occur because of the training sessions, where the aim is the development of each of the energy pathways. The development of them is known as total endurance and is shown in Fig. 25.

To ensure that the correct levels of intensity are adhered to when undertaking the following training sessions, the use of a heart-rate monitor can be of

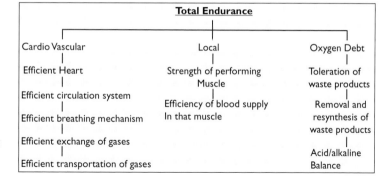

Fig. 25. This table shows the interaction between cardiovascular endurance and respiratory endurance (aerobic efficiency), with local muscular endurance (strength endurance) and anaerobic endurance (speed endurance) and their training effects.

Total Endurance		
Cardio Vascular	Local	Oxygen Debt
Efficient Heart	Strength of performing Muscle	Toleration of waste products
Efficient circulation system	Efficiency of blood supply In that muscle	Removal and resynthesis of waste products
Efficient breathing mechanism		
Efficient exchange of gases		Acid/alkaline Balance
Efficient transportation of gases		

value. It has a number of functions. First, it is a check to ensure that the required heart rates mentioned in the following training sessions are met. This allows the training session to be correctly controlled. If the heart rate is too high, the level of training intensity has been set too high for the athlete to reach at this time of the training year. Second, it checks that the recovery time is correct. The more rapid the drop in the pulse rates after a repetition, the better the training condition of the athlete. However, if the pulse rate does not drop quickly enough in the time allowed between repetitions, it means that the prescribed recovery is insufficient. Third, the heart rate for the aerobic-anaerobic threshold is approximately 168 beats/min. Therefore, training just below and above this level involves both the aerobic, but predominantly the anaerobic, energy pathways. Fourth, the resting pulse rate, which should be taken first thing in the morning, is a good indicator of the athlete's state of health. An unusual increase in the resting pulse rate often indicates the presence of a virus or infection. Fifth, the optimum training level, or threshold, can be deduced by subtracting the resting pulse rate from the pulse rate achieved after the greatest maximum effort. The figure remaining is known as the maximum pulse increase and should be used as a guide when setting the levels for the training programme. An example of this would be as follows:

- maximum pulse rate: 215
- resting pulse rate: 35
- maximum pulse increase: 180.

If the maximum training heart rate is required it can be estimated as follows:

- maximum heart rate = 215 − age in years, for example: maximum heart rate = 215 − 28 (age) = 187 beats/min.

Although not as scientifically accurate as lactate or laboratory testing, the use of heart rate monitors is a useful guide to ensuring that the levels of intensity and recoveries are being correctly adhered to. One of the aims of endurance training is to increase the volume of the flow of blood, through increased capillarization, opening up the existing capillaries, and a more effective redistribution of the blood. This is achieved by a greater stroke volume and a stronger heart, allowing for greater oxygen utilization. A highly trained endurance runner could have a resting heart rate as low as, or lower than, 30 beats/min. However, a high performance long-distance runner who has accrued many years and miles/kilometres in training will be able to read how his body

is reacting to a particular session, volume of training, or the type of training for a particular point in the athletic year. He also has the benefit of a second pair of eyes and the opinion of his coach, who will have obtained a great knowledge of his athlete through years of close observation.

TRAINING METHODS

Aerobic System

It is essential, when devising a training programme to improve aerobic capacity, to understand the responses and adaptations of the cardio-respiratory system to exercise and training, as well as its role in oxygen transport. This type of training is the staple diet of the long-distance runner's training programme. It is important that, when the training programmes are set, the lactate threshold and lactate turning point are taken into account when required. High performance long-distance runners will have high annual training volumes and the further their racing distance, the higher these volumes will be. However, these volumes have to be progressed over a number of years and throughout a season. The peak annual weekly mileage should not be kept constantly high, week in, week out, without reducing the volume at least every third or fourth week. If this is not done, the athlete is likely eventually to break down through an injury – for example, 140 miles/225km over a sustained period of time is likely to lead to overtraining and injury.

The following types of training should be incorporated into the training programme. It is noticeable with high performance long-distance runners that whatever type of training they are doing, it is always of a higher intensity than the norm. Marathon runners and 10,000m runners will do a good percentage of their training near to the required race pace; when in full training, they are never more than five weeks from racing fitness.

The main duration aerobic training methods involving the oxygen transportation system are:

- continuous long-distance run
- continuous steady-state run
- recovery run
- fast aerobic or tempo run
- lactate threshold run
- alternating pace run
- *fartlek*
- mixed training session
- repetition/interval training.

These training methods have a marked effect on both the athlete's respiratory system and cardiovascular system. Before any training phase is undertaken the athlete should take an aerobic fitness test. If he has not got access to a treadmill and scientific laboratory there is a variety of field tests available. He also may have a particular session or training run that he uses as a key indicator of his fitness levels. One such test should be over the duration of an hour, run at maximum speed, on a flat course. From the distance covered during this run the speed per kilometre can be calculated. Using this as the basis, all the aerobic training methods can then be developed and the percentages they need to be run at for maximum effect can be determined. To ensure that the aerobic training is progressing correctly, the athlete should be retested over the same duration and course every four to five weeks. This test is known as a VCR test (velocity of controlled running). Once the test is undertaken using the chart shown (Fig. 26) it will indicate the athlete's running velocity at this stage of his preparation. Using this test, it is then possible to determine the following percentages for the main training methods:

- repetitions = 100 per cent of test fitness level speed
- tempo run/fast aerobic run = 95 per cent of test fitness level speed
- long-distance run = 90 per cent of test fitness level speed

Table for the determination of prescribed velocities inbasic edurance training

Test			Vcr CALCULATIONS			TRAINING METHODS				
30 Min Test	45 Min Test	60 Min Test	Velocity	Time per km	Time per 400 m	Endurance run for Regeneration	30-90 min endurance run, or 30-60min tempo run			Extensive interval
						70%	85%	90%	97%	>100%
(m)	(m)	(m)	(m.sec)	/1km	/400m	/1k	/1k	/1k	/1k	/1k
5400	8100	10800	3.0	5:33	2:13	7:56	6:32	6:10	5:44	5:13-5:23
5580	8370	11160	3.1	5:23	2:09	7:40	6:20	5:53	5:33	5:03-5:13
5760	8640	11520	3.2	5:13	2:05	7:26	6:08	5:47	5:22	4:53:5:03
5940	8910	11880	3.3	5:03	2:01	7:13	5:57	5:37	5:12	4:43-4:53
6120	9180	12240	3.4	4:54	1:58	7:00	5:46	5:27	5:03	4:34-4:44
6300	9450	12600	3.5	4:46	1:54	6:43	5:36	5:17	4:55	4:26-4:36
6480	9720	12960	3.6	4:33	1:51	6:37	5:27	5:09	4:46	4:18-4:28
6660	9990	13320	3.7	4:30	1:48	6:26	5:18	5:00	4:39	4:10-4:20
6840	10260	13680	3.8	4:23	1:45	6:16	5:10	4:52	4:31	4:04-4:13
7020	10530	14040	3.9	4:16	1:42	6:06	5:02	4:45	4:24	3:56-4:06
7200	10800	14400	4.0	4:10	1:40	5:57	4:54	4:38	4:15	3:50-4:00
7380	11070	14760	4.1	4:04	1:38	5:43	4:47	4:31	4:11	3:44-3:54
7560	11340	15120	4.2	3:58	1:35	5:40	4:40	4:25	4:05	3:38-3:48
7740	11610	15480	4.3	3:53	1:33	5:32	4:34	4:19	4:00	3:33-3:43
7920	11880	15840	4.4	3:47	1:31	5:25	4:27	4:13	3:54	3:27-3:37
8100	12150	16200	4.5	3:42	1:29	5:17	4:21	4:07	3:49	3:22-3:32
8280	12420	16560	4.6	3:37	1:27	5:11	4:16	4:02	3:44	3:17-3:27
8460	12690	16920	4.7	3:33	1:25	5:04	4:10	3:56	3:39	3:13-3:23
8640	12960	17280	4.8	3:28	1:23	4:53	4:05	3:51	3:35	3:08-3:18
8820	13230	17640	4.9	3:24	1:22	4:52	4:00	3:47	3:30	3:04-3:14
9000	13500	18000	5.0	3:20	1:20	4:46	3:55	3:42	3:26	3:00-3:10
9180	13770	18360	5.1	3:16	1:18	4:40	3:51	3:38	3:22	2:56-3:06
9360	14040	18720	5.2	3:12	1:16	4:35	3:46	3:34	3:18	2:52-3:02
9540	14310	19080	5.3	3:09	1:15	4:30	3:42	3:30	3:15	2:49-2:59
9720	14580	19440	5.4	3:05	1:14	4:25	3:38	3:26	3:10	2:45-2:55
9900	14850	19800	5.5	3:01	1:13	4:20	3:34	3:22	3:07	2:41-2:51

Jonathu, U.; Krempel, R.; Haag, E.; Müller, H.: Leichtathletik 1 Rororo, Reinbek 1995, (Angaben nach Lange. G.; Pohlitz. L.)

| 9540 | 14310 | 19080 | 5.3 | 3:09 | 1:15 | 4:30 | 3:42 | 3:30 | 3:15 | 2:49-2:59 |

Fig. 26. This chart shows the results of VCR testing.

- steady-state aerobic runs = 85 per cent of test fitness level speed
- recovery runs = 70 per cent of test fitness level speed.

The test can be repeated at various important stages and phases of the season to ascertain adaptation and progress. Assuming everything is progressing correctly, it can also be used to recalculate the running speeds for each training method.

Other simple field tests that can be used to test an athlete's current fitness level, without entering a scientific testing laboratory, are the Balke, Billat and multistage fitness tests.

The Balke test involves running on a track at maximum speed for 15min. The distance covered is referred to on a chart, which predicts maximum VO_2 to an accuracy of 95 per cent.

The Billat test – devised by exercise researcher Professor Véronique Billat – involves running around a running track at maximum effort for 6min. From the distance covered, it is possible to calculate running velocity in metres per second to determine VO_2. For example, if the athlete has covered 1,800m in 360sec this means their running speed is 5m per second. Billat, after a great deal of research, has shown that 6min is the optimum amount of time that an athlete can operate at VO_2 max. Like all tests, it should be repeated to assess improvement at important stages of the athletic season.

The multistage fitness test involves a series of 20m shuttle runs at increasingly faster speeds, keeping in time to prerecorded signals until the athlete cannot keep pace with the recording. The shuttle runs are structured into a series of progressive levels and the highest level achieved is then referred to a table, which predicts the VO_2 max.

A large proportion of aerobic training will be with heart rates in the range of 120–160 beats/min, known as steady-state running. It is essential, particularly in the preparation phase, that a good aerobic base is built up so that the other training methods that are used later will gain the maximum benefit. The following types of aerobic training, if correctly deployed, will not only build up an aerobic base, but also maximum VO_2. Certain types of aerobic running, such as steady-state, recovery and long-distance runs, can be done in a group with other athletes. However, to get the maximum benefit, the members of the group must be of a very similar ability. Because of the specificity of *fartlek*, alternate-pace runs, tempo runs and repetition sessions it is better to do these individually, or in a very structured, controlled small group situation.

A key, but often neglected, component of long-distance running is rhythm. The long-distance runner needs to have a rhythm to his running when doing aerobic training, as this will assist with running economy and efficiency. It should be at a pace that is applicable to his event and the type of session he is undertaking, but

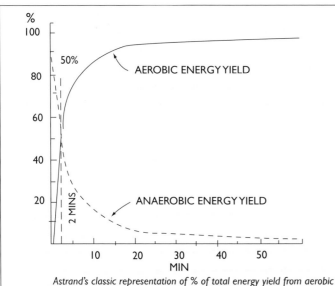

Astrand's classic representation of % of total energy yield from aerobic and anaerobic pathways, during maximal efforts of up to 60 mins duration, for an athlete of high maximal power for both types of energy production

Fig. 27. This graph shows the percentage amount of the aerobic and anaerobic energy pathways' yield during maximum effort up to 1hr in duration (after Astrand).

with the high performance long-distance runner this will be at a higher velocity.

Continuous Long-Distance Run

This will be carried out over times ranging from 45min to well over 2hr, depending on the runner's event. It is therefore advisable to do this run in the daylight and away from traffic in a stress-free environment. The speed determined by the chosen base fitness test will be at 90 per cent of the runner's maximum, with heart rates in the 140–165 beats/min. Because of the duration of the training run and the speed, this is a medium to high intensity training session, as it will not be too far away from race pace. Fig. 27 shows how the three energy systems are utilized in an hour's training run at this type of intensity.

Continuous Steady-State Run

This is the staple diet of aerobic training. It will be over distances of 10–15km, or longer, with a heart rate of 120–160 beats/min. The speed will be at 85 per cent of the athlete's fitness level. It is a medium-intensity session and is important to building up the aerobic base and running economy, and also in developing maximal VO_2. Because throughout the year this is the most repeated training unit it helps to vary both the surface and training environment where possible (see Fig. 28). What makes the high performance long-distance runner different from other long-distance runners is that he will, because of his VO_2 max and running economy, run his steady-state runners much faster than they will while still remaining inside the set parameters. Because of this ability, over a number of years of constant training at this level and intensity he will also improve both his lactate threshold and lactate turning point levels. For example, the African male runners do one-third of their total mileage running at 80 per cent to 100 per cent of VO_2 max., where 21km per hour would be 8 per cent pace. European runners tend to do only 10 per cent of their total mileage at 80–100 per cent.

The steady-state running speed – lactate below 4mmol – in high performance long-distance runners varies between 2min 50sec and 3min 10sec per kilometre. As well as being the highest percentage of an endurance runner's training programme, steady-state running close to the threshold level has the following effects:

- the improvement of blood supply through the development of the capillaries
- an increase in the mitochondrions
- the capacity to eliminate any accumulated lactate faster during work
- an increase in the contraction capacity of the heart muscles.

Fig. 28. Off-road steady-state running.

Recovery Run

This is an essential pert of aerobic running. It is of low intensity, run at 70 per cent of fitness level. The heart rate will be low, at 110–130 beats/min. This session should always follow a high intensity session such as a tempo run, a repetition session or a race to help the body recover and adapt. The distance covered in a recovery session should be no more than 40–50min of running time. If possible, it should be done on a surface that will not impact too much on the already fatigued legs. The aim of the session is to recover and refresh both physically and mentally.

Fast Aerobic/Lactate Threshold Run

This type of training is also known as tempo running. It is used once a week or every ten days, if there are no race commitments, and is done at 95 per cent fitness level, with heart rates of 160–175 beats/min. It is used to replicate the demands required in the race situation, raise the intensity level and also include a small anaerobic effect. This is a reasonably intense session, but should not stress the athlete, and is usually followed by a low-intensity recovery run. The distances covered in this type of session will vary from between 10–20km depending on the athlete's endurance event. In many cases, the speed of the run will be close to race pace.

Alternate-Pace Run

To ensure that all the training is not done at a similar pace, sessions such as an alternate-pace run can be introduced. This type of training will be used during a long-duration run, with the pace alternating every half-mile/kilometre, from steady to hard, to hard to steady, and so forth. Heart rates will fluctuate from 120 beats/min on the steady part, to 170 plus per minute during the harder bursts. This means that there will be a little anaerobic work on the faster sections, with the steady sections helping the recovery. This type of training is very beneficial in developing VO_2 max. The steady sections of the training run will be at 85 per cent of fitness level, whereas the faster sections will be at nearer 95 per cent. Distances will vary from 10–20km plus.

Fartlek

This is another similar session to the alternate-pace run. It is a Swedish word meaning speed play and involves all the energy pathways. It will involve short sprints, easy running, hill work, long sustained bursts and steady-state running all mixed together. The duration of the training session will be anything from 45min to well over an

hour. This type of training session will usually be run in a forest, on a golf course, on playing fields, canal paths or on parkland. The demands of the environment will affect the training response (see Fig. 29). Because all the energy pathways are being developed, there will be some high-intensity work involved. The heart rate will fluctuate from a 100 beats/min on the easy jog, up to 180 beats/min on the long sustained bursts of 1,000m plus. Like the alternate-pace run, if done correctly this is a medium- to high-intensity training session. Similarly, it is a beneficial training method for improving maximal VO_2 and, depending on the undulations of the environment, strength endurance as well.

This type of training is advantageous in four ways. First, it will help to develop all three energy pathways. Second, it will simulate the race conditions that the high performance athlete may expect when racing against runners from Africa. Third, because it covers so many units in one training session it frees up time later in the microcycle for more aerobic running. Finally, because of the duration of the session it keeps the volume of miles/kilometres high.

Over the years, variations of true *fartlek* training have evolved. The following type of *fartlek* is one that I have devised and used for a great many years. An example of this is as follows: a 60min *fartlek*, including fifteen bursts within the 60min, over different types of terrain, with a maximum hard burst of 1,200m and a minimum hard burst of 80m, all the other hard bursts being within these set two parameters. The athlete then chooses any other distance between the parameters for his other thirteen hard bursts; the recovery matches the distance run. Therefore, if a burst is 90sec long, the recovery will be 90sec.

The following variable examples of *fartlek* all have as part of the prescribed training a 10min warm-up and a 10min cool-down as a minimum:

• The Watson *fartlek* includes a 10min warm-up, followed by a 4min hard burst, followed by a jogged 1min recovery, repeated eight to ten times, and then a 10min cool-down.

Fig. 29. Group fartlek – if on a long burst the group fragments, the leaders can always jog back to the main group.

- The Saltin *fartlek* is a variation on the Watson *fartlek*, with hard bursts of 3min duration and again a 1min easy jog recovery, repeated six to ten times.
- The Astrand *fartlek* has a maximum effort of 75sec, followed by a 150sec jog recovery, followed by a maximum effort of 60sec and a 120sec jog recovery. This is repeated three times, then a 5min minute jog and repeated again twice.
- The Gerschler *fartlek* comprises the following session repeated three times: stride hard for 30sec, easy run 90sec. Then repeat with 15sec decreases in each easy recovery run down to 15sec. Jog 4min and repeat three times, for example 30sec hard/90sec jog recovery, 30sec hard run/75sec jog recovery, 30sec hard run/60sec jog recovery, 30sec hard run/45sec jog recovery, 30sec hard run/30sec jog recovery, 30sec hard run, 5sec jog recovery. Jog 4min recovery. Then return to a hard run of 30sec with 90sec recovery and repeat the set again down to 15sec recovery and then repeat a third time.
- With the Whistle *fartlek*, the coach, using a whistle, controls and dictates the session over a 1,200m circumference grass area. When the whistle is blown, the athlete runs hard until the whistle is blown again. In this way, the coach controls both the length of the repetition run and the recovery. Also the athlete does not know either the length of the burst or how long the recovery will be. This also assists with reinforcing mental toughness. The coach can employ a pyramid-type session of 4min, 3min, 2min, 1min, 2min, 3min, 4min, with a 60sec easy run recovery between each of these hard efforts.

These types of *fartlek* session can also, if required, be employed on hilly terrain using a variety of lengths of hills and gradients.

Mixed Training Sessions

These can incorporate a number of training sessions and energy pathways within a training session, similar to a *fartlek* session. Instead of just a threshold run or continuous aerobic steady-state run, both *fartlek* and mixed training sessions may be incorporated in one training session and more than once. For example:

- 15min steady-state run, followed by 30min run between the LT and LTP, followed by a 15min steady-state run. Total running time: 1hr; or 30min run between LT and LTP, followed by a 20min steady-state run, followed by another 30min run between LT and LTP. Total running time: 1hr 20min.

The distances, or duration, of the sections of the run can be longer or shorter depending on the athlete's event, time of year and fitness level. He can also just run the stated sections at LT pace. An even more complex example of a mixed training session that incorporates LT runs, hills and repetition running is as follows:

- 10min threshold run, 3min jog recovery, 6 × 6min with 45sec recovery between each repetition, jog 3min, 6 × 3min with 30sec recovery between each repetition, jog 3min, 6 × 1min hills with jog back recovery between each hill repetition, jog 3min and finally a 10min threshold run. Total training time: 80min; total running time including jogged recoveries: 100min plus. This can again be varied in distance and duration, with or without the hills, depending on the athlete's event and fitness and the time of year.

Repetition/Interval Training

This is a high intensity type of training session, which has a number of variables that are determined by the athlete's fitness and the time of year. It is run at 100 per cent of the athlete's fitness level and will involve heart rates in the region of 165–185 beats/min. Because of this, the pace that the repetitions are run at – depending on the time of year – may well be at or above race pace.

The variables available for this particular type of session are the duration of each repetition/interval, the recovery between each repetition, the type of recovery, the number of repetitions or sets, the intensity of the repetitions and the type of environment in which the training session takes place. Because of the variables involved and how these variables are used, there is a variety of training effects. An overview of the many variables used in repetition running is shown in Fig. 30:

- The *duration* of the repetitions can be either a distance, such as 200m intervals, 1 mile repetitions or longer, or a repetition for a certain length of time. The time repetitions will be of short duration (15sec to 2min), of medium duration (2min to 8min), or long duration (over 8min) (see Fig. 32). The high performance long-distance runner will tend to do more long-duration repetition training.
- The *type of recovery* used can be a   half the time of the repetition), a jogged distance recovery (400m jog), or a pulse recovery (once the pulse returns to 120 beats/min the next repetition

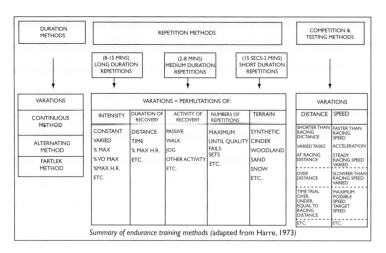

Fig. 30. An overview of the many different types of training methods, terrains, recovery and variety in endurance training (adapted from Harre, 1973).

DURATION METHODS	REPETITION METHODS			COMPETITION & TESTING METHODS
	(8-15 MINS) LONG DURATION REPETITIONS	(2-8 MINS) MEDIUM DURATION REPETITIONS	(15 SECS-2 MINS) SHORT DURATION REPETITIONS	

VARATIONS	VARATIONS = PERMUTATIONS OF:					VARATIONS	
	INTENSITY	DURATION OF RECOVERY	ACTIVITY OF RECOVERY	NUMBERS OF REPETITIONS	TERRAIN	DISTANCE	SPEED
CONTINUOUS METHOD	CONSTANT	DISTANCE	PASSIVE	MAXIMUM	SYNTHETIC	SHORTER THAN RACING DICTANCE	FASTER THAN RACING SPEED
ALTERNATING METHOD	VARIED	TIME	WALK	UNTIL QUALITY FAILS	CINDER	VARIED TASKS	ACCELERATION
FARTLEK METHOD	% MAX	% MAX H.R.	JOG	SETS	WOODLAND	AT RACING DISTANCE	STEADY RACING SPEED VARIED
	% VO MAX	ETC.	OTHER ACTIVITY	ETC.	SAND	OVER DISTANCE	SLOWEER THAN RACING SPEED VARIED
	% MAX H.R.		ETC.		SNOW	TIME TRIAL OVER, UNDER, EQUAL TO RACING DISTANCE	MAXIMUM POSSIBLE SPEED TARGET SPEED
	ETC.				ETC.	ETC.	ETC.

Summary of endurance training methods (adapted from Harre, 1973)

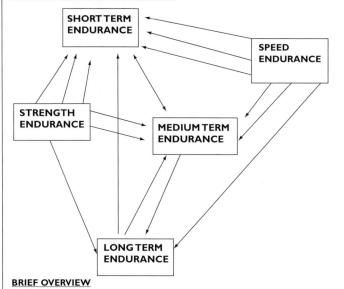

ENDURANCE TRAINING

Certain types of exercise and training will INCREASE certian bodily functions whilst others decrease them. The following is a look at these various methods, and their effects.

CHARACTERISTICS OF ENDURANCE

SHORT TERM ENDURANCE

SPEED ENDURANCE

STRENGTH ENDURANCE

MEDIUM TERM ENDURANCE

LONG TERM ENDURANCE

BRIEF OVERVIEW

1. Short Term Endurance (Aerobic) – 45 seconds to 2 minutes duration
2. Medium Term Endurance (Aerobic) - 2 to 8 minutes duration
3. Long term Endurance (Aerobic) - 8 minutes plus
4. Speed Endurance (Anaerobic) – loads between 85%-100% maximum
5. Strength Endurance (Anaerobic) – loads 4-6 x 25%-50% up to 3-5 x 50%-70%
6. Note the three Anaerobic Pathways – 5 seconds up to 2 minutes

Fig. 31. This schematic diagram depicts the interrelation and interlinking of the various types of endurance training and their importance to each other. The more interlinked they are, the more dependent they become on each other.

can be started). One to one recovery can also be used (the recovery is the same as the time achieved for the repetition). The high performance long-distance runner will tend to use very short jogged recoveries.

- The *recovery* can be passive, such as sitting or lying down, a walked recovery, a jog recovery, or some other active recovery. The most effective is the jog recovery, as this allows the runner to keep warm and get rid of the waste products that have built up in the body, thereby hastening recovery. This is the type of recovery the high performance long-distance runner will employ.
- The *number of repetitions and sets* used in any particular session will be determined by fitness level, the time of year and the required effect of the session. Once fit, the high performance long-distance runner will expect to do a large number of repetitions in sets initially, then as one set.
- The *intensity* of the session will be a set constant speed, a variable speed, or at a percentage of the runner's maximum heart rate, fitness level or VO_2 max. This will be dictated by the time of the year, the runner's event and his fitness level.
- These types of repetition sessions can be done on any *type of terrain*, such as a synthetic track cinder track, woodland, canal paths or forest paths, parkland, golf courses, sand or road.

The main aim of these types of sessions is to build up the athlete's aerobic base and maximum aerobic capacity, and to get his body to adapt to the requirements of his event.

Please note that throughout the following pages the suggested training session examples will be written as follows:

(sets × repetitions) × (distance) × (intensity or pace) × (recovery between repetitions) × (recovery between sets).

Three examples for a 5,000m runner are:
15 (repetitions) × 400 (metres) in 60 (sec) with 1 (minute recovery between each repetition)
3 (sets) × 5 (repetitions) × 300 (metres) in 42 (sec) with 40 (sec) between each repetition and 5 (minutes between each set)
2 (repetitions) × 1,500 (metres) at (100 per cent effort) with 8 (minutes recovery between repetitions), then 20 (minutes) recovery before 5 (repetitions) × 200 (metres) in 26 (sec) with 2 (minutes recovery between each repetition).

The following are examples for a 10,000m runner showing how a repetition session, using the same distance, can be progressed throughout the season. As the number of repetitions is increased and the recoveries are reduced, the speed will remain constant, or be increased due to an improving fitness level.

For a 10,000m runner in late November during the mid-preparation phase:

- 6 × 1,500m, on grass, with 3min jog recovery, with the intensity at 100 per cent of fitness level.

Late January during the early part of the specific-preparation phase:

- 2 × (5 × 1,500m) on grass, with 1min 30sec jog recovery, and 3m between sets, at 100 per cent intensity of fitness level.

Late March during the mid-specific-preparation phase:

- 10 × 1,500m on grass, with 1min jog recovery at 110 per cent of fitness level.

Fig. 32. An individualized repetition training session.

Fig. 33. An individualized repetition training session with athletes of different abilities. The athletes in the foreground are doing parts of the same session as the athletes who are chasing them. In this way, the training emphasis and needs of each athlete are maximized.

A world-class 10,000m runner covering 170–180km per week in winter would include the following types of repetitions during this period:

- 5–20 × 300m 48–50sec target 100m, jog recovery between repetitions in 40sec; or
- 15–20 × 400m 64–66sec target 200m, jog recovery between repetitions in 50sec; or
- 10 × 1,200m 3min 30–35sec target 400m, jog recovery in 90sec.

During summer:

- 12 × 300m 44–46sec, with 100m jog recovery in 30sec; or
- 25 × 400m 62–64sec, with 200m jog recovery in 50sec; or
- 6 × 1,000m 2min 35sec, 1,000m jog in 4–5min; or
- 5 × 2,000m 5min 30sec, 800m jog in 3min 15sec; or
- 4 × 500m 61/62sec; 5 × 300m 45sec; 10 × 200m 28sec, all with 100m jog recovery, for example 40sec.

As well as using single or multiple sets, there is a number of other variables on repetition running, four examples of which are shown here:

- A pyramid-type session for a 10,000m runner on grass during the specific preparation phase (February/March) could be: 2min; 4min; 6min; 8min; 6min; 4min; 2min repetitions, with either 2min recovery between repetitions, or half the previously run repetition, which would be 1min, 2min, 3min, 4min, 3min, 2min for a combined repetition running time – not including the jog recoveries – of 32min.
- Using a mixture of longer repetitions on grass with shorter repetitions during the specific preparation phase will involve a session as follows: 6 × (5min/1min) with 20sec between each repetition and 90sec between sets. This gives an overall running time – not including the jog recoveries – of 36min.
- Because of the impact involved when running on a track, it is sometimes advisable to devise a session that involves both track and grass repetitions, or at least the recovery jogs done on grass. However, the proximity of the grass to the track is of great importance for this session to be possible. The session is as follows: 5 × 3min on grass, with 1min recovery, followed by 10 × 400m on the track, with 30sec recovery, followed by 5 × 3min on grass with 1min recovery, with 2min recov-

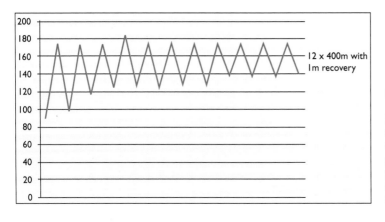

12 x 400m with 1m recovery

Fig. 34. Session of 12 repetitions × 400m, with 1min recovery between each repetition. The graph depicts the training heart rates after each repetition. This session took place at the end of the specific preparation phase. Because it is an early track session it would be done in racing flats, not spikes.

Fig. 35. Heart rates for a session of 5 × 800m, with 2min recovery. The training chart is during the pre-competition phase.

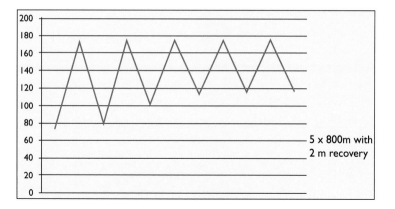

ery between sets. The approximate running time, depending on the speed of the 400m repetitions, would be between 40/41min of running, not including the jog recoveries.

- A beneficial session involving a group of athletes of varied ability and gender that will ensure they run to their maximum is the following grass session known as 'out and back', a couple of examples of which are shown here: 3 × (2 × 6min) with 5sec turn-round between repetitions and 3min jog recovery between sets (running time, excluding jog recoveries - 36min); or (2 × 6min) (2 × 5min) (2 × 4min) (2 × 3min) (2 × 1min), with 5sec turn-round and 3min, 2min 30sec and 2min respectively between each set. Running time excludes jog recoveries of 38min. In each of the two examples, the first repetition of each set is run outward. In the first example, this would be for 6min. Therefore, the strongest, fastest and most able athlete will lead the way on the outward leg, with the others following relative to their ability and fitness levels. The athletes then have a 5sec turn-round to run the second repetition of each set – in

the first example this again would be 6min – back to the starting point. We now have a situation where the fittest athlete, instead of being chased out by the other athletes, will now have to pursue them on the return to the start point. If all have run each repetition as required on the way out, the athletes should all finish together, or nearly together, at the end of each of the second repetitions in each set. This makes it fun, competitive and involves all the athletes. It also allows those who are not as strong or fit to miss a set and still be competitive on the repetitions they take part in.

A world-class marathon runner or 10k runner could run 5 × 2,000m with a 40sec recovery, during which period lactate samples are taken to monitor the training sessions. These set repetition times would be on either side of the season's goal pace (6min 10sec), decreasing by 5sec on each repetition, from 6min 20sec down to 6min. This would be a key training component and the results of the training session progressions leading to a marathon in late August showing lactate and heart rates are below:

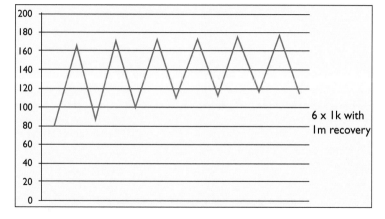

ig. 36. Heart rates for 6 × 1km, ⱴith 1min recovery. The training chart s at the end of the pre-competition ⱷhase about to enter the competition ⱷhase. The repetitions are run t – because of the length of the ⱸcovery – slightly quicker than the ⱸquired race pace.

5 × 2,000m	Test in June	Test in July	Test in August
6min 20sec	1.9mmol/171beats/min	1.3mmol/167beats/min	1.1mmol/167beats/min
6min 15sec	2.5mmol/175beats/min	2.0mmol/171beats/min	1.4mmol/168beats/min
6min 10sec	3.1mmol/177beats/min	2.5mmol/175beats/min	2.0mmol/172beats/min
6min 5sec	3.8mmol/178beats/min	3.1mmol/179beats/min	2.1mmol/174beats/min
6min	5.9mmol/185beats/min	5.0mmol/182beats/min	2.8mmol/172beats/min

Fig. 37. Table showing marathon test progressions in lactate/heart rate and velocity at key parts of the pre-competition and competition phases (Dr D. Faraggiana, EACA Congress, 1991).

As with all the above training sessions, the distances or duration of each repetition, the number of sets, the number of repetitions, the length and type of recoveries, the terrain and total training time involved are all determined by the high performance athlete and his coach with the time of year and the demands of the event uppermost in their planning process.

By progressively improving his maximal oxygen uptake, the athlete will also improve the function of the cardiorespiratory system and his capacity for aerobic work. Appropriate aerobic training will produce the following changes, which combine to improve VO_2 max:

- increased utilization of oxygen in and out of the lungs
- increased diffusion of oxygen from the lungs into the blood
- a more efficient transport of oxygen by the blood
- a more effective circulation of blood to the muscles
- an increased number and efficiency of capillaries
- an increased size and number of mitochondria
- an increased concentration and activity of aerobic enzymes.

Therefore, the greater the amount of oxygen (VO_2 max) that can be utilized, the more efficient and effective the athlete becomes, particularly when he has an excellent running economy. Females will have a VO_2 max approximately 10 per cent lower than that of their male counterparts. This is due to the following factors involved in the transport and uptake of oxygen:

- smaller lung volumes
- lower stroke volume
- smaller heart size and stroke volume
- lower blood volume
- lower levels of haemoglobin.

The three energy systems do not work independently. All of them are active during exercise to a greater or lesser extent. In this context, the aerobic system uses oxygen to provide energy for the resynthesis of ATP.

Alactate (ATP-CP) System

Training the ATP-CP system will involve maximum efforts of between 1–9sec in duration. This is because of the amount of ATP stored in the muscles and the amount that can be resynthesized utilizing the ATP-CP system. Therefore, most of the training will involve maximum efforts (100 per cent) within these time parameters of 4–9sec, or as part of a longer time period where some of the running will be at submaximal level. This type of training is primarily to improve the athlete's pure speed and to assist with his acceleration and change of pace. It should always be done when fresh and with focus on technique and relaxation.

A good retest of an athlete's speed to see if there has been an improvement is the 'flying speed' test. The test is conducted over 40m from a standing start. Times are taken at 20m and 40m, to indicate how good his acceleration is. However, the key time is between 20m and 40m, which is deduced by deducting the two times from each other; this is the called the 'flying 20m'. This is because this 20m segment is when the athlete is at his maximum speed and is an indicator of his sprinting ability. It is important that some element of this type of training is incorporated into the high performance long-distance programme, to ensure that the athlete's ability to react, accelerate and change of pace is developed. At the highest level of competition in all endurance events the ability to accelerate, increase speed, or at least main tain it at the end of a race, is paramount. The following are some of the methods that can be used to improve this energy system:

- sprint drills and dynamic stretching
- pure speed sprinting
- up-the-clock session

- down-the-clock session
- pyramid training session
- downhill sprinting
- acceleration sprinting
- zigzag run
- skills sprinting.

Sprint Drills and Dynamic Stretching

These are a good introduction to training this energy system. Both are progressive, culminating in explosive movement over a short period of time. This type of training should be done at the start of the training session. As in all the training methods used for this energy system, an emphasis on technique is essential. A high performance long-distance runner should ensure that he includes these both in his warm-up and training programme (see Figs 38–39 on drills and dynamic stretching).

Pure Speed Sprinting

Pure speed sessions commence from either a rolling or standing start over distances of 30–70m. It is preferable for the long-distance runner to employ a rolling start, as this is less explosive and so less likely to cause injury. The efforts are at maximum velocity, with a complete

Fig. 39. This side view depicts the driving and bouncing off the rear foot, with the high knee action work in tandem with the active arms. These exercises should take place between 10–30m, with emphasis on good technique and relaxation. The drills are progressed through walking, hopping and skipping to ensure that the body is thoroughly warmed up and stretched.

recovery between each repetition, a small number of repetitions in each set and a reasonable number of sets in total. This type of session should be done when the athlete is fresh and with an emphasis on technique and relaxation. An example of this type of session is as follows: 2 sets × 4 repetitions × 60m; recovery: 2–3min between repetitions and 8min between sets.

Up-the-Clock Session

An up-the-clock session is run at maximum velocity, with a complete recovery between each repetition, progressing as follows: 30m/40m/50m/60m/70m/80m; recovery: 2–3min between each repetition.

Down-the-Clock Session

A down-the-clock session is the same session as up-the-clock but in reverse, culminating with the shortest sprint: 80m/70m/60m/50m/40m/30m; recovery: 2–3min between each repetition.

Fig. 38. A drill as part of a dynamic stretching programme warm-up. With this drill, which is done with a bounce, is far more active and more relevant to running. The knees are kept high, driving from the rear foot with a bounce action and active arms. These types of exercises have been proven to prepare the athlete better for a demanding training session.

If more than one set of either the up-the-clock or down-the-clock sessions are undertaken, there should be at least 8–10min between the sets.

Pyramid Training Session

A pyramid training session would commence with the shortest sprint and progress to the longest sprint before returning back down to the shortest sprint. As in each of the other activities the repetitions should be run at maximum velocity, with the emphasis on technique and relaxation and a complete recovery between each repetition and each set. A typical example of a pyramid session is follows:

50m > 60m >70m > 80m > 70m > 60m > 50m;
recovery: 3min between each repetition.

If the high performance long-distance runner wishes to improve his change of pace by making the pyramid repetitions longer, in order to get the maximum alactate affect he should build up the pace on each repetition so that he is only at maximum velocity for a maximum of 80m. This could apply to any of these sessions: 140m > 160m >180m > 200m > 180m > 160m > 140m; recovery: 3min between each repetition.

Downhill Sprinting

To improve leg cadence it is occasionally worth doing a downhill sprinting session. This type of session should be done on grass, with a downhill gradient of no more than 15 degrees over distances ranging from 30–80m, with a complete recovery in-between each repetition. The idea is to get the legs moving much quicker than would be achieved on a straight surface. However, care must be taken with both technique and safety to ensure that the runner does not overbalance.

Acceleration Sprinting

Acceleration sprints are an important part of the long-distance runner's equipment. There are different methods in which acceleration can be included in the training sessions to replicate the race situation. The following two examples and skills sprinting are some of the methods that can be included to both improve the ATP-CP system, but also the ability to accelerate, either during or at the end of a race.

In order to get a progressive feel for how acceleration is occurring, a distance of between 150m–400m is ideal, with a complete recovery between each repetition and up to six to eight repetitions in total. Both the 150m and 400m would be broken down into 30m and 80m segments respectively and the pace would accelerate as follows: the first 30 or 80m would be run at marathon pace, the next 30 or 80m segment at long-distance pace, the third segment at 800/1,500 pace, the fourth segment at 400m pace and the final segment at sprint pace (see Fig. 40 below).

Even though the training duration is longer than the time it takes to break down the ATP-CP system, this only happens in the final 30m or 80m between 120–150m, and 320–400m respectively, as this is the only segment where the runner will be operating at maximum velocity.

A similar type of training method to improve acceleration would be to stride at submaximum or cruising pace around the track and on a given command or blast on a whistle react by accelerating for 60m. The number of repetitions would be quite low, with four to six the maximum; recovery: complete recovery required between each repetition.

Zigzag Runs

These can be either a speed and acceleration drill, or a strength-endurance training session (see Chapter 4). A series of six markers (see Fig. 41) is placed at 30m interval in a zigzag pattern. Six 30m sprints are made, with five 90-degree turns round each marker. Because the runner has to decelerate round each marker and then accelerate to the next, this improves both co-ordination and his ability to accelerate. There would be only a few repetition in each set – between four to five – and two to three set with a walk-back recovery between each repetition and complete recovery between sets. This ensures maximum intensity for each of the repetitions. The runner will also replicate the proximity of a race field by constantly checking, decelerating and accelerating again.

Skills Sprinting

The aim of skills sprinting (see Fig. 42–45 opposite) is to get the runner to replicate the possible race situations,

Marathon Pace	10k/5k Pace	800m/1,500m Pace	4,000 Pace	Sprint Pace
30/80m >	60/160m >	90/240m >	120/320m >	150/400m >

Fig. 40. Acceleration sprints using the different race paces.

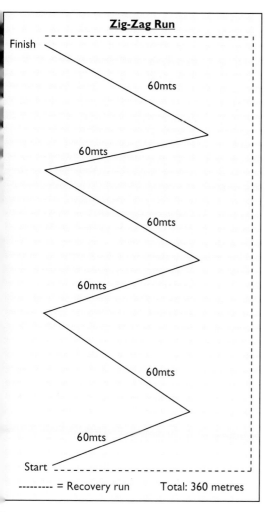

Zig-Zag Run

Finish

60mts

60mts

60mts

60mts

60mts

60mts

60mts

Start

-------- = Recovery run   Total: 360 metres

Fig. 41. A zigzag training drill is used as a strength-endurance session with elements of speed. The dotted line the short jog recovery. Each of the lengths of the individual gs can be altered to meet the demands of the event and e requirements of the session being undertaken.

ork on his acceleration and also to train the ATP-CP stem. The training distance would be over 60m, split to three segments of 20m. With this type of training cover all the racing requirements, there are four sets, ith two to three repetitions in each set, 2min between ach repetition and between 8–10min between sets. he first set is a progressive acceleration through each f the three segments; the second set is at maximum eed for the first segment, then 90 per cent effort for e second segment, before returning to maximum eed for the final segment. The third set is at 90 per

cent effort for the first segment (cruising pace), followed by maximum speed for the second segment and a controlled 90 per cent effort (cruising pace) for the final segment. This has to be controlled, as the temptation is to ease off too much and not run at the required speed. The final set is at maximum velocity throughout the three segments for the whole distance. With a long-distance runner, the segments between each section should be no less than 50m and no more than 80m. The examples below illustrate the various types of skill sprints with variable distances.

All of the methods, as mentioned, can be done over slightly longer distances, ranging from 60–240m. However, anything longer would then also involve the anaerobic energy pathway and would not be a pure speed training session, because of the duration involved and the intensity of the repetition. It would also involve some speed-endurance training. This type of session can be used if a combination of both of the energy pathways is required for the training programme.

Set 1		
80% velocity	90% velocity	100% velocity
50m >	100m >	150m

Fig. 42. Skill sprints 1: increasing the pace each segment through acceleration.

Set 2		
100% velocity	90% velocity	100% velocity
60m >	120m >	180m

Fig. 43. Skill sprints 2: accelerating – cruising in the middle – accelerating again.

Set 3		
90% velocity	100% velocity	90% velocity
80m >	160m >	240m

Fig. 44. Skill sprints 3: cruising – accelerating – cruising.

Set 4		
100% velocity	100% velocity	100% velocity
30m >	60m >	90m

Fig. 45. Skill sprints 4: controlled – relaxed – full pace.

Obviously, a high performance long-distance runner will need to be judicious in which of these types of training is done, and when he does it in his training programme, without affecting his mileage and volume of training. A simple way of involving this session is to do it – after the warm-up – before a steady-state or long run, as two different energy pathways, the alactate and aerobic systems, are being used in different parts of the training session and will not therefore affect each other. Similarly, the session can be used after the warm-up and before a track session.

Long-distance runners quite often neglect these types of training sessions. The key is working at maximum intensity for between 4–9sec and ensuring that the recovery is adequate enough to allow for the full resynthesis of the system. It is important that both correct recovery and adequate warm-up and cool-down sessions are included. This is because, with this type of training, there is a high demand on the muscles and a relatively high potential for injury. The aim of these sessions is to improve and maintain maximum speed and the fast-twitch fibres, employ good technique and relaxation, but also to improve the ability to react, adjust, change pace and accelerate, as well as limiting the effects of the endurance factors. It is important that the high performance long-distance runner does some of this type of training throughout the year and on the odd occasion when fatigued.

Anaerobic (Lactate) System

This system is of varying importance to the long-distance runner, depending on his event (see Fig. 46) and makes a significant contribution during short-term and maximum efforts. It is often referred to as speed-endurance training. It is the predominant supplier of ATP during efforts up to 45sec and also up to 2min, whereupon the aerobic system has an increasing input.

Therefore the long-distance runner's training should include work in this range of 10sec to 2min+ in duration at high intensity. During this type of training the body adapts and creates a tolerance to the build-up of lactate in the blood. At rest, lactate levels are about 1 mmol/L of blood and can elevate to values in excess of 25mmol/L during intense exercise (see Fig. 46).

There is a point, as the intensity increases, where there is a rapid rise in the levels of blood lactate. This point is referred to as the onset of blood lactate accumulation (OBLA). Blood lactate accumulation is the lactate that builds up in the blood, minus the lactate that the athlete is able to remove from the blood. Once this point is reached it is referred to as the lactate threshold (LT). As the intensity continues to increase and it goes beyond the lactate threshold it will reach the lactate turning point (LTP). To determine the lactate threshold, as previously stated, blood samples can be taken by an exercise physiologist during high intensity training sessions. However, to get the most valid results these samples should be taken as field tests at critical times during the training session and at a predetermined time after the conclusion of the training session. The lactate threshold is usually expressed as a percentage of the VO_2 max. With training, the LT level and LTP level can be improved because the training has improved the efficiency of lactate removal. In high performance athletes their LT will be as high as 70–80 per cent of their VO_2 max.

The LT is a good indicator of performance. If two athletes have, as stated previously, a similar VO_2 max, it is usually the athlete with the most efficient running economy who will produce the better performance. High performance 5,000/10,000m runners will be performing at levels of 20mmol/L+ of blood lactate and a marathon runner at 18mmol/L of blood lactate. Therefore, high performance long-distance runners need to consider training methods that will raise both LT and

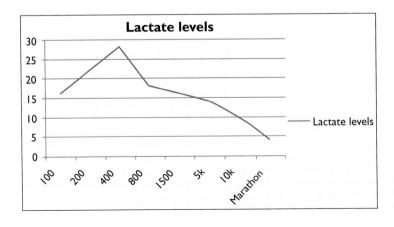

Fig. 46. Lactate levels of all running events and levels for long-distance events.

Fig. 47. Load monitoring for a session run at a certain levels of velocity.

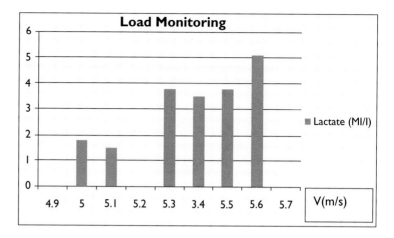

-TP, so as to improve performance, build up a tolerance to the accumulation of lactic acid and develop running economy, as well as training to raise VO_2 max.

When doing anaerobic repetition work it is essential that the athlete remains relaxed and concentrates on his technique. This type of training session is very individual and specific to the athlete and his event. Therefore group training is not recommended. This is because each training programme should be tailored for each individual athlete and it is likely that only one of the group would get the maximum benefit from this specific training session (see Fig. 47).

The following are some of the types of training that are used to develop this energy pathway and can be done on track, road, canal paths, grass, forest paths or a mixture:

    quality repetitions
    pyramid training
    up- and down-the-clock sessions
    differentials/split intervals
    pace injectors/tired surges/pace increases
    high intensity repetitions
    time trial.

ome of the following sessions are similar to the others previously mentioned, but will differ in the duration and umber of repetitions and the length of the recovery eriod. The key to training the lactate system is to run a smaller number of repetitions at maximum speed, with sufficiently long recovery to maintain the quality. With all the following lactate (speed-endurance sessions), the heart rates will be over 170 beats and up to 200+ beats/min. This is because this type of training is anaerobic.

Quality Repetitions

A quality repetition session for a female 5,000m runner with a personal best of 14:35min would be as follows:

- 3 × 1,000m in 2m 45sec (faster than the race pace of 2min 55sec); recovery: 4–5min recovery between each repetition; or
- 6 × 500m in 85sec (race pace 87.5sec); recovery: 5min recovery between the repetitions.

This type of training will help the body's adaptation to both the speed of the repetition and how to cope with and tolerate the build-up of lactic acid in the system. Once the long-distance runner goes on the track for repetition training, it is wise for the first few sessions to wear their racing flats until they are used to the impact, then they can move into their spikes.

Pyramid Training

A pyramid session to train the lactate system (or for speed endurance) would involve longer distance repetitions with longer recoveries. There will be some repetitions run at faster than race pace. Using the same 14:35min 5,000m female runner, a typical pyramid session, at quicker than race pace, is shown in Fig. 48.

Up- and Down-the-Clock Sessions

Again, these sessions involve longer repetitions in duration and fewer repetitions in total, with long recoveries. An example of both these types of training sessions are as follows in Figs 49 and 50 for a 13min male 5,000m runner.

200m (33sec)/400m (51sec)/600m (68sec)/800m (2min 17sec)/1,000m (2min 50sec)/800m (2min 17sec)/600m (2min 17sec)/400m (67sec)/200m (33sec); recovery: 1min/1min 30sec/2min/2min 30sec/3min/2min 30sec/2min/1min 30sec.

Fig. 48. Pyramid session for a female 5,000m runner with 14:35 personal best.

400m (58sec) > 600m (1min 28sec) > 800m (2min 0sec) > 1000m (2min 33sec) > 1200m (3min 4sec); recovery: 1min/3min/5min/7min

Fig. 49. Up-the-clock, male 5,000m runner, 13min personal best.

1,200m (3min 4sec) > 1000m (2min 33sec) > 800m (2min 0sec) > 600m (1min 28sec) > 400m (58sec); recovery: 7min/5min/3min/1min

Fig. 50. Down-the-clock, male 5,000m runner, 13min personal best.

Both of these sessions are structured to ensure that the body develops a tolerance against the build-up of lactic acid. Of the two, the down-the-clock session is slightly easier, both physiologically and mentally, because the distance of each repetition is diminishing as the session progresses. With the up-the-clock session, as the body gets more fatigued and there is a build-up of lactic acid, the repetitions are becoming progressively longer.

Differentials/Split Intervals

These are used to improve both speed endurance and pace judgment. With these sessions the repetition is split into half and both sections are either run at the same pace or the second section slightly faster. It is possible to do both these types of differentials in the one session, alternating them each repetition. To help with the runner's pace judgment, the coach may use a whistle to signal when the target time has elapsed. Fig. 51 is an example of how the session could be run, with the second part of the repetition run quicker for a 27min male 10,000m runner.

Fig. 51a. Differential repetition training session showing three athletes running the same session. However, the front one is running the 400m as split intervals and the other two athletes are running at even pace.

6 × 800m in 2min 8sec, the first 400m in 65.5sec, the second 400m in 62.5sec or for even-paced running two laps each in 64sec; recovery: 4min recovery between each repetition.

Fig. 51. Differential interval training session.

Pace Injectors/Tired Surges/Pace Increases

Pace injectors, tired surges and pace increases are not only speed-endurance sessions that train the anaerobic lactate system, they are also excellent sessions for both simulating race situations and improving acceleration. The following are examples of these three types of training sessions:

Pace injectors Race pace of 30min female 10,000m runner: 4 × 1,200m; recovery: 4min recovery between each repetition. The three 400m sections are broken down as follows: first 400m in 72sec (race pace), second 400m 68sec (faster than race pace) and the third 400m in 72sec (race pace).

Tired surges Race pace for a male 13min 5,000m runner: 3 × 1,000m/200m; recovery: 100m stride between each repetition and 3min recovery between each set. 1,000m in 2min 28sec (faster than race pace), stride 100m, 200m in 26.5sec (faster than race pace).

Pace increases Race pace for a 27min male 10,000m runner: 4 × 1,500m; recovery: 2min recovery between each repetition. First 500m in 81sec (race pace), second 500m in 78sec, third 500m in 75sec.

Each of these sessions helps the athlete to cope with the race situation. The pace injectors prepare him physically to be able to react to any sudden injection of pace. The pace increases prepare him for making a long sustained run to the finish if this is what is required. The tired surges simulates the conclusion of the race, for there will still be some lactic acid in the legs that the 100m stride will not have had time to disperse.

High Intensity Repetitions

High intensity repetitions are only to be used with mature high performance athletes. The aim here is get the athlete to run repetitions at a high intensity when there is lactic acid still in his system. The repetitions are run at maximum intensity, with a short recovery between the repetitions and a longer recovery between sets. With this particular type of training, there is a high degree of lactate in the system and the pulse rate could be as high as over 200 beats/min. The distances that are most effective for this session are over 200m or 300m.

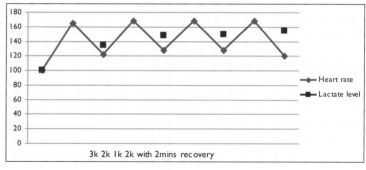

Fig. 52. Graph to show the effects of different training loads and distances at various levels of intensity.

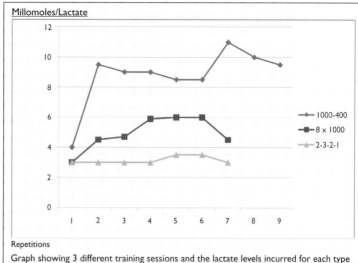

Graph showing 3 different training sessions and the lactate levels incurred for each type of them.

Session 1: 1000metres/ 400metres x 4 sets with 30 seconds recovery and 3 minutes Jog between sets.

Session 2: 8 x 1000 metres (1K) with 1 minute jog recovery

Session 3: 2000metres/3000metres/2000metres/1000metres x 2 with 1 minute and 3minutes Jog between sets.

Fig. 53. Graph to show the effects of different training loads and distances at various levels of intensity.

The following example is a combination of both distances for a 3,000m male runner with a personal best of 7min 30sec: 4 × (300m/200m); recovery: 15sec between each repetition and 5min between sets. The 300m would be run in 42–43sec (faster than race pace) and the 200m in 27–28sec (faster than race pace).

Mixed sessions A 10,000m runner may well include some of the above type of training, along with 1:1 recoveries, to ensure that there is still an endurance element in a training session, as well as touching on the anaerobic and alactate energy pathways. The training table in Fig. 54 shows three examples of an Olympic female champion's training sessions of either 6km in total or 4km or 2km, depending on what effect is required, and is made up of 400m, 300m, 200m, with

the same repetition as a slow recovery. These sessions are used the whole year round.

Time Trials and Tests

These should be used sparingly and at particular stages of the training programme. They are used as an indicator of how the training has progressed. However, the phase of the training, the weather and the athlete's health should be taken into consideration when undertaking them. Because they are run at maximum effort, the time trials are a good indicator of his current race speed. Most time trials are not over the race distance, but are either under or over it. A 5,000m runner may therefore have a time trial in the pre-competition phase over 10,000m to check on his endurance. To check how his speed-endurance is progressing, he may test

Distance	400m	300m	200m	100m
6km session	69sec 400m slow rec	51sec 300m slow rec	33sec 200m slow rec	16sec 100m slow rec
	70sec 400m slow rec	49sec 300m slow rec	32sec 200m slow rec	16sec 100m slow rec
Total time + **recoveries = 19:55**	70sec 400m slow rec	49sec 300m slow rec	32sec 200m slow rec	16sec 100m slow rec
4km session same **slow recoveries**	70sec	50sec	32sec	16sec
Total time = 13:15	70sec	50sec	32sec	16sec
2km session same **recoveries Total** **time = 6:38**	68.7sec	50sec	32sec	16sec

Fig. 54. Three training sessions using 400m/300m/200m/100m varying in total from 6km, 4km and 2km for a 5,000m/10,000m runner (V. Bondarenko).

himself over 3,000m, or 1,500m at the commencement of the competition phase. Similarly, the 10,000m runner would use distances of a 10-mile road race or half marathon to check the progress of his endurance and a 1,000m time trial to gauge how his speed endurance is progressing.

The high performance long-distance runner may well use more repetitions – because of his race distance – with shorter recoveries. This will still be a speed-endurance training session, but the intensity

levels from both a lactate level (millimoles) and heart rate perspective will not be as high as they would be with a lower number of repetitions and longer recovery between repetitions. Once the high performance long-distance runner is into his training programme, he is never more than five weeks away from being in 'race shape'.

All these training sessions are designed to train the energy pathways and make them more efficient in the race situation. Within each of the three energy

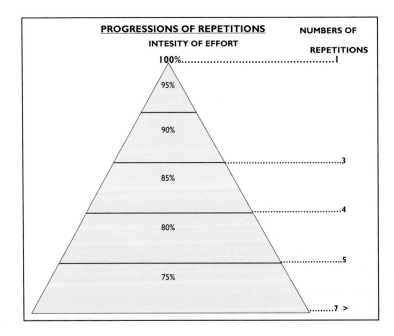

Fig. 55. Overview of how repetition training – in all its forms – should be progressed with regard to loadings, intensities and recoveries.

pathways there is a great deal of variety, race simulation and an overlapping of each of the pathways, which are performing at different levels depending on the type of training session. It is essential that the intensities and progressions are correct (see Fig. 55).

Once the types of training mentioned above have taken place, it is very important during the pre-competition phase, and particularly during the competition phase, that *event-specific training* takes place once a week or every ten days. This type of training is a mixture of the other three types of training, therefore there is an element of alactate, lactate (anaerobic) and aerobic training involved. This is because the event-specific training is the culmination of the year's training and is also simulating the race's requirements. Event-specific training has three key areas – the total in each of the two sets always totals the race distance; the second set of repetitions are always shorter; and every repetition in each set should be at race pace, with short recoveries between the repetitions and longer recoveries between the sets.

Therefore, a male 5,000m runner aiming to run 13min would undertake the following event specific session with all the repetitions run at race pace:

Set 1
1,800m (4min 39 sec) 45sec recovery; 2,000m (5min 12 sec) 20sec recovery; 1,200m (3min 7 sec); recovery from Set 1: 8–10min.

Set 2
10 × 500m (78sec); recovery: 1min between repetitions.

It is important that all the energy pathways are trained and at the correct stage of the year. Progression is the key throughout the year and the repetitions should be progressed as indicated below, so that they move from being aerobic-based in the preparation phases to becoming more anaerobic and event-specific in the competition phases. This means that as the season progresses quality is introduced as well as quantity, short recoveries replaced by nearly complete recoveries and low intensity training replaced by much higher intensity training. However, unlike his high performance middle-distance counterpart, the high performance long-distance runner will have a much greater emphasis on aerobic endurance running. If he is doing two repetition sessions per week or every ten days in the pre-competitive and competitive phases, one of them will still be a high volume session (number of repetitions) with short recoveries.

High performance marathon and 10,000m runners may well break down their training repetitions into the following four areas:

- long variation repetitions
- medium variation repetitions
- short variation repetitions
- mixed variation repetitions.

Fig. 56 shows how these methods are constructed by a world-class long-distance runner, showing the variations, volume, intensities and examples of the training sessions.

Fig. 57 shows the different types of interval (repetition) methods and their training effect. Figs 58 and 58a show how the three energy systems are developed

Construction of the Repetitions	Long Repetitions	Medium Repetitions	Short Repetitions	Mixed Repetitions
Distances for repetitions	3–7km	3–5km	1–3km	400–500m > 2–3km
Total volume	15–21km	12–15km	10–12km	10–12km
Speed	3–7% faster than marathon pace	5–8% faster than marathon pace	6–10% faster than marathon pace	7–12% faster than marathon pace
Examples of training sessions	1 × 5km 3 × 6km with 3min rec	1 × 5km; 1 × 4km; 1 × 3km with 3min rec	10 × 1km or 5 × 2km or 3km/2km + 5 × 1km all with 3min rec	1 × 3km with 4min rec+ 1 × 2k with 4min rec+ 1 × 400m

Fig. 56. Overview of repetition running in a season's training plan.

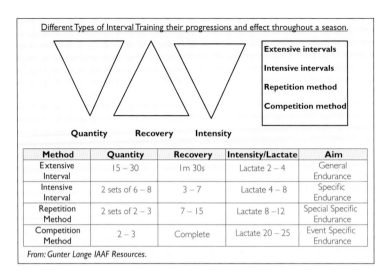

Different Types of Interval Training their progressions and effect throughout a season.

Extensive intervals

Intensive intervals

Repetition method

Competition method

Quantity   Recovery   Intensity

Method	Quantity	Recovery	Intensity/Lactate	Aim
Extensive Interval	15 – 30	1m 30s	Lactate 2 – 4	General Endurance
Intensive Interval	2 sets of 6 – 8	3 – 7	Lactate 4 – 8	Specific Endurance
Repetition Method	2 sets of 2 – 3	7 – 15	Lactate 8 –12	Special Specific Endurance
Competition Method	2 – 3	Complete	Lactate 20 – 25	Event Specific Endurance

From: Gunter Lange IAAF Resources.

Fig. 57. Chart showing the progression of repetition training, how the loadings (quantity), recoveries and intensities progress throughout the season from the general to the event-specific phase, and the lactate effects.

DEVELOPMENT OF THE
THREE ENERGY SYSTEMS

	Anaerobic Alactic	Anaerobic Lactic	Aerobic
Duration	0 – 8 secs	8 secs – 1 min	1 – 60 mins +
Distance	20m – 80 m	80m – 400m	300m – 15Km or continuous runs
Intensity	maximal	90% –100%	50% – 75%
Repetitons	3 – 4	1 – 5	3 – 20
Recovery	1½ –3 mins	2 – 10 mins	1 – 3 mins
Sets	1 – 4	1 – 4	1 – 4
Recovery	8 – 10 mins	10 – 20 mins	5 – 8 mins

Fig. 58. Chart showing the recommended duration, distance, intensity levels, volume and recovery for how to train the three energy pathways.

through training at the correct intensities and with the correct recoveries. Fig. 59 is a summary of the inter-relationship of the three energy systems and how the training methods affect their development.

It can be seen that there is a multitude of training methods available. It is in how and when these methods are used by the high performance long-distance runner

that the key lies. Over a period of time he will understand which of the above methods benefit him. He needs to maximize his training through these methods to ensure that his training meets not only the demands of the event, at the correct stages throughout the season, but is also best tailored and suited to him as an individual.

Loading	Running time (RT)	Recovery time	Recovery activity
Estimation of Recovery Times Between Running Intervals			
Short speed (all-out) (anaerobic capacity training)	10 sec	3 × RT	Walking and/or stretching
	20 sec	3 × RT	Jogging
	30 sec		
Long speed (35%-100% of maximal effort) (anaerobic capacity training)	30 sec	3 × RT	Jogging
	60 sec	2 × RT	Jogging
	80 sec		
Speed + endurance (90%-95% of maximal effort) (VO$_2$max to aerobic capacity training)	80 sec	2 × RT	Jogging
	2 min 40 sec	1 × RT	Rest
	3 min		
Endurance (80%-90% of maximal effort) (anaerobic conditioning)	3 min	1 × RT	Rest
	4 min	0.5 × RT	Rest
	20 min		

Fig. 58a. Chart showing the recommended recovery times when training the energy pathways.

A Summary of the Interrelationship of the Three Energy Systems and the Running Activities for their Development							
RUNNING TERMS	SPEED	SPEED ENDURANCE			INTENSIVE REPETITIONS	EXTENSIVE REPETITIONS	CONTINUOUS
CONTRIBUTION OF THE ENERGY SYSTEMS	ATP-CP SYSTEM	ANAEROBIC LACTIC SYSTEM				AEROBIC SYSTEM	
INTENSITY	95% - 105%	95% - 105%			80% - 90%	60% - 80%	40% - 80%
DISTANCE OF RUN	20m - 60m	60m - 600m			up to 1200m	up to 1200m plus up to 5000m Continuous	5000m +
No. OF REPS/SET	3 - 4	1 - 5			3 - 12	6 - 30	-
No. OF SETS	3 - 4 (5)	0 - 3			1 - 3	1 - 3	1
TOTAL DISTANCE OF SET	80m - 120m	180m - 1800m			Long	Long	-
TOTAL DIST. IN SESSION	200m - 600m	300m - 1800m			600 - 5000m	Long	Long to Very Long
RECOVERY / REPS	[2' - 3']	Incomplete, Nearly complete and Complete [2' - 20']			Pulse 50-60% max [3' - 5']	Pulse 60-70% max [1' - 3']	-
RECOVERY / SETS	[8' - 10']	[8' - 10']			Nearly complete [7' - 20']	Incomplete [5' - 7']	-

After McFarlane, B. *The Science of harding 1988*

Fig. 59. Table showing a different form the interrelationships of the three energy systems. The loadings and intensities are specific to the individual athlete (after B. Mcfarlane, 1988).

CHAPTER 4

CONDITIONING TRAINING

Success in a major championship long-distance competition can be determined by how strong the athlete remains in the latter stages of the competition. Strength training through conditioning can greatly enhance both an athlete's training programme and his ability to compete at the highest level. The dilemma for the high performance long-distance runner is how important this element of training is to him and how he incorporates it into his programme, given the number of miles/kilometres he has to fit into his microcycle. If he feels it is not important to him, the two key areas he needs to ensure are included in his training programme are core stability and leg strength. Strength or conditioning training falls into five major categories. These are:

- gross strength
- elastic strength, also known as power, fast strength or strength at speed
- strength endurance
- resistance training
- core strength.

The high performance long-distance runner can use all of these types of strength and conditioning in his training programme. However, strength-endurance training – which could include resistance training – and elastic strength work should be inculcated into the training programme along with core stability/strength. But he may decide not to use all of them and will use some more than others. Some high performance long-distance runners will neglect conditioning work in favour of more miles/kilometres. However, this is not wise, as conditioning is not only strengthening work, but is also preventative to stave off the injuries that are common with such constant impact work. A well-conditioned runner will also recover quicker if they do suffer any injuries, or from intense training. What he must ensure is that any conditioning programme he undertakes must involve some core strength training and that any other conditioning programmes employed must be predominantly leg-orientated. This is because of the high mileage/kilometres he will undertake during his weekly and annual training cycles often on unforgiving terrain. His legs must be strong enough to accept the constant impact they will receive.

CORE STABILITY

It is crucial that a long-distance endurance runner should ensure he has good core stability. This will not only make him strong in the core area, but also will help when he is fatigued, aid his posture and underpin his technical running model. It important that his core strength/stability work becomes part of his training regime.

Why is building core strength important? Most runners – as previously stated – will tend to have overlooked core stability in favour of increasing their miles, believing that running is the only way to become a better runner. However, quality core strengthening sessions offer the following benefits:

- better posture, which in turn will lead to a more consistent technique
- improved efficiency, which will enable the athlete to run for longer and faster and to be able to tackle hills while being unaffected by the terrain
- increased stability, which will help to reduce stress on individual muscles that can lead to injury
- improved balance, which will help with off-road running, even when its uneven underfoot
- greater abdominal strength, which not only links into all the other benefits listed, but is also where a runner's strength emanates from.

Where exactly is your core? Fig. 60 explains The core section – your torso or trunk – is made up of more than thirty separate muscles across your back, stomach and hips. The following are the five key muscles that need strengthening with core stability training:

Transversus abdominis Think of this as an internal weight belt that wraps around the torso, providing support and stability.

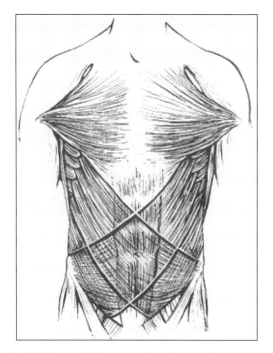

Fig. 60. Schematic diagram to show the area of core stability.

Rectus abdominis   The abdominal muscles are primarily responsible for flexing and curling the torso as well as providing core support.

Spinal erectors   These muscles strengthen and stabilize the spine for balance and posture.

Obliques   These are the muscles that rotate the midsection and provide support when twisting and bending.

Hip flexors and rotators   A key area in stabilizing the running technical model, as they pull and lift the thigh muscles with each stride. This area tends to be very neglected, tight and stiff in long-distance runners.

The further and longer the long-distance runner is performing for, the more important his core stability/ strength becomes. For core strength, as with most strength training programs, strengthening exercises specific to the muscles in the core area should be performed, for example, the abdomen, buttock, back and hips. Most of these exercises will isolate a particular muscle group in order to develop specific strength in the selected area (for example, back extensions, curl-ups). Core stability, however, is the integration of strength and coordinated movement. Specifically, therefore, core stability is the interaction of coordination and strength in the abdomen, back and buttock muscles during activity to ensure that the spine remains stabilized and provides

a firm base that will support both powerful and very basic everyday movements of the arms and legs.

The neutral spine should be located and the deep abdominal muscles activated prior to each core stability exercise. Core stability training is an essential component of endurance performance and plays a key role in injury prevention. The primary function of the body's core muscles is to stabilize the spine, pelvis and shoulder blades, thereby providing a strong postural foundation for movements of the arms and legs. The deepest layers of muscle in the torso are the core muscle and include the abdominal muscles, lower back muscles as well as buttock and hip muscles, which surround the pelvis. Developing a solid foundation within the torso muscles will allow powerful movements to be generated from the trunk outwards. In sum, core stability:

• improves posture
• maintains healthy and balanced muscles
• enhances physical functioning in everyday activities (that is, functional fitness)
• facilitates powerful movements such as those executed during training
• helps to protect joints and muscles from injury, by locating the neutral spine.

The idea of the neutral spine simply relates to setting the trunk before beginning a core stability programme. By locating the neutral spine position, the key core muscles are activated within the torso, which need to be 'turned on' prior to executing coordinated movements. The following exercise example will help you in locating the neutral spine:

a) Start by lying flat on your back on a mat or comfortable carpeted floor with your knees bent.
b) Place your arms by your sides so that your elbows are straight and your shoulders relaxed.
c) Slowly take three deep breaths in and out to try to release any stress and relax your body.
d) Gently and slowly tilt your pelvis so that you are flattening your back into the floor. Do not lift your buttocks. Try to isolate the movement so that only your pelvis is moving.
e) Now tilt your pelvis in the opposite direction so you are arching your lower back. Again try to keep the movement isolated to your pelvis.
f) Repeat steps (d) and (e) a few more times. By tilting your pelvis you are performing what is called an anterior pelvic tilt (arch back) and a posterior pelvic tilt (flatten back).
g) You can now locate your neutral spine, by finding the middle position between flattening and

Fig. 61. Front crawl exercise to strengthen and stabilize back, abdominals and buttocks.

arching your back. (To do this: place the heel of your hands on the hip bone of the same side and place your fingertips on your pubic bone located at the very bottom of your stomach.) Your hands are making a triangle shape on your lower abdomen. The fingers and heels of your hands should all be level.

The following is a set of core stability exercises to cover the abdomen, lower back, buttocks and hip areas, with instructions and illustrations of the exercises. It is crucial that technique and activation of the correct muscles is employed with core stability exercises.

Each exercise should be started by finding the neutral spine and drawing in the lower stomach. It is important to remember that these exercises are working the postural and endurance muscles surrounding the trunk, so the workout will not be at the intensity of the running workouts. Relaxation is a key part of this programme, which can take between 30–40min to complete.

The following is a sample of core stability exercises. Please note that all the exercises, including those illustrated, are working not only the areas mentioned, but are also interlinked and strengthening and stabilizing other parts of the core area.

Stomach Exercises

Lower stomach to spine:

- lying flat on your back
- feet on the floor, knees bent to 60 degrees
- find your neutral spine position
- holding that position, gently draw lower stomach to spine (30–40 per cent effort only)
- hold 5sec, keep breathing
- repeat ten to fifteen times.

Leg movements:

- continue in the same position as the exercise above
- keep that neutral position and draw in the lower stomach
- slowly lift one foot off the floor, keeping knee bent, and return
- hips should stay level and not drop as you lift your foot
- breathe in as you lift your foot and breathe out as you place it down
- repeat with the opposite leg
- repeat ten to fifteen times each side.

Fig. 62. Foot lift exercise to strengthen and stabilize abdominals, buttocks and legs.

Fig. 63. Toe pointing exercise to strengthen and stabilize buttocks, legs and abdominals.

Abdominal controlled curls:

- same position as above
- find neutral spine and draw in the lower stomach
- hands/arms by your side, slowly curl up, lifting your shoulder blades off the floor
- as you lower, do not let your stomach muscles go – keep that lower stomach drawn in
- breathe in as you curl up and out as you lower
- repeat twelve times; complete three sets.

Advanced roll-ups:

- lying flat on the floor, knees bent, feet on the floor, arms and hands along your sides
- gently/slowly lift your head off the floor and draw your lower stomach to your spine as you slowly start to sit up

- slowly breathe in as you continue sitting up until you are straight
- pause when you are straight, begin rolling back down, breathing out
- start at the pelvis and slowly unfold your spine as you return to the starting position
- repeat twenty times.

Buttock and Back Exercises

Bridging:

- lying flat on your back, find your neutral spine and draw in the lower stomach
- slowly push down through your feet and lift your bottom right up so that your trunk is straight (shoulders, hips and knees in line)

Fig. 64. Abduction exercise to strengthen and stabilize the lower back abductors and abdominal muscles.

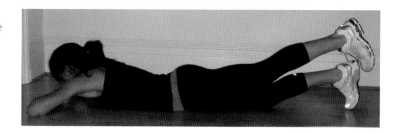

Fig. 65. Reverse leg extension exercise to strengthen and stabilize the lower back, abdominals and hamstrings.

Fig. 66. Bridge exercise to strengthen and stabilize the back and abdominal muscles.

Fig. 67. Single leg extension exercise to strengthen and stabilize the back, buttocks and abdominal muscles.

Fig. 68. Side kick/stretch exercise to stabilize and strengthen the back, abdominals and hip-flexor muscles.

Fig. 69. Hip flexor exercise to strengthen and stabilize the buttocks, abdominals and hip-flexor muscles.

- breathe in as you lift and out while lowering the bottom
- hold the lift for 5–10sec, squeezing the buttocks while holding
- repeat ten to fifteen times.

Front plank:

- place your elbows on the floor shoulder-width apart and directly under the shoulders
- supporting yourself on your elbows and toes, be sure your body is in a flat line (no dip or arch in the spine and bottom tucked in)
- keeping your spine neutral, and drawing in the lower stomach, hold this position 20–30sec

Fig. 70. Hip flexor leg extension exercise is to strengthen and stabilize the buttocks, abdominals, hamstrings and hip-flexor muscles.

- rest for 30sec
- repeat three times.

Trunk and Leg Exercises

Wall squats:

- stand with your back to the wall
- take one step away from the wall, but still leaning against it (toes should be in line and slightly turned out)
- find your neutral spine position and draw in the lower stomach
- holding this position, slowly perform a ½ squat (your bottom should stay in contact with the wall)
- hold the squat for 5sec, then return to the start, and repeat 3–5 times.

Hundreds plus:

- start in a prone position
- instead of keeping your feet on the floor, lift the lower legs so that hips and knees are at 90 degrees and shins are parallel to the floor
- drawing your lower stomach in, perform a curl-up so that the shoulder blades are off the ground
- holding this position, perform five beats per inspiration and five beats per expiration
- continue for 60–100 beats, rest and repeat.

Trunk and Full Body

Side plank:

- lying on your side, prop yourself on your right elbow placed directly under your shoulder

Fig. 71. Plank exercise to strengthen and stabilize the whole back, buttock, abdominal and upper thigh area.

Fig. 72. Plank extension exercise, which also requires good coordination, strengthens and stabilizes the whole back, buttock, abdominal and upper thigh area.

place your right knee and hip in line with your shoulder
lift yourself off the ground, supporting your body on your right elbow and knee, your body should be in one flat line
hold for 20–30sec, then repeat two times each side.

Lunges:

stand in the walking stride position, with your feet hip width apart
find your neutral spine and draw in your lower stomach, thinking of stretching from the trunk
with 90 per cent of your weight on the front leg, bend your knee, keeping the knee and hip at 90 degrees, and the trunk directed straight down, not forward
your back heel should come off the ground; keep your arms by your side for balance straighten your knee

• repeat fifteen times on each leg, doing two to three sets.

GROSS STRENGTH

The area of strength training that is used the least, or not at all, by long-distance runners is gross strength training. It is often referred to as maximum strength training. This type of training is defined as the greatest force the neuromuscular system is capable of exerting in a single contraction. Free weights are predominantly used, with the occasional use of machines. Therefore, the force lifted is of a high resistance and weight, and the number of repetitions utilized is low. The loading will be in the range of 90–100 per cent of the maximum lift, with few repetitions and a higher number of sets (example: bench-press 8 sets × 2 lifts × 95 per cent loading). Most of the exercise used in any form of weight training should be predominantly for the legs. The effect of this type of training is to increase muscle

Fig. 73. Lunge exercise to stabilize and strengthen the groin, buttocks and abdominal areas.

quadriceps (antagonist), should also be strengthened. Whichever muscles are being strengthened, a team of muscles called synergist muscles will be supporting them.

It is advisable, where possible, always to do the weight training strengthening work in a purpose-built fully equipped weights room (see Fig. 75), which adds not only safety and good quality equipment to the session, but also has equipment to help the novice lifter (see Fig. 76) and more advanced equipment to help with other strengthening activities (see Fig. 77).

When weight training is used as part of a conditioning session, the same principle with the number of repetitions and the level of intensity applies as with repetition running training (see Fig. 55).

bulk; it therefore slows movements and has little effect on fast strength. From the long-distance runner's perspective, this type of training is best used in rehabilitation after injury and to eradicate any areas of weakness. Because it is carried out with free weights, it is of paramount importance that the lifter's technique is correct to avoid any injury. When undertaking the lifting session, he should always be accompanied by 'spotters' on either side to ensure that the weighted bar is not dropped, potentially causing injury.

As with all types of strength training, it is important that each activity is compensated by the next activity. This means that if the first exercise involves strengthening the active muscle, known as the agonist, the following exercise will be to strengthen its partner support muscle known as the antagonist. For example, if the exercise involves activating the hamstring muscles (agonist), its partner support muscle, the

Fig. 74. Lunge exercise shown from the side with arms extended to strengthen and stabilize further the groin, buttocks and abdominal areas, as well as the core area.

Fig. 75. Fully equipped weights room.

ELASTIC STRENGTH

Elastic strength is the ability of the neuromuscular system to overcome resistance by employing a high speed of contraction. It may also be referred to as power, fast strength or strength at speed. This type

Fig. 77. Sophisticated apparatus to help with abdominal and core activities.

Fig. 76. Support rack for athlete who is just commencing weight training or is a novice lifter.

of training aids performance in the explosive events. Here again, free weights are predominantly used, with a loading of 75–85 per cent of maximum. The lifts are done faster than with maximum-strength lifting, but the same ground rules of technique, safety and 'spotters' applies. The number of repetitions will vary from six to ten, with the number of sets from three to four, with short recoveries between the sets. The effect of this type of training is some bulking of the muscle and increase in contractile speed. Elastic strength training not only underpins the other aspects of the training programme, it is also very beneficial in the shorter endurance events, particularly with the assistance of acceleration.

An aspect of elastic strength is plyometric training. This reactive strength type of training can easily be developed through incorporating ballistic, rebound activities such as hopping, two-footed jumping, skipping and bounding into the training programme, particularly emphasizing technique to ensure that each foot contact is 'active', with a pre-tensed calf muscle. Plyometrics have been an integral part of conditioning training since it was introduced by Vladimir Zatsiorsky in 1966. The more advanced form of plyometrics is 'depth jumping',

Fig. 79. Learning to lift and do the technique with a bar only and no weights attached. The weights can be attached once the correct technique has been learned.

Fig. 78. The squat exercise is good for all-round conditioning. Great care needs to be taken when lifting – it needs spotters and good technique, otherwise it can cause damage to the knee and tendon areas. It balances the body using the major muscle groups of the legs in the correct sequence, gluteus > hamstrings > quadriceps. The back has to be kept straight, with eyes looking straight ahead with the knees bent to or just below the horizontal. With all activities, it is wise to start with just a bar and then add weights progressively once the correct technique has been achieved.

which involves jumping off and on benches and over hurdles. It was proposed by Yuri Verkhoshansky in the same year.

Plyometrics is now perceived as any explosive-reactive training comprised of muscle stretch-shortening cycle actions that are aimed at improving reactive strength. With appropriate training, there is an increased mechanical efficiency in the muscle for creating power and the rate of force development. The long-term effects include greater control of muscle stiffness and coordination of the neuromuscular response.

Plyometrics should be introduced into training very gradually, starting with relatively low-intensity exercises

Fig. 80. This shows the athlete in an extended snatch position. Weights can be added when or if required. Holding these positions with just a weight bar is demanding.

Fig. 80a. Shows the athlete in the same position from a different angle. As well as assisting technique, these exercises also help the athlete with conditioning and getting in the correct position.

uch as skipping with a rope, hops on the spot and clap press-ups. These can progress through more intensive bounds and jumps to the highest-intensity exercises uch as depth jumps. This progression, however, should take years, rather than months, and only athletes with a high training age should consider using depth jumping. Squat jumps with weights can be used – though are not advisable for the long-distance runner – but too heavy a loading should be avoided, as this would slow the movement. Squat jumps for reactive strength should use 30–40 per cent of the athlete's one-repetition maximum, but should also take into account the athlete's body weight, since he is leaving the ground. If the athlete's body weight is 80kg and his one-repetition maximum is 140kg, the total 'system maximum weight' is 220kg. Since 40 per cent of 220kg is 88kg, this particular athlete only needs to carry 8kg over his body weight while performing jump squats.

To summarize, plyometrics fall into the following categories of difficulty:

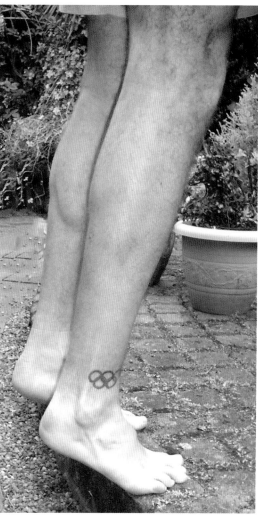

Fig. 81. Calf raises using a patio – or any raised area - with no weights on the shoulders to achieve the correct position and technique. This activity is ideal for an athlete who has no time to go to a weights room, as it strengthens the calves if done regularly. To aid support initially, one hand can be against the wall. A bar, then weights, can be added when required. The amount of time off the ground should be controlled by time.

Jumps – the least demanding activity, which can involve jumping for distance (horizontally), or on the spot (vertically), usually with two feet. The

exercises will be in sets of five to eight repetitions and can include skipping. Could be used by the long-distance runner.

- Hopping – usually for distance over a set distance (for example, 40m), or for a set number of hops, with the exercise again being in sets of five to

Fig. 82. An arm exercise to aid running technique. Arm exercises are not incorporated into the training programme as much as leg exercises. If used, they must assist the running action. In this exercise, note the driving action of the arms while carrying the dumbbells, the extension of the rear leg. This exercise also strengthens the biceps (agonist) muscles.

eight. The exercise can be performed on single legs only, alternate legs or a combination of both. A low- to medium-intensity set of exercises. Good for long-distance runners.

- Bounding – a medium-intensity exercise using alternate legs, landing from one leg to the other, in a repetitive sequence. These exercises also try to achieve greater height than in the hopping exercise. The aim is distance (for example, 60–80m), trying to go as far as possible with each bound. Again, these exercises will be in sets of five to eight exercises. To be used, if at all, with caution by the long-distance runner and on forgiving surfaces.

- Depth jumping – a high-intensity exercise that is not recommended for long-distance runners, because it places significant stress on the neuro-muscular system and connective tissues. The jumps are from height and will have either a verti-

Fig. 83. To assist leg strength balance and coordination, the athlete, while still carrying dumbbells, balances on one leg for a certain time and can increase the pressure on the leg by raising and bending the free leg at the knee so that the leg is parallel to the ground. He then changes legs. The number of repetitions is determined by the abilities and requirements of the athlete.

Fig. 84. This figure depicts an elastic-explosive strength exercise, in which the athlete, with the weightlifting bar as the force above their shoulders, is in a semi-squat position and is about to explode into the air. The exercise is repeated as needed to gain the required benefit. Extra weight can be added.

cal component – jumping down and then up – or a horizontal component – jumping down and then out. The number of sets and repetitions will be less than for the other types of plyometric training.

ig. 85. This is a continuation of Fig. 84, with the athlete moving into the upright phase, with legs shoulder-width apart.

Fig. 86. The athlete is now in the final explosive phase – driving as far upward as possible. All the three phases (Figs 84–86) are done as one movement so that the athlete is generating explosive strength from the squat position, through the upright position and into the air. This dynamic explosive exercise is good for developing leg strength, which is of paramount importance to the long-distance runner.

Similarly, medicine ball work and hurdle jumping are an integral part of plyometric training (see Figs 87–88). The mature athlete may also include depth jumping but there are enough options without including this activity in the programme. These activities involve jumping off benches, gymnastic half and full boxes. The landing surface needs to be cushioned to avoid injury. The effects of plyometric training are that it improves the speed of the muscle contraction, elastic strength and can aid speed endurance. It is very beneficial to long-distance runners, but must follow other forms of strength training. It is advisable with plyometric and bounding exercises to ensure that they are done on a soft, forgiving surface such as grass, parkland or golf courses. Plyometric training can be involved in the athlete's training programme from an early age, whereas bounding should only be introduced with the mature

Fig. 87. This activity can be started in the standing position, with the athletes the appropriate distance apart to accomplish the exercise. In this kneeling activity, the athletes cannot use their legs and so they have to work their arms and abdominal muscles harder and therefore strengthen them more. The distance between may be shorter than in the standing position.

Fig. 88. This is a continuation of the same exercise, in which the athletes have been sitting with their legs apart, again working on strengthening their arms and abdominal muscles. They have now progressed to lying on their back, where they also require coordination as they have to release the medicine ball as they move into the upright sitting position.

athlete who is strong enough to cope with this type of training.

The long-distance runner has to be judicious in deciding which parts of the elastic strength training programme will benefit him as an individual, taking into account his own strengths and weaknesses. Plyometrics and hurdle work are excellent for not only strengthening the legs, but also for improving and aiding the finishing sprint at the end of a race. He can also fit this in alongside a track session. He may decide that the weight-training and medicine ball work are not going to be an integral part of his training programme.

The use of hurdling drills is to be recommended for long-distance runners. It aids mobility, coordination, range of movement, suppleness and helps strengthen weak areas. It is also very good for working areas in which long-distance runners are notoriously stiff, such as the hip flexors. Following are the basic hurdle drills that can be used.

Coordination Drills

- place the hurdles × 8, with the base of each hurdle touching the legs of the next hurdle.
- walk down the side of the hurdles, with the left trail leg going over each hurdle. The action over the hurdle is very slow; repetitions × 3
- repeat with the right trail leg, as above; repetitions × 3
- step over each hurdle in the middle with the right leg lead. The trail leg comes through to join the lead leg. Then repeat over each hurdle; repetitions × 3
- as above with the left leg lead; repetitions × 3
- stand square to the hurdle with the right leg to the nearest hurdle and skip/swing the right leg over each hurdle with the left leg following; repetitions × 3
- repeat with left leg square to the hurdle × 3

- bring the hurdles closer together. Step over the first hurdle in the middle and then bring the trail leg through. However, the trail leg will not land next to the lead leg but will extend and step over the next hurdle and so on over each hurdle; repetitions × 4.

See Figs 13–15 in Chapter 2.

STRENGTH ENDURANCE

Strength endurance training involves using lighter weights, with either free weights or machines, with a loading of 60–75 per cent of maximum lift, but can also be included in running training and circuit training. The methods will vary depending upon the required training effect. The effect of this type of training is to increase muscular endurance, which can either be general or very specific. It is appropriate to all endurance events and can be used for general all-round conditioning or is specific to certain aspects such as speed. The effect of strength-endurance training is to ensure that the muscles continue to perform at the same rate once they become fatigued. This is an element essential to the long-distance runner. However, he may decide that he can gain a similar effect by employing circuit training, stage training or an Oregon circuit in his training programme.

Circuit and stage training can either be general or very specific. A general conditioning circuit is used to develop overall general condition during the preparation phase. A far more specific circuit will replace this during the specific preparation phase. However, to get the maximum benefits for his athlete, the coach should design an individual circuit that is tailored to his needs. The type of exercises, arms, legs, abdominal and general exercises are denoted on the illustration, as are the number of circuits and the times and recoveries for each exercise. With the long-distance high performer this will include a number of general exercises, for example, star jumps, and abdominal exercises, for example chinnies, a few arm exercises, for example press-ups, but will be predominantly leg exercises, for example, high knees. The exercises involved are as follows:

- chins on a gymnastic beam, either under-grasp, or the more difficult over-grasp. Raise the body up using the arms until the chin is above the beam, then lower and repeat (arms)
  step-ups onto one bench, then with the other foot onto a second bench, two benches high; reverse back down to the second bench, then the floor and repeat (legs)

- chinnies, a type of sit-up – while sitting up, twist the body so that the alternate knee is touched by the opposite elbow, hands clasped behind the head. Returns to the prone position and repeat (abdominal)
- star jumps – squatting, with hands between feet, spring up legs apart, return to the start position and repeat continuously (general)
- press-ups (arms)
- jumping to touch a gymnastic beam placed at an appropriate height; upon landing bounce back up to touch the beam; repeat continuously (legs)
- inclined sit-ups – with the feet attached to a bench that is fastened to the gymnasium wall with bars at a suitable angle, the hands are clasped behind the head (abdominal)
- burpees – starting from a press-up position, the legs come forward toward the arms; at this point, jump up into the air as high as possible. On landing, shoot the legs back into the starting press-up position, then repeat the exercise (general)
- rope-climb to the top of the gymnasium, with either a double rope using both arms only with no assistance from the legs, or with a single rope using the arms and feet (arms)
- bent knee sit-ups – instead of starting from a prone position, the exercise starts with the knees bent with the body moving from the floor to the knees, then returning to the floor before repeating the exercise; the hands are clasped behind the head (abdominal)
- shuttle run – fetching, carrying and returning two medicine balls in turn over a set distance (legs)
- star jumps – as previously, but with legs split one in front of the other (general)
- tricep dips, either on the parallel bars or on a single bench. The arms are at full extension, then lowered to a 90-degree angle and held. Return to the full extension position and repeat the exercise (arms)
- jumping over a row of hurdles, either with a single- or double-footed take-off, or a mixture of both. It is essential that the hurdles be on gymnastic mats to avoid any impact injuries (legs; see also Figs 85 and 86)
- leg raises, lying flat on the back, arms at the side with the legs held together 6in off the floor for the whole of the allotted time (abdominal)
- beam traverse, hanging from a gymnasium beam move along it, one arm following the other until the other end is reached and then returning using the arms only (arms)

- squat thrusts – in a press-up position, both legs move to the arms and then back to starting position repeatedly (legs)
- bench jumps – holding a medicine ball, with a leg either side of the bench, jump up onto the bench with both feet, then back to the floor; continue to repeat the exercise (general)
- bench raises – the bench is hooked onto the wall bar at the appropriate height. Start with the bench at full extension from the wall bar against the chest. From here, go down into a squat position and then drive upward into the original position, at the same time lifting the bench above the head with arms fully extended. Continue to repeat the exercise.

These are just some of the many exercises that can be incorporated into a circuit. The high performance long-distance runner and his coach can devise their own general circuit, then make it more specific to the athlete's individual requirements.

Stage training is an extension of circuit training, in which the emphasis is on specific exercises and the time spent on each activity. In a normal circuit the athlete would rotate from exercise to exercise for three circuits. Therefore, after completing a leg exercise (for example, step-ups), he would move to an exercise on his arms (for example, triceps dips), then to an abdominal exercise (for example, press ups) and finally a general exercise (for example, burpees). However, with stage training the athlete would remain at the same exercise for all three circuits – three leg exercises – before moving to the next three exercises on his arms. In this way, there is a great build-up of local muscular fatigue in a specific part of the body, such as the legs. With a general circuit the build-up of local muscular fatigue will not be as acute, because the athlete will move next to an arm exercise, then to an abdominal exercise and finally to a general exercise and the local muscular fatigue in the legs will have been dispersed by the time he returns to the next leg exercise.

A long-distance runner, because of time, may prefer to do a circuit requiring no gymnastic apparatus that can be done in at home, in the carport, or at the track. This circuit is very convenient as it saves time travelling to a gymnasium or fitness centre, and can easily be adapted to stage training as he gets fitter. Similarly, as he enters the specific preparation phase, the circuit can be made more specific to his individual needs as long, as there is no gymnastic equipment required. It may be that the long-distance runner will devise his own circuit, with a few exercises covering one arm exercise, for example,

tricep dips, one abdominal, for example inclined press-ups, one general, for example, burpees, and three leg exercises, for example, donkey kicks, high knees and squat thrusts, interspersed with the other three exercises. In this way, he is covering the main requirements and as it is being done at home he may do it three to four times a week.

These are some of the exercises in the non-apparatus circuit he could select:

- press-ups (arms)
- squat thrusts (legs)
- chinnies (abdominal)
- star jumps with the legs split (general)
- triceps dips (arms)
- donkey kicks – squat thrusts with legs alternating (legs)
- inclined sit-ups (abdominal)
- burpees (general)
- inclined press-ups (arms)
- high knees (legs)
- half sit-ups (abdominal)
- star jumps with the legs together (general)
- V position – lie prone, then come to the sit-up position with one foot in the air and the opposite arm and hand touching the toe to form the V position (abdominals)
- one leg, then alternate leg, then two-legged skipping (leg exercise)
- lunges – without weights (core area)
- high leg crunches – legs in the air, raise the body so that extended hands can touch the toes (abdominals).

This seventeen-exercise circuit – they do not all have to be included – should build up to a maximum of three circuits, with 1min on each exercise, a 30sec recovery and 1min 30sec between sets.

The Oregon circuit was devised at Oregon University specifically for endurance runners, and was popularized by Joaquim Cruz, the Olympic 800m champion. With this type of circuit, the exercises are predominantly leg exercises, as are all the recoveries. This is ideal for the long-distance runner, who is constantly on his legs when training and competing and therefore wants to make them as strong, durable and resilient as possible. Unlike the normal indoor circuit training, both between exercises and between circuits all the recoveries are run at a brisk pace. This makes the circuit specific to endurance runners, as it improves the muscular endurance of the legs, but also improves the cardiovascular and respiratory systems. There are nine exercises involved. Two are for general mobility, two are for general endurance, out still with an element of leg work, and the other five are leg exercises. The exercises are as follows:

- side swings (general mobility)
- side stretches (general mobility)
- burpees (general conditioning)
- star jumps (general conditioning)
- high knees (legs)
- shuttle run (legs)
- donkey kicks (legs)
- knees to chest (legs) – standing straight up, feet on the ground, bring the knees up to the chest while remaining as straight as possible; back must not be bent to meet the knees
- leg claps (legs) – bouncing on one foot with the opposite leg extended in front as near parallel to the ground as possible with the upper body

remaining upright. In this position the arms and hands come together under the extended leg to perform the clap. On the next bounce the legs change position with the clap taking place under the other extended leg. The activity is repeated with the legs alternating positions.

With all conditioning work it should be progressed – as shown in the matrix below – throughout the athlete's career until he is able to manage event-specific exercises and has devised a structure that meets his requirements. With the long-distance runner, if he has not previously done any conditioning work it is essential to follow the strength matrix, as follows:

- general preparation exercises
- specific preparation exercises

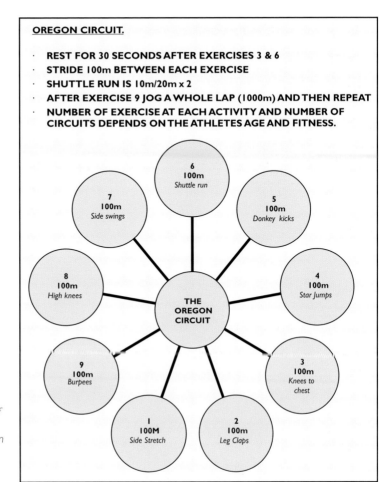

OREGON CIRCUIT.

- REST FOR 30 SECONDS AFTER EXERCISES 3 & 6
- STRIDE 100m BETWEEN EACH EXERCISE
- SHUTTLE RUN IS 10m/20m x 2
- AFTER EXERCISE 9 JOG A WHOLE LAP (1000m) AND THEN REPEAT
- NUMBER OF EXERCISE AT EACH ACTIVITY AND NUMBER OF CIRCUITS DEPENDS ON THE ATHLETES AGE AND FITNESS.

6 100m Shuttle run
7 100m Side swings
5 100m Donkey kicks
8 100m High knees
4 100m Star Jumps
THE OREGON CIRCUIT
9 100m Burpees
3 100m Knees to chest
1 100M Side Stretch
2 100m Leg Claps

Fig. 89. The Oregon circuit is done outdoors over a 1,000m grass or easy running terrain circuit, with 100m between each exercise. After exercises three and six, there is a 30sec recovery before moving on to the next exercise. If a large suitable area is not available, a football pitch can be used to get the 100m stations, with the recovery between each activity also being the length of the pitch, and three whole laps of the pitch between each circuit. The number of repetitions at each station and the number of circuits, as in all similar activities, is determined by the athlete's fitness level.

- specific development exercises
- event development exercises
- event exercises.

Strength endurance can also be developed through running training. The main methods are as follows:

- repetition work
- hill or step work
- turnabouts
- back-to-back training
- zigzag runs.

Three examples of strength-endurance repetition sessions for a long-distance runner are as follows:

- 20 × 400m in 64–66sec with a 45sec jog recovery; female in 72–75sec; same 45sec recovery
- 20 × 300m in sub-48sec with a constantly reduced recovery; female in sub-55sec; same reduced recovery. The recovery for the 300m session would commence at 1m 45sec, each recovery reducing by 5sec until the final recovery is only 15sec (1minute 45sec > 15sec)
- 10 × (5 × 100m), with 10sec hold between each repetition and 1min 30sec jog between sets.

All of these three sessions, while looking reasonable on a training schedule, are indeed very challenging and should only be attempted by the high-performance long-distance runner.

Other running sessions to improve strength endurance are hill running, step work, turnabouts, back-to-backs and zigzag runs. Hills can be done up an incline of up to 20–30 degrees, either on a road, parkland, forest, grassland or golf course. Hill training is great conditioning and strength work and is perhaps the closest of any of the types of conditioning – outside of repetition running – that resembles the event. Hill training is also an excellent way to work on relaxation, postural control and maintaining a good technique and technical model. The distance of the hill and the number of sets and repetitions will vary depending on the event and the time of year. However, the long-distance runner's hill repetitions will be longer in duration than those of his middle-distance counterpart. Once he is into the specific preparation phase, the number of repetitions will be quite high and the total distance of the repetition equivalent to his race distance. For example, a 10,000m runner would run over a distance totalling 10,000m. This could comprise ten repetitions of 1,000m. The recovery between repetitions would be a jog-back recovery. If the recovery needs to be shorter to get a more specific effect, the recovery back-down could be on a bicycle, on a shorter route back, or even in the coach's car! This is not only to make for a shorter recovery, but to also ensure that the athlete does not have to run back down the hill, thus avoiding any braking action, which can lead to injury.

Step running can be done in a stadium, at a multi-storey car park or in an office building. It is a similar method to hill running, but is done in a more controlled

Fig. 90. Hill training can be used to improve either strength endurance or speed endurance. What effect is required, and which energy system is being trained, will determine the length of the hill, the number of repetitions and sets, as well as the recoveries. The picture shows Jo Pavey on a long hill in Richmond Park working on strength endurance. Whatever the type of hill, there should always be an emphasis on technique and relaxation.

environment. It is also invaluable if the athlete lives in an environment where there are no hills. The principle of ensuring that he has a high knee lift, drives off his rear leg and has active arms is the key to good technique and ensuring that the maximum benefit is derived from the hill or step sessions (see Fig. 90).

The following sessions, while useful to improve strength endurance and coordination, are likely to be used sparingly, if at all, by long-distance elite runners, who are more likely to focus on the Oregon circuit, hill running, plyometrics and specific circuits to improve their conditioning. However, it is good to understand the impact of the following types of training sessions so that they can be used on occasions to add variety to the training programme.

Turnabouts are similar to a shuttle run, in which the athlete will run a large number of repetitions or for a given time over a short distance, and has to keep turning to run in the direction he has just come from. For example, the athlete would run 12 × 120m, with a turn at each end, or run round a post. With a back-to-back session, the athlete runs for a given distance, has a short rest and then repeats the distance again. The number of repetitions will be small, but with a reasonable number of sets. In a back-to-back session, he would run 5 (sets) × (3 × 100m); 10sec recovery with 1minute 30sec between the sets, the total adding up to his race distance. Zigzag running (see Fig. 41) is over distances between 180–210m, but the athlete does not run in a straight line. The distance is split into 30m legs, each at 90 degrees to the last leg and marked by posts or cones. Therefore, the athlete has to continually slow down to check his speed, turn and begin to work hard on the next leg. The recovery is a jog recovery down the side of course and the number of repetitions is high. This also simulates a race situation, in which he will never have a clear run and is being constantly checked and blocked by other athletes.

RESISTANCE TRAINING

Resistance training is a versatile training tool that adds variety and spice to the normal training regime. It is also another form of conditioning training. It can either be utilized against the natural environment, such as mud, wind, snow, sand, surf, altitude and water. Or it can be used against a force, such as towing, harness running, weighted belts, power suits and medicine ball work. The resistance training can be used with any training method, such as a steady-state run, hill work and repetition work, wherever the coach feels it is applicable. The effect is an increase in muscular endurance and coordination. It applies to all endurance events, but should be used selectively with the long-distance events. It can be both general and specific, depending on the phase of the periodized year during which it is employed. Resistance training adds variety to the training programme – it is a different challenge, with good physiological benefits as well as psychological ones. It does not have to be used every week, but is very beneficial during each of the preparation phases.

Using the natural resources of the environment as a resistance is both cheap and effective. Wind and mud are regularly available throughout the year; however, snow is not available as frequently as in the past, but when available has the same conditioning effect. Using surf training and sand dune running may require a certain amount of travelling, unless the athlete happens to be fortunately placed geographically. Simple things like running into the wind and over muddy terrain makes the athlete much stronger and these elements are easy to

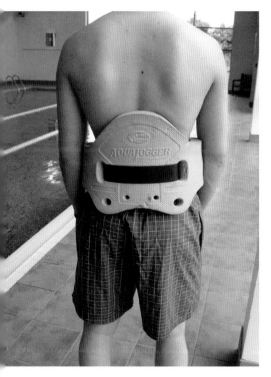

Fig. 91. Wet-vest training is excellent for maintaining aerobic fitness levels. This type of training can be used as part of an overall training programme to take the pressure off the legs and do some non-weight-bearing training. It can also be used in the case of injury. The photograph shows how the wet vest will keep the athlete buoyant in the water and therefore allow him to maintain his correct running technique while doing the training.

find. He has to work much harder than in normal conditions, which accentuates both the arm and leg action. He must, however, ensure that with this type of training his technique does not suffer and he maintains a good technical model. This means a slight shortening of his stride and ensuring a good foot placement.

A mini-parachute, with an attached harness, can be purchased, then fitted to his body. He can then run into the wind catching the air in the parachute, which will act as an extra resistance and force to work against it. He must ensure, however, that he modifies his technique slightly.

Similarly, when running on sand dunes, the athlete must ensure that he has a high knee lift to drive out of the sand and ensure that his landing foot is secure. When running on mud, he must not slip backwards. Sand dune running can be incorporated with hill running. This is an excellent form of resistance training, ensuring good strength endurance. Areas such as Methyr Mawr (South Wales) and Southport (Lancashire) are ideal for this type of training. Sand dune running can also be used for normal repetition work, again putting extra emphasis on the athlete's ability to keep driving through and out of the sand. This helps with his conditioning programme and makes his legs much stronger. Another type of training that can be utilized on the sand is to have a circuit of approximately 1min in length and see how many circuits can be completed in a given time of 10min, 15min or 20min. The terrain, in conjunction with the competition element, will not only train the lactate threshold of the athlete, but also the lactate turning point.

Normal hill training, whether on grass, road, steps, parkland or in forests, is an excellent form of resistance training, but it is particularly applicable to sand hill running, with the extra underfoot resistance added to the resistance of the hill itself. Running in the surf, up to mid-calf in height, is not only good conditioning work, it is also invigorating and therapeutic for the legs.

Altitude training is another type of conditioning and resistance training, but one that should be used carefully and at specific times of the year. The best effects are obtained when the length of stay at altitude is for a minimum of three weeks, repeated often throughout the year and at a height of between 2,000–3,500m. The initial training should be of low intensity until the body has acclimatized to this different environment. The more frequent the visits to altitude, the quicker the acclimatization. It is particularly effective during the competition period and will achieve the best effects up to twenty-one to twenty-eight days after returning. Altitude training effects can work for up to six weeks after returning to sea level. After an initial uplift in performance upon returning to sea level, there will be a dip in performance before returning to the high performance levels. Precautions at altitude should be taken with regard to sleep, hydration and exposure to the sun.

Water training – in a swimming pool – can also be very beneficial for the long-distance runner. Because of the high volume of his training, the number of training sessions involved and the surfaces he trains on, it is good to do some aerobic water training every three to four weeks to take the pressure off the legs and revitalize them. Because of their psychological need to keep their volume high, some high performance athletes do their water training on their rest day. It is very useful when the athlete is injured, but is also very good for building and maintaining the oxygen base. Because there is no weight-bearing, there is no stress on the legs. With water training, the athlete may replicate an aerobic run, spending the same duration in the water, or may do a repetition session. The same technique as running should be employed with a vigorous arm and leg action to keep the torso as high above the water as possible. A wet-vest or buoyancy aid can be used if required (see Fig. 91).

Similarly, for the same reasons as he would use water training, the high performance long-distance runner can supplement his training with a static, racing, spin or mountain bike, depending on the training session and the effect he wants to gain from it. Although it may be difficult from both a time and access point of view, it is better, if possible, to use the wet vest.

Harness running and towing exercises have to be used very judiciously and correctly so that there is no injury to the athlete and no risk of impairing his technique. With both these methods, the harness or weight being towed can either be fixed to a static object, or pulled by the athlete. Examples used with these exercises are harnesses, tyres, wall bars, parachutes or rollers. The emphasis at all times is on correct technique and the driving phase of running. Unless he feels this is the best conditioning method for him, it is unlikely that the long-distance runner would employ this as his chosen conditioning method in his training programme.

When a belt around the waist containing weights is used, the athlete can do any of his normal training accompanied by the belt. This could include steady-state training repetition work, hill training or circuit training. The coach will decide the amount of weight placed in the belt, which can be increased or decreased depending on the time of the year and the desired training effect. These particular training methods are very good for strengthening the abdominal and lower back muscles. But because training with an additional weight can affect his centre of gravity and his technique, the athlete must ensure that he is totally concentrated on running correctly at all times in training. Once the weighted belt is removed, not only is the athlete stronger, but more powerful because he is no longer carrying the additional weight.

Similarly, with hill training to improve his arm strength and arm drive, the runner can carry small dumb-bells or pebbles in his hands to increase the local muscular endurance in his arms. The athlete can wear a power suit similar to an underwater swimsuit, containing pockets around the major muscle group areas where weights can be inserted. Like the weighted belt, the amount of weight inserted will be determined by the athlete's fitness, the time of year and the effect required. Most training aspects utilizing the power suit can be undertaken. However, this suit can get quite hot and the training sessions undertaken with it should be not too long, as it is very demanding and tiring training in this suit.

All of the above methods may be employed by the long-distance runner, but are more likely to be used to improve a specific weakness that needs addressing and strengthening, rather than as the specific chosen conditioning session. The aim of all these types of resistance training, as well as bringing an element of variety, is to make the athlete work harder against a given resistance or force.

All conditioning work should be introduced during the general preparation phase. The greatest intensity of conditioning work will be during the specific preparation phase. It is important that conditioning or strengthening training is continued throughout the whole season. This will not entail as much strength or conditioning sessions as during the specific preparation phase, nor will there be as many exercises or repetitions involved. Far too many athletes and coaches stop all strength and conditioning work as they enter the pre-competitive phase, with the result that all conditioning and strength work done since October, and the accumulative effects they have gained by stopping in May, will be lost by the time of the competition phase in late July and August. This type of training must be continued in a reduced form to carry the effects through into the pre-competition and competition phases.

While not undertaking and placing quite as much importance on conditioning as other on other types of training, it is essential that it is not neglected by the high performance long-distance runner. It is important that the conditioning work he does includes core stability and a predominance of leg conditioning work, as well as some general and arm conditioning. Any weaknesses should be addressed in order to make him a better all-round, well-conditioned athlete.

Fig. 92. The use of compression socks – support socks – which are designed to support and increase blood circulation through graduated pressure on the lower leg and foot, ensuring that there is no pooling of blood in the lower limb.

Fig. 93. Rear view of the sand pit showing the muscles in action from the hip downwards.

Fig. 93a. The same exercise in the sand, with the leg about to drive forward followed by the free leg. Each leg will be strengthened alternately over a set number of repetitions and set distances.

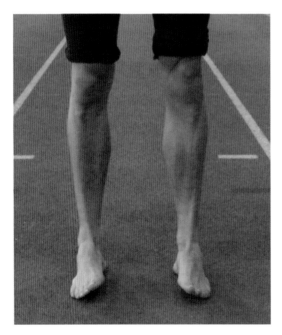

Fig. 93b. The key areas of the leg which are susceptible to injury can be strengthened by a variety of methods, one of which is to work bare-footed on a variety of surfaces. A good practice is to wear no footwear whilst at home. This exercise guards against over-pronation whilst also strengthening the ligaments, muscles and tendons of the leg, ankle and foot by walking on the outside of the foot, on the track.

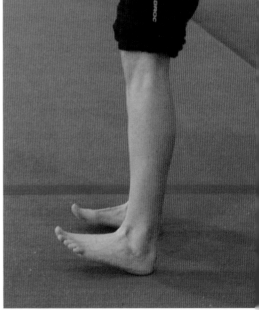

Fig. 93c. On an indoor surface, this exercise is to strengthen the tendons, ligaments and muscles around the Achilles tendon by walking on the heels. The exercise impacts all the way up through the knees to the hips. The number of repetitions and the distance will be determined by the athlete/coach.

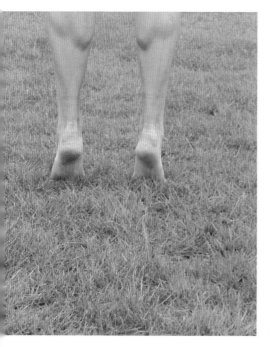

g. 93d. The strengthening effect on the calf muscles and ankle area. As with the sand pit, the grass area should be ecked thoroughly first for any objects which could cause ury.

Fig. 93e. This is the same exercise viewed from the side. The length of each repetition, and number should be determined by the athlete/coach.

CHAPTER 5

INJURY PREVENTION

The long-distance runner, because of the volume of his training and the number of weekly sessions he accumulates over many years, will be vulnerable to both injury and illness. It is important that everything possible is done to ensure that this double threat is minimized and, where possible, neutralized. Statistically, 70 per cent of injuries will occur in training. Therefore, the following chapter looks at several methods of avoiding or minimizing injury and also ways of monitoring the training programme so that potential injuries, stresses or overtraining are spotted early enough and are avoided. It also illustrates that if one of these problems arises or appears imminent, the correct support structure needs to be in place to deal with any likely outcomes. It also aims to raise the awareness of both the long-distance runner and his coach of the problems, possibilities and pitfalls that they may encounter and how to be best placed; first, to prevent them, or, second, to be prepared for them.

Being Proactive

The long-distance runner can help himself by having his own self-monitoring sheet covering daily body weight, daily sleep patterns, nutrition, resting heart rate and his attitude to training. This sheet can easily be adapted to be part of his daily training diary. The following illustrates how he can be proactive, not reactive, and ensure that nothing is left to chance.

No athlete likes to be inactive, therefore to ensure that all the planning, preparation and training reach fruition, the athlete and coach should be proactive and not reactive in ensuring that any missed training due to injury or illness is kept to a minimum. There are simple, but often overlooked, aspects in a training programme that need to be adhered to if injury is to be avoided. These include: not running in worn training shoes (whether the wear be on the heel or sides); not racing in new training shoes, particularly in

a marathon; adhering to a correct diet, with plenty of hydration; incorporating off-road running as part of the training process; always doing a full warm-up and cool-down; employing a good technical model; moving into track sessions in flats or racing shoes before progressing into spikes; and including a daily stretching programme. These are just some of the ways to nullify the chance of injury.

There are three key proactive areas that should be put into place. The first area is to ensure that the training is not only correctly balanced, but also includes plenty of off-road running, non-weight-bearing training, rest and regeneration. The second key area is having in place the correct support systems, which are not only instantly available if there is a problem, but especially are utilized to avoid any minor problems becoming major ones. The third key area – which is covered in detail later in the chapter – is to allow the athlete to work hard, then recover thoroughly and with care.

It is essential that any training programme is progressive and well-structured in order to ensure there is the minimum chance of injury. Therefore, it is crucial that a good conditioning programme is in place (see Chapter 4) particularly core stability and leg strength. Good conditioning will also ensure that the athlete's basic technical model can hold up under the constant impact it will undergo during the many training sessions and miles accrued over the years. To support the technical model, running drills are essential. However, the running drills are not effective unless the long-distance runner has a good strength and core base to work from. Therefore, it is important that all these aspects of his training, which fit together and complement each other, are not neglected.

Due to the high mileage they undertake, endurance runners often complain of lower back pain, tightness in the hips and shin, and foot pain. In order to ward off injuries in areas of the body that are crucial for endurance success, the following five conditioning drills are essential

- dynamic stretching – prepares the joints for the rigours of distance training
- skipping hurdles drills – assist in strength development for the gluteous muscles, hip flexors, back and abdominal muscles. These can be supported by advanced training drills using a medicine ball to strengthen further the core and build a better running posture
- lower leg conditioning – drills for conditioning the lower leg to allow the athlete to sustain a greater training load
- core stability – exercises designed to develop the entire core rather than just focusing on the lower abdominals
- skipping drills – an exercise sequence designed to tie together all of the components of the entire programme.

These drills will allow a distance runner to improve fundamental skills and lower the risk of injury. They will also help the coach to check for any imbalance in the running technique.

There is a variety of ways to ensure that athletes are not subjected continually to high-impact road training. The first method is to make sure that training is not all done on the same surface and that a proportion of it is done off-road, on more forgiving surfaces than constantly running on tarmac or hard synthetic tracks (see Figs 94 and 95). Constant training on hard surfaces can lead to injuries such as shin splints and stress fractures. Surfaces that can be utilized as an alternative to road running include grassland, forest paths, parkland, canal paths, playing fields, sand, surf and golf courses. These surfaces are much easier on the legs and therefore there is less chance of injury. They also bring variety and a change of environment to the training programme. By watching the volume of miles run by his athlete and ensuring that there is a variety of different types of terrain and environments for him to train on, the coach is being proactive in ensuring that his athlete is less likely to pick up an injury.

Similarly, when training at high intensity on the track – particularly in the early season pre-competition sessions – it is advisable for the runner to train in his racing flats. This way, his legs do not suffer as much and allows them to get used to both the intensity of this type of training and the surface. Then, later in this phase of training or in the competitive phase, when his legs have adapted to the work and surface, spikes can be introduced into the training routine.

There are other methods which the coach at times can include in the training routine to ensure his athletes do not get injured. These activities are sometimes referred to as 'cross-training', because they ensure that an athlete maintains his aerobic base and cardiovascular

fitness while having no weight-bearing on his legs. With this type of training, all the aerobic training methods covered in Chapter 3 can be used. The two main non-weight-bearing exercises are water training and cycling. In both instances, a large amount of aerobic training can be done with no impact-loading stress being put on the legs. The cycling can be done on a racing, mountain or static bike. Water training, in particular, can be utilized if the athlete has a leg injury and needs to maintain his aerobic fitness base while keeping off the injured leg.

Another type of cross-training is cross-country ski-machine training, in which the legs move in a skiing motion on a static machine. Once the technique has been mastered, heavy sessions can be used, although because of the technique it is difficult to do high intensity sessions on this machine. However, because it is so smooth, the machine avoids any jarring or impact problems. Many of these machines can now be found in fitness centres. This type of training is very good for maintaining a good aerobic level; cross-country skiers have some of the highest VO_2 max readings in the world. However, cross-country ski training is not a substitute for running training, because the action required with ski training differs from that used in the normal running

Fig. 94. An example of off-road running, which is fundamental to the high performance long-distance runner in safeguarding his legs from constant high-impact pounding. All types of endurance running training can take place off-road.

Fig. 95. Another example of an off-road running environment showing the variety of endurance training terrains that are generally accessible to all.

action. It is best, particularly with the injured athlete, to use ski training in conjunction with water training or cycling in order to get the higher intensity sessions into the training programme. It is also possible to use the machine to strengthen the upper body against different resistances. Used in conjunction with a heart rate monitor, it is an ideal way of maintaining aerobic fitness.

Running in water is nearer to the actual technique of running. If possible, it is preferable to train in the water without a buoyancy aid or wet vest, unless the athlete is not a good swimmer. The technique is to keep as high as possible in the water, using the arms as a driving force and with the knees in a high driving position. It is similar to running on the spot, but in the water (see Fig. 96). In this way, he can either work for a given time, such as 45min, to simulate an aerobic run, or he can do repetition sessions of 6 × 3min, with a 1min recovery (still in the pool). As an alternative, he can also swim a large number of lengths to build up his aerobic base and give his legs a rest from the constant pounding on the roads. Heart rate monitors can be used in these water sessions so that a comparison of readings can be made with normal training loads to ensure the work rates are at the correct level.

With cycling, the athlete can use a static bike, found in most leisure centres, or a normal bike to use on the road, or a mountain bike for a rougher terrain. Once again, a high number of miles can be achieved without much stress on the legs and a very high aerobic level maintained. A cycling training session can either be for a set time or a set distance. With a normal cycle training session, the different types of terrain, such

Fig. 96. The wet vest is worn in a pool in a depth of water that the athlete cannot stand up in. Here, a normal running action, aided by the wet vest, allows the athlete to do normal running training in a non-weight-bearing environment. The upper body has to remain high above the water to allow for the normal running action.

as hills and undulations, will provide the resistance required to make the runner work harder. With a static bike, the resistance is provided by the controls on the machine.

Another excellent way of maintaining fitness levels, with again no stress on the legs, is to use a spin bicycle (see Fig. 97). Here, the athlete can go through his normal training programme of repetition work, steady running, *fartlek* training, or a tempo/lactate threshold run. He sits with the spin wheel in front of him and propels it with his feet. Coming inside and doing 10–15min on a spin bike is also an excellent way to aid recovery after a steady-state, long run, or repetition session. If used regularly, it will also improve the athlete's cadence.

All of the above methods not only stave off possible injury, they also add variety to the training programme and freshen up the athlete's legs. They can be used as the second session of the day in conjunction with a normal running type of session, so that the athlete does not feel he is missing out totally on his running training.

A correct warm-up is essential if injury is to be prevented. It is of the utmost importance that the body is thoroughly warmed up and mobile prior to the commencement of the training session, particularly if it is a high intensity session. The warm-up should include jogging, stretching or dynamic stretching, strides and acceleration runs. Similarly, it is of equal importance that a thorough cool-down routine – including stretching and strides – always concludes each training session.

The long-distance runner must ensure that he is supple, flexible and lacking in tension. This is to ensure

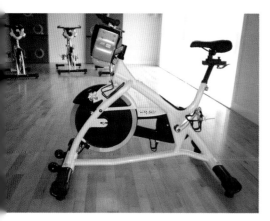

Fig. 97. A spin bike allows the athlete to again use a non-weight-bearing activity as part of the training programme. It is particularly beneficial at the end of a normal training session to loosen off the legs and assist with the athlete's running velocity.

that he remains injury-free and that his stride length is not impeded. The loss of a single centimetre on each stride can be the loss of well over 100m in a 10,000m race and much more in the half or full marathon. A new concept which relieves tension in every part of the body is the foam roller.

SMR Techniques

Foam rollers, tennis balls and other such implements are used in self-myofascial release (SMR), a technique designed to release the build-up of tension in the muscles and tendons that could lead to injury. While stretching will improve the length of the muscle, SMR and massage adjust muscle tone and help with the breakdown of soft-tissue adhesions and scar tissue. As in stretching, foam rolling does not show marked improvement overnight, but requires a period of constant use. As well as breaking down adhesions and scar tissue, foam rolling will improve mobility and range of movement, decrease the tone of overactive muscles and improve the quality of movement. It is cheaper than massage, but should not be used on an injured area.

The SMR techniques either utilize pressure or density. With density, there are three options: increasing the mass of the area being worked upon; decreasing the volume; or increasing the mass while decreasing the volume The easiest option is to increase the mass, for example, when progressing from a tennis ball to a lacrosse ball, or from a lighter foam roller to a heavier foam roller. Similarly, if the aim is to increase pressure, either the force needs to be increased, or the area being worked on decreased.

A foam roller is the largest implement used; the smallest is a tennis ball. The foam roller is very versatile, as it can work almost every muscle group using the foam roller alone. The rollers also come in varying densities, which allows for progression as well (for example, white roller – less dense; black roller – more dense). The rollers are best used for the large muscle/fascial areas such as the gluteal, quadriceps and the iliotibial band. The IT band is one of the main areas of injury for the endurance runner around the knee. It is a superficial thickening of tissue that extends from the thigh through the hip to below the knee, and is crucial to stabilizing the knee during the running action.

The medicine ball may actually be a more versatile tool for SMR purposes. Not only is it more focal when compared to the roller (the surface area being worked is smaller, which increases pressure), but it also allows more three-dimensional working. Any muscle group that can be used with the foam roller can be used with the medicine ball.

White Roller – less dense

Sticks

Black Roller – More dense

Fig. 98. The diagram shows the different types of implements used in self-myofascial work – in addition to tennis, lacrosse and medicine balls, also the less dense white roller, the denser black roller and the stick.

A tennis ball is generally the smallest implement used for SMR purposes and is very convenient for muscle/fascial groups with smaller surface areas (for example, the plantar fascia and the calves), as well as upper body muscles where the ball must be placed against a wall (for example, the pectoral muscles). The tennis ball progression, once it becomes easily managed, is to move on to a lacrosse ball, then on to light and then dense rollers.

The stick is another implement that can be used in soft tissue work. While neither better nor worse than the other mentioned implements, its narrow diameter allows work on tendons (for example, hamstrings and quadriceps) at a much better level than either the foam roller or medicine ball. This is particularly true of the hamstrings, because when using the foam roller the hands are employed in taking the rest of the body's weight.

When using any of these implements – foam roller, medicine ball, lacrosse ball, tennis ball or stick – it is important that the correct position for each exercise is taken up, otherwise it will cause stress and undue fatigue. It is best to work each area for between 1–2min more if very tense, less if lacking in tension. The longer an athlete has been working on this type of programme, the less time he will require on each exercise, as the tissue tension and quality will have improved and therefore each area will require less time and attention.

Rest and Regeneration

A key area in aiding recovery and often neglected by a great many athletes is rest and regeneration. Too many athletes continue to train hard, when a rest day would be far more beneficial and productive. This rest day may mean doing only one training a session a day instead of the normal two, or a complete day off once per week, once every ten days or once a fortnight depending on the length of the microcycle. Increased training loads require an increased recovery to ensure the appropriate adaptation. This is particularly important after high intensity training sessions (see Figs 100 and 107). Failure to restore the body to its normal values (homeostasis) results in overtraining and the incorrect training effect.

After a high intensity training session there will be an increase in the pulse rate, body temperature and muscle soreness, as well as an accumulation of metabolic by-products. There will also be a decrease in fluids, energy reserves and a reduction in the immune system, therefore the sooner the body is returned to homeostasis, the better. It is important that immediately after a high intensity training session, the lost fluids are replaced and that a low intensity cool-down of jogging and stretching takes place. This will help the utilization of lactate and its removal along with waste products from the muscle tissue. It will assist the gradual return to normal of both the body's core temperature and the pulse rate. It will help to prevent blood pools occurring at the body's

Fig. 99. In this picture, we see the less dense white roller in operation helping to ease and stretch the muscles around the hip-flexor area

Recovery Process	Minimum Recommended Time	Maximum Recommended Time
Restoration of ATP and PC	2min	3min
Repayment of alactic acid O_2 debt	3min	5min
Restoration of myglobin	1min	2min
Restoration of muscle glycogen	10hr	46hr, after prolonged exercise
Removal of lactic acid from the blood and muscles	30min–1hr, depending on type of recovery	1hr–2hr, depending on type of recovery
Repayment of lactic acid O_2 debt	30min	1hr

Fig. 100. Recommended recovery times after intense training.

extremities. In addition, it will lower both the hormonal levels and the psychological levels of arousal, which have been brought about by the high intensity training. It will also assist in the removal of muscle spasms and the effects of muscle soreness.

Rest is a specific training unit that allows the body to recover and recharge, ready for the next training unit. It can either be a passive rest, in which no physical activity takes place and with plenty of relaxation and sleep, or it can be an active rest, in which another physical activity, such as orienteering, swimming or cycling, can be undertaken. It is important therefore that it is included in the training programme to aid the recovery phase. As can be seen from Fig. 100, after intense exercise it takes certain areas a long time to return to normal levels. To speed up this process, the recovery times for different types of interval sessions are recommended in Fig. 100a.

Regeneration is an additional aid in accelerating the body's recovery so that it returns to normal as quickly as possible. Regeneration can be covered in a variety of ways, from simple rehydration to massage, sauna, ice therapy, hydrotherapy, acupuncture/acupressure, or, possibly, hyperbaric oxygenation therapy.

Rehydration

With rehydration, the aim is to replace the depleted energy reserves, fluid electrolytes and carbohydrates as quickly as possible.

Massage

Massage increases the muscle blood flow, simulates the nervous system, reduces muscle tightness, reduces anxiety levels and gives the athlete a feeling of well-being. It also reduces pain, disperses scar tissue and adhesions, and also realigns muscle fibres, all of which speed up recovery. For these reasons, and for any early warning signs of injury that the treatment may detect, massage is very beneficial in quickly restoring the athlete to normal and has both a physical and psychological effect. These early-warning signs can allow him to back off training and manage the problem quickly instead of wasting weeks of training if the problem is allowed to develop. Massage should be undertaken as often as finances allow, but particularly after high intensity training sessions.

Fig. 100a. This chart shows the recommended recovery times for high intensity training sessions. The recovery should be aided by hydration and recovery nutrition. The high intense session should always be followed by a low intensity session, whether later in the day or the following day.

RECOVERY TIMES AFTER INTENSE TRAINING:	
Area of Recovery	Time Required
Creatine Phosphate (CP)	4 – 6 minutes
Heart Rate and Blood Pressure returns to Normal	20 minutes
Blood Glucose improves after Carbohydrate intake	20 – 30 minutes
Homeostasis and lactate below 3mmls	30 minutes
Increased protein re-synthesis	60 – 90 minutes
Neuromuscular/sensor motor recovery of muscle	2 Hours
Normalization of Hema tokrit (Blood Ratio Components)	6 Hours - 1Day
Restoring of Glycogen stores in the Liver	1 Day
Refill of Glycogen in high loaded Muscles	2 – 7 Days
Refill of Fat in the muscles	3 – 5 Days
Regeneration of proteins in muscle fibres	3 – 10 days
Structural repair to mitochondria	7 – 14 Days

There are five terms describing the different massage techniques: vibration (shaking); tapotement (percussion); petrissage (kneading); effleurage (stroking); and friction (small-range intensive stroking). Depending on his needs at the time, the long-distance runner may find a combination of these techniques being used on him during his massage session. Massage treatment will be used in three distinct ways:

• during a training session to help with high loads and training intensity and to increase training potential
• preparatory massage as part of a warm-up 15–20min before a competition or training session. Techniques here will vary, depending upon the athlete's needs, either to relax him if overstimulated, or arouse him if subdued and lethargic. Sometimes it may be localized if there is a minor injury or soreness. However, it should be part of the warm-up process and not replace it.

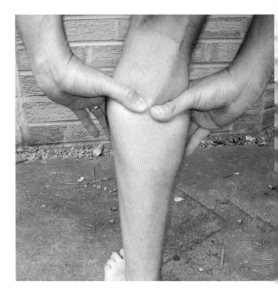

Fig. 102. The gastrocnemius and soleus muscles, the two major muscles in the calf, meet at the heel – the Achilles' tendon – and because of the constant wear and tear all this area needs attention and care. Similarly, the muscles and tendons attached to the knee need care also, because of the constant stress. The aim of self-massage is to maintain and, where possible, repair these hard-worked muscles. They are often stiff, sore and tender from the constant pounding on hard surfaces. In this picture, the thumbs are drawn outward across the muscle towards the fingers. This is done all the way up the calf. Then it is done in the opposite direction across the fibres of the muscles. It is repeated on each leg. Also, the fingers can be used gently to straighten and realign the bulky muscles back into their correct position. In this way, any soreness or swelling is dissipated and it opens up the muscles for normal movement.

• restorative massage is given after a high intensity or loading in a training session or after competition. The techniques used here will be to lower stress levels and reduce muscle tension and stress

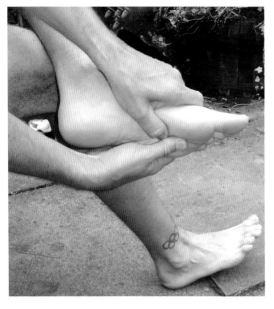

Fig. 101. With the long-distance runner, the feet have to absorb the shock from the consistent pounding they take each day, sometimes up to three times a day. They are also – unless blistered – very neglected. As shown in the picture, it is easy to massage the underside of the feet, by simply sitting with one foot over the other. In this way, both hands are free to massage the feet. Use the fingers and thumbs, first with small circular movements on the sole of the foot, including toes and heel. Then repeat with a clenched fist across the sole and arch on both feet. The toes can be massaged separately too.

The length and number of massage sessions required weekly will depend upon the type of training the athlete is undergoing during a particular microcycle. However, a high performance long-distance runner, because of his high volume of training, needs at least two massages per week. This will allow him to get rid of any soreness, stiffness or tightness in the muscles and flush out the waste products ready for his next training session. Another benefit of massage is that the long-distance runner will begin to become more aware of his body, knowing which of his muscles and tendons are stressed or sore.

Self-massage is another option, which can be done straight after training, late in the evening before going

therapy and/or an ice massage reduce fluid build-up in the muscles and alleviate post-exercise soreness. Cold baths, where the legs and other parts of the body are wholly or partially immersed in the water for up to

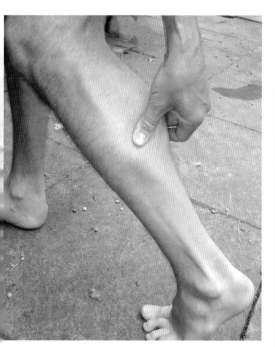

Fig. 103. In this picture, the calf muscle is being squeezed. Handfuls of muscle are taken into the hand and the fingers and thumbs are kneaded into them, then they are released. This again is done systematically working from the bottom of the leg to the top, constantly squeezing with both hands and then letting go. It is then repeated on the other leg. This sounds difficult and painful but once a method has been found and a rhythm set up, it is very beneficial. Both legs should be done twice with the emphasis on the second occasion being on working towards the bone. To warm up the muscles, the flushing method is employed. With this method, the leg is stroked using a flat hand one after the nother for approximately 30sec, all around each leg. Flushing and friction are also useful for working the Achilles' area.

to bed, or first thing in the morning if there is a stiffness, soreness or tightness in the muscle (see Figs 102–104). Massage is highly beneficial, restorative and highly invigorating, especially when used in conjunction with hydrotherapy.

Saunas

Saunas are an excellent form of regeneration and therapy. A sauna should be followed by a cold plunge. This is because the heat from the sauna has stimulated the blood to help reduce the waste products in the system, muscle soreness and muscle tightness; the body is then reinvigorated by the cold plunge. Ice

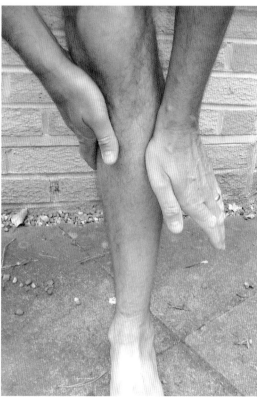

Fig. 104. The shin area is very susceptible to injury. This is because the one major muscle in this area – tibialis – is placed under great stress and pressure. There is also a low blood supply to this area, therefore injuries are not only painful but slow to heal. The massage along this area should be slow and gentle, avoiding lumps and bruises and using flushing strokes towards the body, with one hand following the other. Circular friction movements will reduce swelling. Shin splints is a painful injury that runs up the side of the shin and can be aided by using flushing and circular movements with the pad of the thumb. It will not pass immediately and may take several days. However, if this method is used regularly it could prevent shin splints. The knuckles may be used on less sensitive areas of the leg in order to get deeper. Other methods of massage for this part of the leg that can be used are shaking – taking the muscle in both hands and shaking the leg – and tapping, which involves tapping the length of the muscle from the ankle to the knee using alternate hands held as a loose fist. These two methods are to be used prior to a race or training and should not be used afterwards.

1min, have a similar effect, depending on how used to this method the athlete is. The current recommendation is to have the cold bath at normal temperature as it comes from the tap, without the addition of ice.

Hydrotherapy

Hydrotherapy involves the use of either hot and cold showers, or hot and cold spas or baths, and has the same principle as the other regeneration methods. It is therefore ideal for recovery, stretching and also for performing self-massage. The shower method – preferably power jets – which can be used at any time of day, should involve using the warm/hot shower for 1–2min, then the cold shower for 10–30sec, depending on how used to this method the athlete is. The process should be repeated three times. This method enhances muscle relaxation by stimulating light muscle contractions. Collectively, this promotes both physiological and neurological recovery.

If a hot spa is used in conjunction with a cold plunge pool, it provides an increase in peripheral circulation and neural stimulation. With the spa or bath method, the athlete should stay in the warm/hot spa or bath for 3–4min, and the cold one for 30–60sec. The process should be repeated three times. This method is best used at the end of the day. However, it should not be used if the athlete has a cold or virus, or has had a recent soft tissue injury.

Guidelines for bath/shower recovery Before the recovery exercise, the athlete should be well-hydrated and ensure he has cleaned his skin with soap and showered beforehand. These recovery strategies should not be used if he has a cold or virus, or a recent soft tissue injury (see table below).

Acupuncture and Acupressure

Acupressure – which uses finger pressure – may often be used as an accompaniment to massage. Acupuncture involves the use of needles and requires a specialist with the correct skills and training. Both employ similar techniques, however, in that their aim is to balance the energy fields within the body, based on the fourteen meridian points that pass through the body. The acupuncture points have lower electrical resistance and therefore can be measured and evaluated. Because it relaxes the muscles, acupuncture claims to have a positive effect on respiration, oxygen uptake and the immune system. It also has a good success rate with injuries. However, there are few qualified specialist practitioners to be found and they are expensive.

Hyperbaric Oxygenation Therapy

A new innovation in the search to get injured athletes back running again quickly is hyperbaric oxygenation therapy (HBOT). It is a means of increasing the availability of oxygen in the body. This is achieved by inhaling gas with a high oxygen content in an environment – chamber – with an increased atmospheric pressure, the premise being that this increase in partial pressure in the body will allow oxygen to reach damaged and fatigued parts of the body much quicker than under normal conditions. It therefore speeds up the healing or recovery process. It can also be utilized to accelerate training adaptations. However, there are only a few of these chambers available and they are very expensive.

All of the above methods of rest, whether active or passive, and regeneration are vitally important in helping the athlete's body return to normal as quickly as possible, to avoid injury and be mentally ready and physically refreshed for the next training session. To be proactive, these therapies should not be used randomly, but should be built into the training programme as specific sessions. It is also crucial that the training programme does not cause the athlete to overtrain, strain, reach a plateau or become stale. The coach must be constantly monitoring his athlete to ensure that this does not occur. The coach should also be acutely aware that any signs of stress may not only be due to overtraining or straining, but may also be linked directly to the Triad (see opposite). This is where checks regarding weight, pulse, training levels and diet, as well as coach observation, are crucial in the coaching jigsaw, in order to help monitor not only the athlete's training progress, but also his state of health. In this way, any possible major

Alternate	Hot (35–38°C)	Cold (10–16°C)	Number	Time of Day
Shower	1–2min	10–30sec	three	anytime: before, during or after a session
Bath/spa	3–4min	30–60sec	three	preferably at the end of the day

problems can be caught early and dealt with by the appropriate members of the support team.

The Triad

In the early 1990s, 'the triad' became part of the athletics vocabulary and subsequently an integral part of an athlete's development and long-term plan. Invariably, it is referred to as the 'female triad', but certain aspects are just as applicable to men. These areas refer to the harmful effects of excessive energy deficits on the reproductive and skeletal systems of highly trained athletes. The triad, as the word indicates, refers to three distinct areas of development, which, if not strictly monitored, can become areas of concern. The three areas are:

- eating disorders: including 'disordered eating' and energy availability
- osteoporosis: reduced bone mineral density
- amenorrhoea: absence of menstrual function.

However, monitoring these three areas can be extremely difficult, because high performance long-distance runners, because of the volume of their training and resultant physical make up – lean, gaunt, under normal body weight and so on – could quite easily be perceived to fall into the symptoms of the triad without this actually being the case. The evidence can be conflicting – symptoms not related to the triad – not apparent, not visual, or, even if positive, the athlete may be in denial and not accept the advice given. It is a very delicate issue that needs handling with care, with the correct agencies and experts involved where appropriate.

Eating Disorders

Energy availability is the amount of fuel or dietary energy that is available after training for all the other functions required by the body, such as growth, cellular

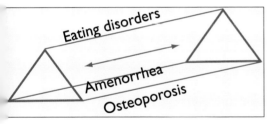

Fig. 105. This picture shows the main three elements of the Triad: eating disorders; osteoporosis; and amenorrhoea.

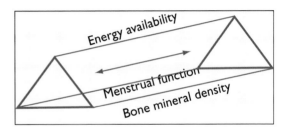

Fig. 106. Showing the continuum of the Triad and its effects on the high performance long-distance runner – energy availability, menstrual functions and bone mineral density.

maintenance and repair, thermoregulation and the menstrual cycle. With a high performance long-distance athlete, the increase in training and mileage does not necessarily increase appetite, therefore he may inadvertently not be eating enough. He must therefore eat to a plan – the more miles run, the more fuel/food required, otherwise energy intake may not match energy expenditure.

Eating disorders affecting the amount of energy available are a problem and there are a number of types, all with attendant features and effects. They tend to manifest themselves because of low self-esteem and high levels of perfectionism. They are apparent in both female and male endurance runners and are the result of a desire to control eating and weight. Some of the main types of eating disorders are as follows:

Anorexia nervosa This is a refusal to keep the body weight at or above the 85 per cent minimum body-weight requirement. There is an extreme fear of weight gain. In women, it can lead to amenorrhoea.

Bulimia nervosa This involves repeated bouts of binge eating, in which large amounts of food are consumed, followed by vomiting, laxatives, exercise, fasting or diuretics to then purge the body. It is a separate disorder to anorexia nervosa.

Eating disorders not otherwise specified (EDNOS) These are other eating disorders that do not fit into the above two categories, but can be as high as 50 per cent of eating disorders. They tend to have symptoms similar to the other two, but do not fit typically into one or the other.

Because athletes with eating disorders are compulsive about their eating, weight gain and shape, but are also involved in high mileage running, it makes any eating disorder all the harder to detect and treat.

Therefore; the amount of training involved for an athlete with one of these eating disorders will impose serious physiological and psychological demands on him. Endurance runners with eating disorders believe that reduced body weight/fat will enhance their performances. Coupled with this is usually a compulsive drive to train and succeed, perceiving running success as important to self-worth.

Although difficult to detect, there are certain warning signs for an endurance runner with eating disorders. These must not be ignored, even if it means a long, painful process of acknowledgement. The warning signs tend to be behavioural, psychological or physical.

Behavioural signs   In isolation, behavioural signs could mean nothing, but collectively a pattern will emerge, including extreme compulsive training, trips to the toilet post-eating, baggy tracksuits, eating tiny pieces of food, remaining alone, being secretive and a reluctance to socialize within the group. Similarly, observed direct evidence of fasting, vomiting, laxatives, diuretics is a sign.

Psychological signs   These include an obsession with gaining weight, mood swings, changes in personality, too much emphasis on diet, anxiety, withdrawal, depression, isolation, low self-esteem, unrealistic goals and wrong perception of body shape.

Physical signs   These include, poor circulation and feeling cold, recurrent injury, dry, rough skin, dizziness, amenorrhoea, poor sleeping patterns, sore throat, fluctuations in weight, damaged knuckles, swollen ankles, stomach, glands and face, and downy body hair. They are perhaps the easiest signs to recognize by the coach, training group, family or support team.

The major problem when faced with eating disorders is not only recognizing the symptoms and pattern, but also to get the athlete – particularly if he is being successful at that time – to confront the issue, as he will invariably have a completely different perception of both his behaviour and somatotype – body shape – to the person who is challenging him. It is a very sensitive issue, which needs handling very delicately indeed. The situation – particularly with younger high class performers – can be further clouded by **disorderly eating**. This is where athletes have 'fads' about certain foods, eat intermittently, eat foods that are lacking in energy value, or avoid food. This situation can be rectified more easily than the effects of an athlete with an eating disorder, although it is recognizing the symptoms and cause that is the key. External help from the support team, such as a doctor, psychologist, nutritionist or all three, may be necessary to rectify the problem.

Osteoporosis

Osteoporosis is a skeletal disease characterized by low bone mass and changes that increase fragility and susceptibility to fractures. Healthy bones are vital to a high performance long-distance runner. If he has a good, healthy diet, there should be no problems. The peak bone mass for a female is between twenty-five to thirty years of age. Healthy bones are constantly changing and adapting to the loads that the high performance long-distance runner imposes upon them. This is called remodelling and as well as the loadings, it is also affected by nutrition, lifestyle, medical support and hormonal and growth factors. Bone health can be measured by a DEXA scan (dual energy X-ray absorptiometry), which measures bone mineral density (BMD) for the whole body, hips, spine and the arm (radius). This provides what is known as a 'T' score. The World Health Organization defines osteoporosis as a bone density 'T' score of -2.5, but states that any score of -1 warrants investigation.

The DEXA scan should, if possible, be done annually, particularly with a high performance long-distance runner, and using the same scanner each time. Other methods of X-ray can be negative in the early stages, a bone scan is not specific, an MRI (magnetic resonance imaging) scan is expensive but has quick results, while a CAT (complete assisted tomography) scan can be detailed and accurate. The quicker the diagnosis and treatment, the quicker the athlete can return to training, so long as the result is not indicative of other attendant triad problems.

Other factors that influence bone healing are age, genetics, hormones, smoking, nutrition, circulation and poor technique. Blood tests can also be used to check on blood count, ferritin levels, thyroid, hormone levels, menstrual cycle and vitamin D (calcium, phosphate, and magnesium). Any bone can be affected. However, because of the loadings, mileage and overuse of specific areas by the high performance long-distance runner, it is more likely to be in the lower leg, shin area or the lower lumbar spine region.

Prevention is the key and must involve the support team, particularly the coach, doctor, nutritionist and physical preparation expert. Calcium, vitamin D and oestrogen levels need to be monitored (the latter is because osteoporosis and amenorrhoea can be interlinked), with possible use of medication. If applicable, the restoration of the menstrual cycle is important. Training should be progressive alongside a conditioning programme. Above all, any energy deficit, whether the athlete is consciously – see eating disorders above – or subconsciously not hungry and not taking enough fuel on board, must be addressed. Preventive intervention could prevent or minimize any major injuries and osteoporosis problems.

Amenorrhoea

This is obviously the one area of the triad that will not affect a male athlete. Sex hormones have a marked effect on the skeletal system and low oestrogen levels can lead to osteoporosis. The later a female athlete in heavy training goes through puberty, the more predisposed she will be to stress fractures. With exercise-associated amenorrhoea (lack of periods), the lack of oestrogen prevents bone resorption and decreases remodelling of the bones. As a result, this leads to a decrease in bone density, osteoporosis, inadequate bone mass and increased stress fractures.

There are three determinants that mainly affect the menses. These are body weight, energy expenditure and stress. Approximately 22 per cent of body fat is required for menstruation; dieting, extensive training, or eating disorders can affect this percentage drastically. An adult high performance long-distance runner needs this amount of body fat to maintain the menstrual pattern. Weight loss accounts for a third of females with amenorrhoea.

Energy expenditure is reliant on the remaining energy after training being added to by energy or fuel intake in the shape of food. Low energy availability appears to be a factor that impairs the reproductive system. High performance athletes will release and increase certain hormones with intense training through stress. These hormones can effect menstruation and treatment may well also cause further stress. Therefore intense training, coupled with disordered eating – food restriction, anorexia nervosa and bulimia nervosa – will lead to amenorrhoea and osteoporosis. The female long-distance runner with a very high mileage is more likely to be susceptible to a lack of periods and stress fractures.

Therefore, as mentioned earlier, the support team, particularly the doctor, psychologist and nutritionist, are key in not only monitoring the athlete, but in educating her – assuming she wants to listen. Fatigue, listlessness, depression and anaemia could be early signs of the triad. If the athlete has not had a menstrual period by the time she is eighteen years old, it should be investigated. If after six months she still has amenorrhoea, treatment should commence with an increased calorific intake, reduced training, vitamins, such as 1,500mg of calcium daily, and hormonal supplements.

The support team has three defined areas to monitor and support. First, nutrition, menstrual health and bone density. Second, injury management of stress fractures, fractures and other musculoskeletal injury risks. Finally, to aid performance through ensuring that consistent training does not delete iron and glycogen stores and that there is adequate recovery, nutrition and hydration.

The triad is difficult to monitor and detect, particularly as the three elements of its symptoms are not interlinked. All, or just one or two of them, could be apparent. Couple this with the athlete who does not want to recognize his or her problem and you have a delicate and dangerous situation that could delay or derail all the planning and preparation that has gone on during the previous years. The triad primarily affects female athletes, but male athletes can be affected by the first two areas just as easily. However, no matter how complex, if the triad is apparent a solution must be found by using the support team to the full. If a high performance athlete has a good diet and intake of food to meet the demands and increases in his or her training, it is more than likely that this will alleviate any problems that may lead to the triad occurring, particularly if much of the training involves a good conditioning programme and off-road running to ensure there is no risk of stress fractures. But it needs careful supervision and consistently monitored checks to ensure that no matter how diligent the athlete may be, there is no inadvertent straying into one of the triad's three areas.

Area of Recovery	Time Required
Creatine phosphate (CP)	4–6min
Heart rate and blood pressure returns to normal	20min
Blood glucose improves after carbohydrate intake	20–30min
Homeostasis and lactate below 3mmols	30min
Increased protein resynthesis	60–90min
Neuromuscular/sensor motor recovery of muscle	2hr
Normalization of hematokrit (blood ratio components)	6hr–1day
Restoration of glycogen stores in the liver	1 day
Refill of glycogen in high-loaded muscles	2–7 days
Refill of fat in the muscles	3–5 days
Regeneration of proteins in muscle fibres	3–10 days
Structural repair to mitochondria	7–14 days

Fig. 107. Recovery times after intense training.

Recovery Strategies

Because of the constant need to fit in each required training session and increase the volume of his training, the high performance long-distance runner can often neglect rest, recovery, nutrition, hydration and regeneration. It is vital that these strategies are in place. As Fig. 107 shows, it is important that they are acted upon immediately after a high intensity of loading, work or competition in order to start the recovery process.

Recovery Nutrition/Hydration

High performance athletes must understand that the further and more often they train and run, the more fuel they will need. Therefore, an athlete who is running over a 100 miles a week will require more fuel – food – than an athlete who is running a mere fraction of that total per week. You would not drive a car without constantly topping it up with fuel, otherwise it will stop. Similarly, the high performance long-distance runner needs to keep his fuel intake topped up to ensure that he does not break down. This has to be done constantly and his intake of food after hard training needs to happen quickly. Essential recovery foods aim to:

- refuel muscle glycogen (energy stores)
- regenerate muscle tissue
- repair muscle tissue
- minimize any disorder or condition by which the immune response has been reduced
- replace any lost fluids or electrolytes.

Timing is key in starting carbohydrate and glycogen resynthesis and should take place within 30min after completing training. This process is twofold, in that it not only helps the body to recover, but also ensures that during this vulnerable period, when the athlete's immune system is low – which can be between 3–72hr – the risk of infection is neutralized. Therefore, immediately post-exercise 1–1.5g carbohydrates (CHO/kg) are required, depending on the intensity and duration of the training session. This can be taken as either high carbohydrate food, which is the preference, or small, frequent carbohydrate feedings. If taken with protein, this will increase the insulin response and help resynthesis. This type of recovery can be achieved through either liquids or solid foods.

It is also important to remember that hydration should be occurring in conjunction with this process. This use of carbohydrates is important for minimizing the time when the athlete is vulnerable and prone to infection, particularly when undertaking double daily training sessions. The lower the stores, the faster will be the recovery. Muscle protein synthesis is the product of essential amino acids such as leucine. Therefore, 15–20g of high protein (6–8g of essential amino acids) assisted by carbohydrates are required to help muscle resynthesis and adaptation. Other nutrients that are important to include in recovery meals/snacks are:

- vitamin A – found in oily fish, fruit, dairy produce, leafy red and orange vegetables
- vitamin C – found in sweet potatoes, broccoli, peppers and berries
- vitamin E – found in nuts, oils, seeds and fish.

It is important that the high performance long-distance runner is aware of this and ensures that during this period of vulnerability when training intensely – whether through the volume of training or the type of session – he replenishes his body with fuel through snacks or meals as quickly as possible. Similarly, he must ensure that he is constantly hydrated, which is achieved through drinks containing sodium, chloride and potassium.

The athlete could bring his recovery snack to training in the form of supplements or foods. It is a good idea to always to have a spare recovery sachet with him in case he forgets to bring his recovery snack. Fig. 108 contains suggestions of foods that aid recovery.

With all individual athletes, their recovery adaptation to the demands of the volume, intensity or competition will be different. Therefore, these individual differences have to be taken into account in any recovery nutrition strategies. Nutrition is one of the key elements in helping support intense, high volume training by

Food	Protein	Carbohydrates
Yogurt × 125g	5g	20g
Skinned milk + raspberries	18g	36g
Chicken pasta salad	24g	50g
Tuna pasta + tomato sauce	21g	50g
Small turkey sandwich	20g	45g
Salmon and cheese sandwich	20g	40g
Glass of fruit juice	–	20g
Cereal bar	–	20–25g
Thin slice of bread	–	15g
Piece of fruit	–	15–20g

Fig. 108. Foods that aid recovery and their intake.

maximizing muscle recovery and adaptation. The recovery snack should include both carbohydrates and proteins, as well as a recovery drink, and should be taken within 30min of the end of the training session.

Recommended drinks that are high in both carbohydrates and protein include ForGoodnessShakes!, Lucozade Pro Muscle Shakes and YAZOO. The athlete will have to initially experiment to see what foods and drinks suit him best and get into a pattern of using this recovery strategy in training, but not on competition day. During the day, because of work commitments, it may be easier for the athlete to fuel up for training with energy snacks rather than try to eat a normal meal. These energy snacks and hydration energy drinks include:

- flavoured milk (YAZOO, ForGoodnessShakes!)
- creamy muesli
- cereal
- cereal bars
- dried fruit
- fruit smoothies
- yogurt
- flapjacks
- fruit juice
- malt loaf.

The high performance long-distance runner's body is a 'Rolls-Royce' of a machine and therefore should be treated like one with regard to fuelling (nutrition and food) and recovery (rest and the many types of regeneration) and therefore recovery nutrition after training and energy fuelling throughout the day is essential, so that he can constantly perform smoothly and efficiently, meeting any intensities and volumes on a regular daily basis.

Nutrition if Injured

The dilemma an athlete faces when injured is that, with the lack of activity, he fears he will become overweight, so his natural reaction is to cut back on his food intake, when in fact he needs to maintain a high intake of nutrients to aid his recovery. The approach to take depends on the type of injury that has occurred and whether there has been surgery. While nutrition alone will not cure an injury, a poor or reduced diet will most certainly hinder or hold up the recovery. If the injury is to the bone, the following nutrients in the diet are essential:

- calcium, magnesium, phosphorous and vitamins D and K.

If the injury is to a tendon, the following should be part of the required food intake:

- vitamin C, zinc, omega 3 and antioxidants.

Muscle injuries require the following nutrients:

- zinc, vitamin B, omega 3 and high quality protein.

Nutrition for the Long-Distance Runner

The high performance long-distance runner runs 100+ miles weekly and can run in excess of 5,000 miles a year. In the process, he will burn countless calories training for the event he specializes in. The more he runs, the more food he will need, therefore, knowing how best to fuel his body – including hydration – so that he can run well is very important. A good diet must include the following key types of food and can be supplemented by vitamins and supplements if required, although if the following recommendations plus constant rehydration are followed, these should not be necessary. Good nutrition is one of the first proactive steps in preventing illness and injury.

Foods are made up of **carbohydrates**, **protein** and **fat**. Endurance runners should eat a diet high in carbohydrates, moderate in protein and low in fat. Another key nutrient that is a must for athletes is **water**. The high performance long-distance runner needs to know why these nutrients are important, how much of them he should eat, and how much water he needs to drink before, during and after training. The following guidelines will ensure that his body will be adequately and properly fuelled, hydrated and able to train and compete at the high intense levels he requires.

Carbohydrates and Muscle Glycogen

The body's preferred fuel for long-distance running is muscle glycogen. Glycogen is the body's storage form of carbohydrate. If, through intense training, muscle glycogen breakdown exceeds its replacement level, glycogen stores will become depleted, resulting in fatigue and inability to maintain high level training and racing intensity. Therefore it will be necessary to replenish and maintain glycogen stores, by means of a diet that is rich in carbohydrates. Carbohydrates should provide 60–70 per cent of the long-distance runner's total calorific intake. To ensure he takes in the amount that is correct for him, a good guide is that he should multiply his weight in kilograms by 7 (in pounds by 3.2) in order to give the number of grams of carbohydrates he should consume daily.

One of the best sources of carbohydrate is grain products (preferably whole grains), such as bread, rice, cereal and pasta, as well as fruits, vegetables and low fat dairy foods. The daily amount required can be calculated by means of the products' food labels, which state how many grams of total carbohydrate are in a serving of each food. If possible, the long-distance runner's daily diet should include fifteen servings of grain products, at least six servings of fruits and six servings of vegetables, and at least five servings of low fat dairy foods. The following show the calorific value in grams of certain carbohydrate foods:

- a grain product, such as a slice of bread or half a cup of cooked rice or pasta, a serving of fruit, such as a piece of fruit or a cup of fruit juice, are all the equivalent of 15g carbohydrates
- a dairy product, such as 1 cup of low fat milk or yogurt, or 1½oz of cheese provides 12g carbohydrate
- a portion of vegetables, such as 1 cup of leafy raw vegetables or half a cup chopped vegetables, provides 5g carbohydrates
- starchy vegetables, such as peas or lentils, provide greater amounts – approximately half a cup serving provides 15–20g carbohydrates.

Protein

Protein is important to the long-distance runner because of the high volume and intensity of training he undertakes. It is needed for muscle growth and repair. His constant physical daily training will tend to reduce muscle protein breakdown and protein loss from the body. While some protein breakdown may occur during training, protein build-up is enhanced during the recovery and the effectiveness of protein synthesis is increased. When muscle glycogen stores are high, protein contributes no more than 5 per cent of the energy needed. However, when muscle glycogen stores are low, such as after intense training due to inadequate calorie and carbohydrate intake, protein is then used for energy rather than for muscle growth and repair and may contribute as much as 10 per cent of the energy needed for exercise. If this happens, the use of protein for fuel is very inefficient. Long-distance runners need up to 50 per cent more protein than the average adult. Protein should contribute 12–15 per cent of the total calories per day. He can work his requirements out by multiplying his weight in kilograms by 1.3 (in pounds by 0.6) to calculate the number of grams of protein he should consume per day.

Good sources of protein can be found in lean meat, poultry, fish, eggs and dairy products, which contain all of the essential amino acids and therefore are complete proteins. Also protein sources can be found in nuts and dried beans. As with carbohydrates, food labels will assist in working out how many grams of protein the athlete is taking in. A long-distance runner should consume three to five servings per day, comprising lean meat, fish or poultry. The following shows the calorific values of protein-rich foods:

- a 3oz serving of lean meat, poultry or fish, for example, one medium pork chop, half a chicken breast or a small fish fillet, provides 21g protein
- 1oz cheese, one egg, two egg whites or 2 tablespoons of peanut butter each provides 7g protein
- a cup of low fat milk or yogurt provides 8g protein
- one serving of a grain product – preferably whole grain – such as a slice of wholewheat bread provides 3g protein.

If the long-distance runner eats more protein than he needs, he either burns it for energy, or stores it as fat. Therefore, carbohydrates are a more efficient and less expensive source of energy. Too much protein increases the body's water requirement and may contribute to dehydration, because the kidneys require more water to eliminate the excess nitrogen load of a high protein intake. A high protein diet after a hard training session is also hard to digest and will not replenish the muscle glycogen stores adequately, whereas a high carbohydrate diet is easy to digest and quickly restores muscle glycogen.

Fat

Long-distance runners should consume less than 30 per cent of total calories from fat and less than 10 per cent from saturated fat. Therefore, if he eats 3,300 calories per day, less than 1,000 of those calories should be from fat. The following are examples of high fat foods:

- chocolate
- fried foods
- ice cream
- bacon
- hot dogs.

Food labels again will advise on the number of grams of fat and percentage of calories from fat per serving. It is prudent to choose foods with less than 30 per cent of calories from fat.

The high levels of volume and intensity of the long-distance runner's training programme can cause fatigue quickly. Planned nutrition and hydration will help him to meet the demands of his training regime. Sports nutrition includes staying hydrated, fuelling before and during exercise and replenishing nutrients after training. A good, well-balanced diet will not need supplements. However, long-distance athletes, because of their high volumes of training, may want to leave nothing to chance and will supplement their diet with vitamins.

Vitamins/Supplements

The water-soluble vitamins (B and C) are not stored to any large extent in the body, so any effects caused by their deficiency will soon be apparent. The fat-soluble vitamins (A, D, E and K) are stored in the body, so it may be advisable to supplement these vitamins prior to the peak high volume training phase.

Perhaps the most important, because of the volumes of training involved, is iron to ensure that the athlete does not become anaemic and prone to infection. This can be supplemented by normal iron tablets, ferrograd C, or in liquid form through such products as spatone. The liquid iron will be absorbed into the system much more quickly and, unlike some tablet forms of iron, will not lead to possible constipation. It is worth checking first, as, for example, ferrous sulphate can, with some athletes, cause stomach upsets.

It is important to note that vitamins should not be taken to excess. An excess of Vitamin A can be fatal and Vitamin C can cause gastrointestinal problems. In any case, there is no evidence that high dosages of any vitamin produce enhanced effects above their normal vitamin function. Fig. 109 is a list of possible suggested daily vitamins that could be taken by the long-distance runner if he wished and what role they achieve.

Some athletes will take beta-alanine, a non-essential amino acid that combines with L-histidine to aid the production of carnosine. The reason for this is that raising the concentrations of carsonine in the muscles is vital, as it can increase the ability of the muscles to work harder and perform for longer. It may also prevent lactic acid build-up during intense work, thus reducing muscle fatigue.

What to Eat Before Running

Before a long training run, many runners will increase their intake of carbohydrates, in order to provide the glycogen that the body needs to burn when exercising. Without this fuel, the body will be lacking in energy and will be forced to run at a slower pace as the run progresses. The high-carbohydrate meal should be consumed 2–4hr before the run takes place and includes pasta, brown rice, oatmeal or sweet potato. Foods that are high in sugar, fat or fibre should be avoided before a workout. Long-distance runners who train in the early morning may not have time to eat and digest a full meal before training, so it is important that a snack or light meal should be consumed about an hour before training, such as a banana, an energy bar, cereal and milk, or a roll with peanut butter.

With regard to a high-fat diet, muscle glycogen is preferred over fat for fuel for high performance long-distance runners, because fat breakdown cannot supply energy fast enough for their needs. Also, fat takes longer to digest than carbohydrates and should be limited or not taken in pre-exercise meals.

Hydration

Possibly the easiest way to prevent fatigue while running is for the long-distance runner to stay hydrated. Fluid loss and dehydration can have serious effects on the body and the runner's ability to stick to his training schedule. He needs to maintain proper hydration levels before, during and after training sessions. He can monitor this by checking his urine, which should be a very light yellow colour, or almost clear. If it is not, he needs to replenish and hydrate with fluids immediately. He must be aware that he needs to replace the fluids he loses during training from sweating, especially in hot or humid conditions. If his bodyweight loss through sweating is 2 per cent or more, it will have a measurable physiological effect on his aerobic output. A simple rule of thumb to follow is to drink 8oz of fluid for every 20min of exercise.

There are many products on the market for high performance long-distance runners, such as isotonic drinks, vitamin water and electrolyte drinks, but water is just as good; it is cheap and easily available and will hydrate him just as successfully. Another good way of hydrating, replenishing and reinvigorating is to drink tea. Mint tea, for example, aids the digestive system, while green tea aids metabolism, therefore taken in conjunction they are very proactive in assisting and revitalizing these areas.

Vitamin	Role
A	Growth, repair, eyes, skin, fights infection and possibly aids energy production
B 1 – thiamine	Energy metabolism and nervous system
B 2 – riboflavin	Energy and protein metabolism
B 6 – pyridoxine	Protein metabolism
B12	Red blood cell production, nervous system, energy and protein metabolism
C	Fights infection and is involved in iron, protein and energy metabolism
B3 – niacin	Energy metabolism, free fatty acid production
Iron	Oxygen transportation
Sodium	Fluid regulation and salt/water balance
Calcium	Bone formation and muscle enzyme activity

Fig. 109. Vitamin intake chart.

With proper fuelling and hydrating, the high performance long-distance runner can maintain his health, train more efficiently, prevent soreness and recover more quickly, leaving him ready for the next training session, which could be later that same day.

Relaxation Techniques

Rest is an important component of recovery strategies and *meditation* can be incorporated into the rest phase. The skill to be able to practise meditation techniques will take some time to master. The idea of meditation is that it allows the athlete to relax by controlling the parasympathetic nervous system, by reducing simulation and noise to the brain. This then will lower his blood pressure, slow down both his breathing and heart rates, relax his muscles and calm the parasympathetic nervous system. Meditation therefore will allow him to control the stresses from training, over-arousal and competition.

Similarly, after training or competition before going to bed he can practise *progressive muscle relaxation (PMR)*. This technique involves tightening and then relaxing certain key muscle groups. It allows the athlete to identify the sensation of muscle tension, improve his awareness of body tension and focus on reducing it. If used regularly. it can have a great impact on performance. Other relaxation techniques include *autogenic training, imagery* and *visualization* (see Chapter 7) and breathing exercises. Breathing exercises, in conjunction with PMR, should lead to a more relaxed state.

Restricted Environmental Stimulation Therapies (REST) involve a degree of psychology. These can range from the athlete just closing his eyes and blanking his mind of everything to music, to emotional recovery, holiday breaks and flotation. Flotation tanks aim to try to reduce the amount of stimulation to the athlete's brain, allowing him to focus effectively on relaxing and becoming emotionally calm. The flotation tank provides this environment with minimal stimulation by reproducing weightlessness and no sight nor sound – music can be utilized if required. Again, this technique will require time before full relaxation is possible, but when this has been achieved it is remarkably effective in reducing stress levels. However, there are only a few flotation tanks to be found and they are expensive to use.

Active rest is a simple way of reducing stress and fatigue, while stimulating the training programme. It can involve a break from running but engaging in other active – non-contact – sports such as walking, swimming, cycling and mountain biking. Or it can be part of the training programme, involving cross-training such as wet-vesting, the Nordic Track or the static bike. The aim of active rest is to aid recovery, while producing both mental and physiological stimulation.

The easiest method of relaxing is to sleep, although this is not always as easy as it sounds. Even though the long-distance runner may be very fatigued at the end of the day because of his hard training regime, he may not be able to get to sleep due to his nervous system being too aroused or his mind too active. Therefore, he must utilize some of the relaxation methods mentioned above to help him to go to sleep quickly and in a relaxed state. Everyone has their own internal body clock – or biorhythms or circadian rhythm – with daily variations such as a fall of 1°C in the core temperature of the body from midday to midnight. Therefore, it is important that the long-distance runner has a regular sleeping pattern that is not interrupted if possible. Irregular eating, time travel, late nights can all have an important effect on the internal body clock and disrupt sleeping patterns. If the athlete has an occasional late social event, he should restrict his sleep-in to no more than one hour.

Similarly, the athlete's internal body clock will also be tuned in to his eating pattern, which will have been determined by his regular training programme. Some athletes will sleep or power-nap – have a short sleep for 20–30min – between sessions or meals to help refresh them and aid recovery. To ensure the best possibility of a good night's sleep, the following, which will upset the sleep pattern, should be avoided before going to bed: caffeine (coffee, tea, cola, chocolate), alcohol and high protein meals. Sleep and rest are the cheapest, most readily available and most beneficial recovery strategies available to the high performance long-distance runner.

Training vs Straining

One of the tests of a good coach is what he does when things are not going well with his athlete. This may be due to injury, in which case there is a variety of specialists to call on, such as doctors, physiotherapists, masseurs, osteopaths, surgeons and so on. However, it is when the athlete loses form that the mettle of the coach is really tested.

Some coaches may see the answer as more training, whether this is more mileage and repetitions, more intense sessions or even more training sessions. This is usually the last thing the athlete requires – sometimes more means less in terms of performance. In any good coach/athlete relationship, a frank, open discussion should pinpoint the problem(s), if the observant coach has not done so already. Fig. 110 is an aid in helping both the coach and athlete to be proactive in seeing the signs and symptoms of non-adaptation at an early stage before the situation has gone too far.

A good coach is constantly evaluating his athlete's progress and must be aware of his strengths and weaknesses. He should ensure that the balance and volume of training meets the requirements of the event that the athlete has chosen. Above all, he constantly monitors his athlete's progress, increasing both loads and intensity progressively. He must set his athlete realistic targets, motivate and support him and ensure that the agreed training programme is implemented correctly. He should ensure that the athlete is eating correctly and often enough to meet the demands of his event. To help him in this monitoring process, the coach can have the athlete fill in his own daily self-monitoring sheet (see Fig. 111), which the coach can constantly check against his own observations and decide if there are any problems. This self-monitoring sheet could be part of the athlete's daily training diary.

Training vs Straining Checklist

If above criteria are adhered to, when the athlete loses form it should help the coach quickly to eliminate certain areas and possibilities and help him to determine why the athlete has lost form or gone stale. It could be one simple reason, or a combination of reasons, as many external factors can influence the athlete's performance and attitude. It could be also complicated by the symptoms of the triad (see

Coaching Observations	Signs and Symptoms of Non-Adaption
Direct communication	Athletes communicate
	Heavy legs
	They don't feel good
	Their legs are sore
	They are tired
Athlete's body language	Facial expression and colour
	The look in their eyes
	Bending over to recover after effort
	Bad technique compared to normal
Physiological	Increase in resting heart rate
	Loss of body weight
	Loss of appetite
Psychological	Low motivation
	Low concentration
	Aggressiveness
	No self-confidence
Others	Poor eating habits
	Poor sleeping patterns

Fig. 110. Coach's observation chart, from Guy Thibault 1993 Canadian Speed Skating Coach).

Body Weight	Resting Heart Rate	Sleeping Patterns	Reaction to Training
Record each morning before eating	Record on waking while still in bed	Record quality of sleep each night	Record feelings about training
Body weight is not a measure of fat stores so there may be small variations	Recommended scale: +/−2–3 beats above normal; OK to train	Regulate daily biorhythms by: Going to bed and rising at the same time each day	Feeling tired after training is normal
	+ 5 beats above normal: light training	Sleep disturbances (+/−2hr) or low quality sleep an indicator	But feeling tired after training for several days = Poor recovery/adaptation
	+ 6–10 beats above normal; no training		
Unexplained weight loss of more than 3% may indicate overtraining		Keep to same wake-up time within an hour if have a late night; Inability to relax	If regularly tired, take a complete day off or try another lighter activity. If not effective, could be a sign of overtraining

Fig. 111. Athlete's self-monitoring sheet.

above). The following checklist is a guideline to some of the reasons that may account for a loss of form and the possible solutions, if the self-monitoring sheet and the coach's own observations have not already detected them. It is also a good barometer by which the coach can monitor his athlete to ensure that he is not overtraining or straining:

Work Stresses
Cause: long hours, physically demanding work, shifts, exams
Solution: training must be tailored to the athlete's demands. Easy sessions should be placed on his demanding work days, double sessions or intense sessions on his less demanding days. The rest and regeneration sessions are invaluable to the athlete in this situation.

Emotional Stresses
Cause: family, work, relationships, money and friends
Solution: maintain a constant dialogue with the athlete. In this way, it may be possible to avoid problems, or at least to be in a better position either to solve them or to be supportive. This helps to take the pressure off the athlete and give him a stable base.

Social Stresses
Cause: peer pressure, religious beliefs, conflict of interests, lifestyle
Solution: encourage the athlete and make him feel valued. Re-emphasize his goals in view of the current situation.

Dietary Stresses
Cause: incorrect eating, for example, at an inappropriate time, incorrect type of food, junk food, not enough food, or vitamins and supplements.
Solution: check the athlete's weekly food intake on a regular basis. Suggest a healthy, balanced diet that will cover the requirements needed to meet his training programme. If they are taking vitamins and supplements, ensure they are the correct ones (see above).

Training Too Intensely
Cause: too much mileage, too many or too intense sessions, no variety in the training, incorrect energy pathways being covered, balance of training is inappropriate, poor use of rest and regeneration.
Solution: one or a combination of the following suggestions should help the situation. Ease back on the mileage, reduce the number of training sessions, lower the intensity and include more rest and regeneration into the training. Re-evaluate the training programme for the time of year, the event and the athlete. Try to add more variety and make it fun! Never follow a high intensity session with another high intensity session. Do not leave all the good work in training, taper for the competition to produce his best.

Health Stresses
Cause: training too hard can exacerbate simple health problems (or minor injuries). Coupled to eating incorrectly and/or any other stresses, it can lead to the athlete breaking down.
Solution: the athlete should not train too hard if carrying an infection or virus; take a few days' rest. Have regular blood checks for anaemia and so on. Periodically check his weekly diet for any signs of incorrect eating (see above for eating disorders and disordered eating).

Environmental Stresses
Cause: city, travel, home, work, facilities, pollution
Solution: tailor the training to meet the demands of the athlete's environment, help them to plan and organize their lifestyle.

Psychological Pressures
Cause: expectations too high from self, family, friends, club, media, governing body
Solution: make the goals realistic and attainable, reassessing them constantly. Be positive. Ensure that the athlete goes into his most important race in the best condition both physically and mentally.

Finance
Cause: lack of financial support could hinder optimal performance and therefore the athlete becomes vulnerable to psychological and other pressures
Solution: try to get a good support system in place for the athlete, to utilize when required, and also actively seek sponsorship.

School/University/Club Pressures
Cause: conflict with institutions demanding his time can lead to a crisis of conscience and an unsettled athlete
Solution: The athlete's aims come first. Ensure that the goals for the season are taking this into account. The club/school/university is only a competition vehicle for the athlete.

Feeling Undervalued

Cause: poor response from club, coach, group, school, community

Solution: build up the athlete's self esteem. Be positive at all times. Nobody competes badly on purpose.

Time Management

Cause: lack of constructive and quality use of time that is available

Solution: sit down with the athlete and help him to plan his time. Maximize the free time he has available for training, resting and socializing.

There are undoubtedly many more causes to add both to and within the list above. However, the points above should give the coach a greater insight into some of the reasons why an athlete may lose form or go stale. A good coach will have an excellent coaching eye that will recognize these symptoms early and he should be able to pinpoint the reason(s) for his athlete's loss of form. He will then be able to eradicate them swiftly.

As defined by POMS (J. Kimiecik, 'Profile of Mood States', 1988):

*   An optimally trained athlete is *low* on tension, depression, anger, anxiety, confusion and fatigue, but *high* on vigour and vitality, whereas an over-trained athlete is *high* on tension, depression, anger, anxiety, confusion and fatigue, but *low* on vigour and vitality.

Support Systems

The coach and athlete should be constantly monitoring for any overuse injuries. Because the legs and feet take the majority of the impact in training this is where most injuries will occur (see section on self-massage above for ways to help avoid this). The most common injuries, apart from muscle pulls, strains or tears, are the following:

*   periostitis – shin splints
*   tendonitis – mainly at the insertion of the tendon
*   knee problems – either to the outer ligaments or wearing at the knee joint (patellar tendon syndrome)
*   foot injuries – mainly to the fore and middle foot
*   sciatic nerve – travels from muscles of the pelvis and buttock down through the legs to the bottom of the foot. Problems caused through slipping, poor surfaces and equipment and incorrect technique. Good core stability, technique and, above

all, posture – particularly in daily life – are key to avoiding problems with the sciatic nerve.
*   Achilles tendon problems.

The athlete should always be proactive in ensuring that he uses dynamic exercise in his warm-up and static exercises at the end of the session to get rid of any stiffness and soreness. Daily mobility is also a good way of preventing minor injuries that could become major. The ideal time to do this mobility session is in the evening when the body is fully warmed up and active, as opposed to first thing in the morning. The occasional aerobic training session in the water (swimming pool), on a cross-country ski machine, or bike to reduce weight-bearing also has its advantages. Similarly, off-road running is an excellent way of avoiding injury, as is rest and regeneration.

However, to ensure that the athlete is constantly monitored and any soreness, strain or impending injury is nipped in the bud, the coach should have in place a network of support systems. This is being proactive and in certain cases reactive. The concept is to ensure that the athlete does not get injured, but, if he does, then the aim is to keep missed training to a minimum so that he will be back running as quickly as possible.

These support systems are to ensure that the early warning signs of injury are acted upon immediately in order to prevent the injury becoming more serious. The support systems should include access to a masseur, physiotherapist, doctor, sports scientist, bio-mechanic, podiatrist, nutritionist, psychologist, conditioner and sponsorship (see Fig. 112).

Because of the amount of training, volume and high intensity work undertaken over many years by the high performance long-distance runner it is of paramount importance that he pays great attention to safeguarding his legs, which take the major strain of his training load. To ensure that the legs are well maintained the athlete and coach can use self-massage and SMR, or have a professional masseuse as part of his support team (see Figs 98 and 99 on SMR release and Figs 101–104 on self-massage).

A good physiotherapist is also an integral part of the support team. If funds will not allow both a physiotherapist and a masseur, it is better to involve the physiotherapist rather than the masseur and to perform self-massage. Unlike a masseur, a physiotherapist can deal with any major strains, stresses, muscle tears and pulled muscles. He will not only be able to diagnose the problem, but remedy it. For any major problems, such as an Achilles tendon injury, he can advise on treatment or a possible operation and recommend who should undertake the operation. In many cases, funded athletes will get financial assistance with both the physiotherapy and the massage.

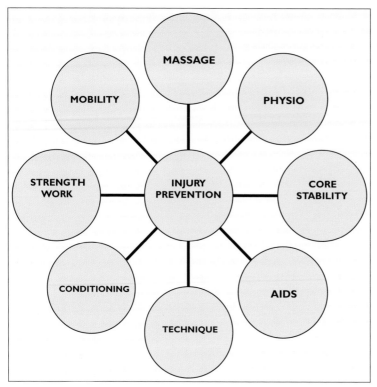

Fig. 112. Injury prevention systems should be in place to support a good training programme and habits, for example, warm-up/cool-down, daily mobility and core work, diet, sleep, rest and regeneration, supplements. These will help to prevent injury and illness and make it easier for the support network to be successful.

A good relationship is required with the local doctor. He will not only be useful for taking blood samples to check the haemoglobin level and for signs of anaemia, but also to advise on and monitor any prescription drugs. This is particularly important for the high performance athlete, who will be regularly drug-tested both in and out of the competition season. In conjunction with the doctor, he can ensure that he is not taking any medicine that contains drugs from the banned list (see below). If the athlete qualifies for therapeutic use exemption (TUE), he will need supporting evidence from the doctor, as this must be submitted to the sport's governing body. This is to ensure that he is covered if the effects of his prescription drugs show up in future testing. The use of asthma inhalers, for example, is covered by this category. If a good relationship is achieved with the doctor, he could be of assistance if any major surgery is required, such as an Achilles tendon operation. The doctor has a large network of contacts that could be accessed by the coach and his athlete.

IAAF/IOC banned drugs:

The IAAF (International Amateur Athletic Federation) and the IOC (International Olympic Committee) identify the following classes of doping. For constant updates and specifics of each category, the coach and his athlete should refer to the national governing body UKA (United Kingdom Athletics):

- stimulants (to increase alertness, reactions and reduce fatigue)
  examples: amphetamines (in some tonics), ephedrine (in some cold cures)
- narcotic analgesics (to manage pain)
  examples: aspirin and codeine (found in cold remedies)
- anabolic steroids (to speed recovery, aid competitiveness, increase muscle bulk)
  examples: stanozolol, nandralone.
- beta-blockers (to manage tension, help hand–eye coordination)
  examples: stenolol, proprandol, oxprendol (in medicines for hypertension)
- diuretics (to manage or lose body weight)
  examples: bumetanide, amiloride and benzthiazide.
- peptide hormones and analogues
  – human chorionic (similar to anabolic steroids); example: pregnyl
  – corticotrophin (to increase blood levels of corticosteroids); example: synacthen

– human growth hormones (HGH) (to increase muscle hypertrophy and reduce aging process) examples: humatrope, norditropin (medication to encourage growth)
– erythropoetin (EPO) (to increase erythrocyte volume/blood capacity).

There are also two important areas on doping methods, which are as follows:

- pharmacological, chemical and physical manipulation
  This is to ensure that there is no tampering or altering of urine samples that would affect the validity of these samples during a controlled drug test
  examples: urine substitution, use of a catheterization.
- blood doping
  A blood transfusion can be taken from an endurance athlete, or another endurance athlete with the same blood group and then reinfused at a later date. The ideal time to take the transfusion is after altitude training. The blood is stored and usually reinfused before a major championship.

To remain constantly up to date with the current prohibited drugs lists and discover whether or not the athlete qualifies for therapeutic use exemption, the coach and his athlete should use the available Inter-net sites. Following are the most useful websites to obtain up-to-date information:

the UK Anti-Doping site: www.ukad.org.uk
the International Association of Athletics Federations site: www.iaaf.org
the World Anti-Doping Agency site: www.wada-ama.org
the therapeutic exemption site (tue@ukad.org.uk) is an email address to which questions may be sent.
another invaluable site is www.globaldro.com, which will help the athlete to check any medication he may be taking. All the ingredients and brands are displayed as follows:

- ☑ **Not Prohibited**
- ⊘ **Prohibited**
- ⚠ **Requires Declaration**

Similarly, supplements should also be checked out, a useful website for which is www.informed-choice.org. A high performance long-distance runner is subject to both competition and out-of-competition testing, which could be either a blood or urine test, so he should leave nothing to chance.

With out-of-competition testing, the athlete has to inform his governing body and UKA sport what time of day he is available for testing and where he will be at the stated time. This has to be done every three months. If he is not going to be at the stated venue, for example, he will be abroad, he has to inform the authorities of his whereabouts and he is just as likely to be visited at a training camp abroad as at home. If selected for the test, whether at home or at a competition, the test follows the same procedure and both are without any warning. If at a competition and the athlete has to warm down or attend a press conference, he will be accompanied by a member of the test team. He can have a representative of the governing body medical team accompany him for testing when at a major championship. He will have to choose a sealed sample collection vessel, which is kept in his and the representative's sight at all times, and is only handled by him throughout so that the receptacles cannot become contaminated.

The athlete then has to produce a sample – which may take several hours, as after a long-distance event in hot/humid conditions he is likely to be dehydrated – and remove enough clothing in order that the drugs official can ensure that it his urine. Once completed, he will be offered a choice of sealed sample bottles. Once he is happy that they have not been tampered with and are clean and empty, he should divide the sample between the two bottles, preferably two-thirds in sample 'A' bottle and the rest in sample 'B' bottle. They will be placed in plastic bags, then into the storage box, which is placed into a cardboard box, then a courier bag and finally dispatched.

If a blood sample is to be taken, once the selected vein has been cleaned and prepared the blood is extracted. The needle is removed, then placed into the storage chamber and sealed. It will be kept at a cool temperature before being sent away. The samples are numbered and recorded on the collection form along with any medication or supplements the athlete has taken in the seven days prior to the test, any therapeutic exemption use he may be on, any blood transfusions in the last six months and any other declaration of use. He is then allowed to add his own comments regarding the test procedure, before checking the details and signing. He must also check the laboratory copy and ensure that his own personal details are not included. He will then be given a copy of the collection form that he should keep.

Access to sports scientists is also invaluable. A high-class performer on funding will have this access. However, if an athlete has not got this type of funding, the coach should negotiate with the local university, which should have a sports science department, to ensure that his athlete is properly tested and monitored. The sort of help sport scientists can give includes blood testing and a range of other tests that include fat content, VO_2 max and lactate tests. The use of a sports scientist is invaluable with monitoring the athlete's training, maintaining the correct balance and ensuring that the correct progressions are properly implemented. These tests should be done at regular intervals throughout the season to help monitor how training is progressing and to make any modifications or changes that are necessary to the training programme. In this way, overtraining, staleness and stress can be either eradicated or spotted early enough for action to be successfully taken.

The coach and his athlete should also ensure that they have the use of biomechanical analysis, in order to ensure that any problems in technique can be eradicated. Many leg problems and injuries are down to poor technique and are exacerbated by the number of kilometres/miles involved in training. The coach should use the biomechanical information and enlist the help of a podiatrist. He will then be able to construct insoles, supports, inserts or orthotics that will give his runner much greater stability, correct any problems and give greater protection to the legs against the constant wear and tear of training.

The coach must ensure that if his athlete is not lottery funded he needs to look elsewhere for alternative methods of financial support. He should approach his athlete's club and employers to see if they can give any support, using the argument that it will be good publicity for them when he is successful. He should approach the local and county sports associations, as well as the local council. Other possibilities include local businesses, established national companies and the major kit manufacturers. It may be that there is no specific financial support forthcoming, but support in terms of kit, time off work to train or go altitude training and help with transport may be given. The more financial support the athlete receives, the easier it becomes to be a full-time athlete. He can then train and recover correctly without the demands of either a full-time or part-time job. It will also allow him to access the support systems already mentioned.

It is useful to have access to a sports nutritionist so that the athlete's diet can be constantly monitored. The nutritionist can oversee the athlete's diet over a period of time. This ensures that the correct fuel is being taken at the correct time and that the calorific intake is correct. It is particularly important that the correct nutrients, carbohydrates, hydration and proteins are taken, particularly after high intensity training or competition. It is essential that the body tissues are repaired and the body returns to homeostasis as quickly as possible. Therefore, if a three-week to monthly check is kept on his athlete's diet, the coach, in conjunction with the nutritionist, can ensure that there is no problem with incorrect food, junk food, rehydration, calorific intake and incorrect nutrients, and that there are no eating disorders or disorderly eating habits. The nutritionist can also recommend if vitamin supplements or other supplements, such as electrolyte drinks and creatine, are required to supplement the athlete's diet. This is particularly important during intense training periods.

A psychologist may only be required by a few athletes who are either lacking in self-confidence, or are not producing the competition results that their training indicates. However, it could also be argued that all high performance athletes should have access to one. A psychologist comes in as a fresh face and helps to build up the athlete's self-esteem. He may get the athlete to go through mental rehearsal exercises, or to look at the positive aspects of both his training and competitions. He may ask the athlete to think of why a particular competition went well and get him to try to create a similar environment at his next competition. Whatever approaches the psychologist takes, in conjunction with the coach his aim is to get the athlete thinking and acting positively in his training and particularly in his competitions. It may be the little bit of impetus or edge that he requires in making the breakthrough or becoming successful.

Most coaches cannot be experts in all the areas his athletes require in order to be successful, therefore they should be prepared to enlist the help and support of other experts who can improve a particular area or requirement. For example, it may mean enlisting the help of a physical preparation expert to improve the athlete's general condition and strength endurance, or a sprint coach to improve basic speed and ability to accelerate, or another coach to check the basic technical model for any flaws or weaknesses, or a fitness instructor to improve suppleness and flexibility.

Support systems and the correct balance to training, including rest and regeneration, have a dual role to play in the athlete's training programme. First, they are put in place to be preventative and proactive in ensuring that the athlete does not get injured, ill or overtrain. Second, they should already be in place to be reactive if injury, illness or overtraining does occur. In this way, the problem can be dealt with quickly and effectively, with the minimum of time lost away from training. It is crucial for the high performance long-distance runner that these support systems and injury prevention systems are in place, and that his whole training programme is constantly managed and monitored.

CHAPTER 6

PLANNING AND PREPARATION

The athlete and his coach should sit down at the end of each season to plan the athlete's training programme for the forthcoming season, first ensuring that they evaluate the programme from the previous season. Even if the athlete is self-coached or has an adviser instead of a coach, he should still go through a review process in order to plan the forthcoming season. From this, it will be possible to deduce whether the athlete is progressing as he is expected to, what elements of the previous season were successful and what areas need development and further work.

This evaluation process is usually carried out during the transition phase, which occurs at the end of the track season when most athletes have a rest phase, before they commence the build-up for the following season. However, with a high performance long-distance runner, particularly a marathon runner, the transition phase may vary from individual to individual. It may take place after a big city marathon in May or December, or after a championship event in September. The transition phase may also be determined by the target competition of the year. The last two Commonwealth Games have taken place in March (Melbourne) and October (Dehli), therefore the transition phase in these two instances could be April and November.

It is also important, while conducting this evaluation, not to overanalyse and become obsessive about it. It is a tool to help define and determine the athlete's ongoing training structure and programme. The high performance long-distance runner, who will attend major championships and races unlike his less talented contemporaries, also has to factor into his preparation and planning such variables as altitude training, jet lag, heat and humidity acclimatization, holding camps and so on. There is also the need to ensure that the athlete is not being affected by the triad (see Chapter 5) and this must be carefully monitored, particularly with the elite-level athlete, where the difference between being supremely fit and only a session way from illness or injury is so acute. Scientific testing too should be built into the training plan at strategic times of the year – usually at the end of a training phase – to monitor how the athlete is developing, progressing and adapting to the training programme.

When doing this evaluation, the coach and athlete should use a checklist or a set of criteria, always remembering that each athlete is an individual and should be treated as one in all respects:

- the age of the athlete and associated issues
- the athlete's strengths and weaknesses
- the event requirements
- the training environment
- aims – short term (season)
- aims – long term (future)
- training required for the event/distance – the year's training for the event and the previous season's training
- time-management skills
- support systems network
- other considerations – nutrition, altitude, the triad, acclimatization to heat, humidity, time travel and so on.

Why do we need to evaluate where the athlete is in his long-term development? It is necessary to evaluate where the athlete is at this point in his athletic development and to examine his strengths and weaknesses. The athlete's progress since the previous evaluation needs to be assessed. It also provides a good cross-reference with the training that was in the yearly training programme, and will therefore help in the evaluation of the athlete's yearly training programme. It commits the athlete and his coach's views to paper and allows for both short- and long-term goals. Finally, it can be used as a motivational tool.

The criteria for this evaluation process need to be objective so that the findings stand the scrutiny of the review process. They need to be reliable so that the evidence gathered is of benefit to the athlete and coach. They need to take into consideration all aspects of the athlete's season. If the athlete has missed a large amount of training through illness or injury this will obviously have an impact on his ability to meet the targets that have been set. The evaluation process should measure more than one factor to give the whole picture. Where possible, it should involve technical input, such as physiological testing procedures.

During this evaluation process the athlete and coach should commit to paper or computer a planning review sheet (Fig. 117) and they should both come to the evaluation with their own views and input. The high performance athlete will have more input than would a younger, less experienced athlete. In many cases, he will be the driving force making most of the major decisions, whether it be the types of training to be incorporated into the training plan or the proposed racing programme This is to be expected, particularly in a long-standing coach/athlete relationship, in which the coach is working towards ultimate redundancy and becoming more of an adviser and sounding board. Using the information from the previous season's training programme and the preceding ones, the athlete's progress can then be assessed.

The assessment should include an examination of the athlete's strengths against the requirements of the event (see Fig. 5). It could be that at some stage the athlete and coach decide they have come as far as they can in a particular event and need to look at changing to another event that is more suited to the athlete's strengths. This is particularly relevant to the high performance long-distance runner, who will move through the events. Some may move from middle-distance events to 5,000m, others may move from 5,000m to 10, 000m and others from 10,000m to the marathon. All have generic endurance training requirements, but they also have their own specific training needs and requirements. An example of this is UK international Jo Pavey, who started her career as the national champion and UK record holder for 1,500m at fourteen, went on to international level at this event, then progressed through the standard distance events to the marathon, gaining international recognition at each event.

The following should be considered in the evaluation process.

AGE

How old is the athlete? How much running or training background has he got? Is he physically mature and strong for his age? How many times does he train a week? How many miles or kilometres has he accrued as his weekly base? How interested or motivated is he? All of these questions are relevant to the development and potential of the high performance long-distance runner.

Training years are also a key component for the high performance long-distance runner. Runners in these events, particularly the marathon, take a long time to mature, build up the required aerobic endurance base, master the event and come to terms with what the event requires of them.

Anatomical Constraints

When planning a programme, the athlete's young career is very relevant. Fig. 114 shows important factors and ages within the athlete's development. The ages cited in the table are approximate and are based on chronological rather than biological ages. Therefore consideration has to be taken of the early biological developer. The statistics contained in the table below emphasize how much more quickly females pass through adolescence and therefore reach their full development earlier than boys. What is important is that when taking into account the high performance long-distance runner's development, these stages are neither neglected nor abused. Even though ultimately high mileage is a requirement, it should not be practised at too early an age through too many training units and too much mileage/kilometres. A large proportion – as when more mature – of this early volume of training should be off-road on forgiving surfaces, so that the growth plates are not damaged. The training should also include a great deal of variety, such as drills, conditioning work, different intensities and loadings, as well as developing the cardiovascular and respiratory systems. It is imperative that from an early age everything is progressed systematically, whether that is mileage/kilometres, number of training units in the microcycle, types of training, intensities of training units and so on.

STRENGTHS AND WEAKNESSES

The athlete's strengths and weaknesses must be pinpointed early. The individual training programme should cater for these strengths to be developed and the weaknesses to be improved. The athlete's strengths

	Girls	Boys
Major height increases	11–12	14–15
Major weight increases	11–12	13–14
Optimum skill age	8–11	8–13
Heart volume (maximum)	11–13	13–20
Maximum volume oxygen uptake	15–16	18–19
Maximum strength	16–17	18–19
Glycogenic system (anaerobic work)	14 earliest	15

Fig. 114. An overview of developmental stages.

and weaknesses can be recognized in a number of ways, such as during a race, training session, scientific testing or field tests. If, for example, an athlete has good endurance, this can be classified as a strength. If the athlete has poor mobility, this is classified as a weakness, particularly in a high performance long-distance runner as it will impact on his range of movement, technique and stride pattern, all of which become more essential the longer the event progresses and fatigue begins to set in. The coach and athlete should also be looking at his strengths and weaknesses in relationship to the qualities required for the athlete's chosen event.

THE EVENT REQUIREMENTS

The long-distance endurance event that the athlete is going to specialize in must be taken into account when planning the season, as this will affect the amount of loading, intensities, bias, balance and the type of training that is included in the programme. The physiological requirements should also be used as one of the main criteria when assessing the athlete's strengths and weaknesses and the needs of the event (see Fig 5). The further the distance the athlete competes at, the more aerobic the event becomes, therefore the more he needs to run and the more time he needs for training. Time management is therefore of particular importance, so that the correct rest, nutrition, hydration and regeneration can take place. It is important that the requirements of the chosen event are blended into the training schedule and that everything is proportionate to the demands of the event.

It is also important that the athlete understands the sort of pace that is required to compete at the highest level on the track (see Fig. 115) or road (see Fig. 116). His training must include specific sessions that help him to adapt to the pace required and allow him to feel comfortable at this level. For a 5,000m runner moving to 10,000m – which is double the distance – or a 10,000m runner moving to the marathon – over four times the distance – he is moving from 'the known to the unknown'. Training and planning should therefore be tailored to ensure that this new challenge can be met and the runner can be confident regarding the planning, preparation and progressions that have been put in place.

THE TRAINING ENVIRONMENT

The coach must know the advantages and disadvantages of his training environment and must utilize the

Split 400m Laps	3,000km	5,000km	10,000km
55sec	6:52.5		
56sec	7:00.0		
57sec	7:07.5	11:52.5	
58sec	7:15.0	12:05.0	
59sec	7:22.5	12:17.5	
60sec	7:30.0	12:30.0	25:00.0
61sec	7:37.5	12:42.5	25:25.0
62sec	7:45.0	12:55.0	25:50.0
63sec	7:72.5	13:07.5	25:15.0
64sec	8:00.0	13:20.0	26:40.0
65sec	8:07.5	13.32.5	27:05.0
66sec	8:15.0	13:45.0	27:30.0
67sec	8:22.5	13:57.5	27:55.0
68sec	8:30.0	14:10.0	28:20.0
69sec		14:22.5	28:45.0
70sec		14:35.0	29:10.0
71sec			29:35.0
72sec			30:00.0
73sec			30:25.0
74sec			30:50.0

Fig. 115. Pace requirements (to the nearest second) at world-class level for the 3km–10km events.

advantages to the full if his programme is to have variety and be successful. He must also ensure that his programme neutralizes the disadvantages. The coach must make the environment work for his athletes. It is the choice of the coach and athlete where and when the training session takes place. The athlete's home circumstances, the physicality of his working day – is he on his feet a lot? – and travel must all be taken into account. The coach must also try to make the sessions varied, creative and, above all, enjoyable for the athlete, particularly if he has been using the same training environment for a number of years.

With the high performance long-distance runner, the coach should minimize the impact on hard surfaces in the training programme and look for as much off-road running as possible, for example in parks and forests, on golf courses, canal paths, disused railway tracks and so on. When doing a high intensity session, it has been scientifically proven that athletes perform better in the early evening, so this should also be factored into the training plan.

Mile Splits	Half-Marathon	Marathon
4:22.5	57:22	
4:25.0	57:55	
4:27.5	58:27	
4:30.0	59:00	
4:32.5	59:32	
4:35.0	60:05	
4:37.5	60:38	
4:40.0	61:11	2:02:22
4:42.5	61:44	2:03:27
4:45.0	62:17	2:04:33
4:47.5	62:50	2:05:39
4:50.0	63:22	2:06:44
4:52.5	63:55	2:07:50
4:55.0	64:28	2:08:55
4:57.5	65:01	2:10:01
5:00.0	65:33	2:11.06
5:05.0	66:39	2:13.17
5:10.0	67:44	2:15:28
5:15.0	68:50	2:17.39
To nearest second		

Fig. 116. Pace required (to the nearest second) for world-class half-marathon and marathon runners.

SHORT-TERM AIMS

Short-term aims usually involve planning the forthcoming season. Therefore, both a winter and summer fixture list are very important to this process. From these fixture lists, the major events that the athlete is aiming toward can be pinpointed and the whole season designed around these. These aims are obviously related to the athlete's ability, as are any specific times that are set as either targets or goals. For a high performance long-distance runner, the result may be a double-periodized year. The 10,000m runner will require two peaks, one for the world cross-country championships in March and a major track championship in August, while a marathon runner may go for a big city race early in the year, followed by a major championship in August or another big city marathon in the autumn, or the world half-marathon championships in October as his twin peaks.

LONG-TERM AIMS

All training programmes should have some general overall plan for the athlete's future development, progression and when and where specific elements should be included within the programme. They should also be looking at the athlete in the long term with regard to future championship aims and target times to be achieved. The athlete should always be setting himself new challenges and targets to help his progression, development and motivation.

SMART

When setting these aims or goals for the athlete, the coach should ensure that they are SMART. This means:

- **S**pecific – to the athlete's needs, development, level, abilities and requirements
- **M**easurable – they can be measured, for example a set time achieved, a medal in a specific championship
- **A**chievable – the aims should be challenging, but realistic and achievable
- **R**elevant – the aims should be relevant to that particular individual athlete and his development
- **T**ime-related – specific dates should be given for when the targets have to be achieved, therefore both long- and short-term aims.

Training Diary and Planning Review Sheet

It is essential that any athlete, particularly a high performance one, has a structured training and racing plan. This ensures that the athlete's strengths and weaknesses are highlighted from all previous seasons and that the correct qualities for the event are being included. It also makes both the athlete and coach commit their plan to paper so that it can be assessed and monitored throughout the season and at the end of the year.

To assist with his review, self-monitoring and weekly and monthly mileage and progress, it is very helpful if the athlete keeps his own personal training diary. Why does he need a training diary, what should he put in it, what form should it take and when should he use it? These are the questions that need answering if the maximum benefit is to be derived from a training diary. The athlete needs to keep one in order to record what training he has done in each training session throughout not only the year, but his career. He needs to note his observations of how he feels these daily training sessions have gone and how, through the season, his training is progressing. A diary will also show the balance between large and moderate volume training weeks and how this impacts upon the runner both physically and mentally. It is a very good tool for reflecting upon both short- and long-term training. If there is a problem in training, the runner can look back over the previous few weeks to see what has caused this situation. In the long term, he can look back at previous seasons and see what training had or hadn't worked to help solve any current problem. It may be that if training or racing is not going too well it is simply down to stress caused by external factors, which will be picked up by the training diary.

Because the high performance long-distance runner will be experienced, the more the diary will aid him and help to provide more structure to his training. The previous year's diary is helpful, as he will be able to develop the positives gained from last year's plan and act to get rid of any negatives. The current diary will help to formulate the plan for the new season and should also contain the proposed racing fixtures for the year.

The more detailed the diary, the greater its use. Therefore, it should be filled in on a daily basis. Everything that is part of the training programme, or may affect the training programme in any way, should be written into it. The runner's actual training session should be written in detail, with the time of day it took place, on what type of training surface and the type of training session. The distance covered, whether in miles or kilometres, and the duration of his training run should all be recorded. This is very useful in adding up his total weekly, monthly and yearly mileage or kilometres. If it is a repetition session, the number of repetitions, distance of the repetitions,

PLANNING REVIEW

NAME:
REVIEW OF SEASON 2010:
WHERE THE AIMS ACHIEVED?
POSITIVE POINTS:
AREAS REQUIRING ATTENTION:

EVENT REQUIREMENT.   ATHLETES STRENGTHS.

SPEED
STRENGTH
ENDURANCE
POWER
STRENGTH ENDURANCE
SPEED ENDURANCE
MENTAL STRENGTH
MOBILITY
TECHNIQUE
TACTICS
SOLUTIONS TO AREAS REQUIRING ATTENTION:
REGENERATION;
DIET;
WARM WEATHER:
RACE REQUIREMENTS:
AIMS:
SHORT TERM:
LONG TERM:

Fig. 117. A blank review sheet.

PLANNING REVIEW SHEET

Name: Margaret Dixon

Age: 30

Review of Season: 2012

Aims:

5,000m: 14m 30sec; 10,000m: 30m 00sec; half-marathon: 66m 55sec; marathon: 2hr 22m 30secs; win the National Championships 10,000m; gain selection for the Olympic Games team and achieve personal bests at 5,000m and at 10,000m in the Olympic final.

Were the Aims Achieved?

5,000m: 14m28.2sec; UK record.

10,000m: 29m 53.6sec; UK record.

Half-marathon: 66m 29sec; P.B.

Marathon: not competed in 2012.

Won the National Championships at 5,000m. Did achieve the Olympic qualifying standard in both the 5,000m and 10,000m, setting personal bests and UK records, and finished fourth in the final of the 10,000m; also set a personal best in the half-marathon.

Positive Points:

Three of the aims were met. The marathon event was not contested because of the heavy mileage required and the effects it would have on the legs and speed. Speed showed a significant improvement. Strength endurance improved – showed in being able to run three races in four days. Endurance improved – a much improved winter's training programme building on previous winter's helped cope with and maintain the higher mileage. Ability to compete at the highest level was another positive point.

Areas Requiring Attention:

Speed endurance still needs attention – particularly repetitions between 500m/600m – to be able to compete at the end of an ever-changing or high tempo race. Self-belief needs some work. Ability to change and maintain pace needs a little more attention and work, as does mobility and tactical awareness.

Scoring: 5* – very important; 1* – minimal importance	Event Requirement	My strengths
speed	***	***
strength	**	**
endurance	*****	****
power	**	**
strength endurance	***	***
speed endurance	****	**(*)
mental strength	*****	***
mobility	*****	****
technique	*****	****
tactics	*****	****

Solutions to Areas Requiring Attention:

Shorter speed endurance repetitions between 200–600m. Constant affirmation of ability to compete at this level, which should have been aided by Olympic position. Tactical training using split intervals, pace surges, alternating pace sessions. To develop both the speed endurance required and the change of pace. Ensure mobility done daily. Look at running shorter distance,s such as 1,500m and 3,000m to try out tactics and change of pace.

Regeneration:

Two weeks' active break from running during the transition phase. Full medical assessment –
set up physiological testing dates for the next season. Every fourth week of each month to be an easier volume and
intensity week. A rest day every ten days. Hydrotherapy – after high loading intense sessions
and high volume weeks. Twice weekly massage.

Diet:

Check weekly diet sheets – make recommendations on diet, supplements and vitamins where applicable.

Warm Weather/Altitude:

Warm weather once a year at the team holding camp in build-up to the World Championships.
Altitude twice at specific times of the year – four weeks in Eldoret, Kenya, from
mid-November to mid-December, and six weeks from early mid-April to end of May
at Font Romeu, France.

Race Requirements:

During the winter the odd cross-country race as a form guide, plus road races including
a half-marathon on returning from the first stint of altitude. Five races prior to World Trials
comprising two 3,000m, two 5,000m and one 10,000m.

Aims – Short Term:

5,000m: 14m 25sec; 10,000m: 29m 50sec; half-marathon: sub-66m 00sec; a medal in the
World Championships in either the 5,000m and/or 10,000m.

Aims – Long Term:

5,000m: 14m 20sec; 10,000m: 29m 30sec; half-marathon: 65m 40sec; marathon: 2hr 17m 30sec;
medals at next Commonwealth/European and World Championships; Olympic marathon gold in 2016.

Fig. 117a. A completed sample review sheet.

...ecoveries and times should be recorded. All his races nd results, with split lap or mile splits where applicable, hould be recorded. This will then show a pattern of how many races he requires to get race fit. Other important nformation he should record is his daily weight, daily resting pulse rate and any health problems that occur. If he athlete has health problems, any course of tablets or ntibiotics should be recorded. If he uses a heart monitor n training, it is a good idea to record the heart rates to nsure that he is not overtraining or training incorrectly nd to compare them to his resting pulse rate for that ay. All rest days or sessions, massage and regeneration f any type should be recorded, to ensure that he is etting enough rest and regeneration. It is also important o note any particularly stressful days at work or home, or ny days where he is finding it difficult to manage his time o meet his training demands.

If all of the above points are recorded, it is much asier to detect a pattern that will help the athlete to olve any problems that may occur with his fitness and raining levels, or confirm why his training is developing ell. It is sometimes difficult to pinpoint either of these,

or to plan a season without the concrete evidence provided in the form of a training diary.

Any type of diary will serve as a training diary, but a desk diary is a good choice as it has more space for all the information the athlete needs to put in it. A year planner can be used to give an instant overview of the whole year's training plan, but must be used in conjunction with the training diary, as the space on a yearly planner is limited and not enough detail can be put on it. Therefore, it is probably best to use one for the year's planned fixtures.

The training diary must be accessible if everything is to be put in it, starting first thing in the morning with the resting pulse rate. It is useful to have a pen clip attached to it so that there is always a pen/biro available and time is not wasted searching for one. Different colours can be used for training, weight, resting pulse rate, regeneration and so on.

When all the aforementioned points have been taken into consideration and evaluated, the coach and athlete should then use the planning review sheet to establish their final aims and objectives. This ensures that the

THE MICROCYLE PLAN

Event(s): _____ Male: ____   ____ Age: _____ years

Best performances: _____ Maturation: Early ☐ Average ☐ Late Developmental Age: _____ years

Pervious year's best performances: _____ Training Age: _____ years

PERIOD							
PHASE							
MESOCYCLE							
MICROCYCLE							
DAYS	SUNDAY	MONDAY	TUESDAY	WEDNESDAY	THURSDAY	FRIDAY	SATURDAY
DETAILS OF SESSIONS							
TRAINING EMPHASIS							
LOADING							

REST LOW MEDIUM HIGH

Fig. 117b. Microcycle sheet to be completed for a week, every ten days or fortnightly depending on the length of the microcycle.

THE MESOCYCLE PLAN

BEST PERFORMANCE(S) _____ PREVOIUS YEAR'S BEST PERFORMANCE(S) _____

MALE/FEMALE TRAINING AGE _____ YEARS

EVENT(S) _____

DAYS	SU	M	TU	W	TH	F	SA	SU	M	TU	W	TH	F	SA	SU	M	TU	W	TH	F	SA
PERIOD																					
PHASE																					
MESOCYCLE																					
MICROCYCLE																					

100%
90%
80%
70%
60%
50%
40%
30%
20%
10%

VOLUME _____ INTENSITY .... LOADING ☐ EXPRESSED AS A PERCENTAGE

Fig. 117c. Mesocycle sheet is the overview of a number of microcycles that form a mesocycle and may vary in number o weeks depending on the required emphasis.

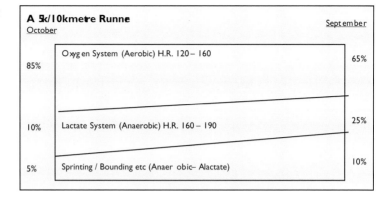

Fig. 118. Training development for a female 5,000km/10,000km runner moving from middle-distance events, showing how the energy pathways are developed during the season.

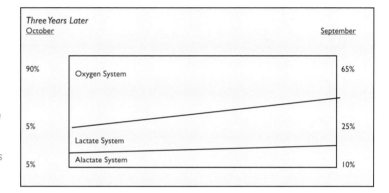

Fig. 119. Training development for a female 5,000km/10,000km runner three years later. This diagram shows how the three energy systems have changed markedly during the three years of training.

thlete's strengths and weaknesses from the previous eason are highlighted. It also ensures that the correct ualities for the event are being included, and that both he athlete and the coach commit their plan to paper so hat it can be assessed and monitored both throughout he season and at the end of the year. Fig. 117 is a blank eview sheet and Fig. 117a provides an example of how : can be filled in. It is a good idea to get the athlete to ll in his views of the previous season and bring this to he review meeting. This should reveal what his views re on which aims he has fulfilled and those he has not; vhat his view is on his strengths and weaknesses regard-1g his event. Does he know what the requirements of he event are? What are his short- and long-term goals? 'hese may well vary to the views of the coach.

Once the review has been agreed and finalized and 1e development phases and progressions agreed, the nicrocycle plans – which can be a week, ten days or a ortnight – can begin to be developed (see Fig. 117b) in onjunction with the mesocycle plans (see Fig. 117c).

It is crucial that the coach and athlete ensure they progress and move through the correct stages at the correct time throughout the athlete's career. They must ensure that no short cuts are taken, nor any key developmental qualities missed. The best maxim is to 'hurry slowly' – that is, the coach must not be in too much of a hurry to achieve his aims at the cost of his athlete's correct development. With a high performance long-distance runner, this means progressing both the miles/ kilometres per week and the number of training units systematically. Nor should the athlete do too much of any of the essential qualities required for his event, otherwise he will become overtrained and stale. Sometimes 'less is more', meaning that better results and benefits are achieved by doing less training, but of the correct type, in the correct proportions.

To show how an athlete's training plan develops and progresses over a period of time, Figs 118 and 119 show how the same athlete's training emphasis will change over a period of three years. It can be seen from these two

Fig. 120. Overview of a periodized year, showing the general breakdown into the three main periods of preparation, competition and transition.

examples how the emphasis in training has shifted from being primarily speed and speed-endurance based, to being endurance based, with an emphasis on developing speed. This is for a middle-distance runner moving events to be a 5,000/10,000m runner. This does not, however, deflect from the continued consolidation of the athlete's overall training requirements for the event.

Once all of the above has been assessed and recorded, the coach and athlete are in a position to start planning the yearly programme. This is sometimes referred to as periodization.

THE YEAR'S PROGRAMME – PERIODIZATION

In a periodized year, which is usually from October until the following September (although with a marathon/road performer their periodized year can have a different climax), the season is basically broken down into four distinct areas:

- preparation phase – general conditioning (approximately November to January)
- adaptation phase – specific conditioning (January to May)
- application phase – competition training and competitions (approximately May to September)
- transition phase – recuperation, rest, recovery (October).

Periodized year – Broken into Phases							
MONTHS **SEPT**	**NOV** **OCT**	**MARCH**	**MAY**	**JUNE**		**JULY**	**AUG**
Phases	1	2	3	4	5		6
Periods		Preparation		Competition			Transition

Fig. 121. Breakdown of a periodized year. This diagram shows how the three main periods are subdivided into the following phases: (1) general preparation phase; (2) specific preparation phase; (3) pre-competition phase; (4) competition phase; (5) competition climax; and (6) transition phase.

Fig. 122. Double periodized year. If the athlete is planning a double competition peak during the year – with a spring marathon and Championship marathon in October – the year would be broken down as follows: (1.1) preparation phase; (2.1) specific preparation phase; (3.1) competition phase (1.2); preparation phase; (2.2) specific preparation phase; (3.2) pre-competition phase; (4) competition; (5) competition climax; (6) transition phase. With this method, each phase is truncated and some athletes may have a short transition phase also after the first competition climax.

DOUBLE PERIODIZED YEAR											
Months: Nov:	Dec:	Jan:	Feb:	Mar:	Apr:	May:	Jun:	Jly:	Aug:	Sep:	Oct
Phases| 1.1	| 2.1	| 3.1	|1.2		2.2 |	3.2 |	4	|	5	| 6	
| Preparation		| Comp. |		Preparation		|	Competition			| Transition	

Fig. 123. The Lydiard (block training) method), or variations of it, is ideal for the long-distance runner. During the duration block of training, the volume of miles/kilometres increases monthly, but at the end of each month there is a smaller-volume week before raising to the next block of training the following month. The volume increases and will then be maintained through the hill and bounding (plyometrics for the long-distance runner). He may decrease his mileage during the track training block and will do so during the competition block.

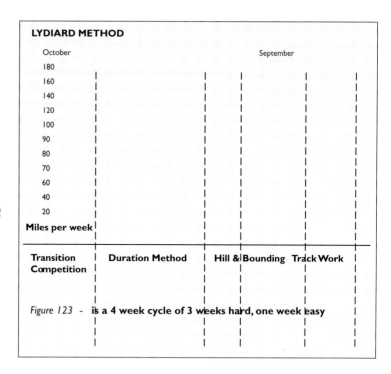

Within these four areas, the long-distance runner's year is then subdivided into the following phases:

general base (endurance, strength, mobility, technique)
progressive development (the above plus strength endurance, conditioning)
progression in intensity (including a little power, speed, speed endurance) leading to low-level competition experience
sharpening towards competitive climax
competitive climax
transition (recovery/rest phase, which can be either active or passive).

These types of periodization are illustrated in Figs 120 and 121. If the athlete is attempting a double periodized year that requires two peaks, one for the cross-country/road season and one for the outdoor season, or a marathon in April and the Championships marathon in August, his periodized year is shown in Fig. 122.

A double periodized year can provide potential for a greater increase in the athlete's performance. However, the athlete and coach have to decide if these benefits, as well as time spent on competition workouts, are worth the loss of endurance, general and specific training time that a double periodized year would involve.

Other Methods to Monitor Progression

There are other methods or overviews of how to progress the athlete's training throughout the year. The first method is by Arthur Lydiard (Fig. 123), the New Zealand Coach who used the method of block training throughout the year. During each block phase of training, he would conclude with one week in which he dropped the volume of miles/kilometres, as a recovery phase, before moving on to the next higher-level block of mileage/kilometres. He followed this large block of endurance training with blocks of hill repetition running and bounding. He then moved on to blocks of track work and downhill running before entering the final competition block. His last three blocks of training, hill running and bounding, followed by track work and downhill running and the competition block all had far less kilometres/miles in the blocks than earlier in the year.

The second method is the Oregon method (Fig. 124), sometimes also called the complex method, which was introduced at the University of Oregon by Bill Bowerman. This shows that the key track session days of Mondays and Wednesdays increase not only the number of repetitions run over a four-week period, but how the recovery time reduces, while still retaining the monthly pace time set. The example here shows 72sec for each 400m, progressing to 71sec for each 400m the

| THE OREGON METHOD | | | | |
Day	Week 1	Week 2	Week 3	Week 4
Sunday	15 miles			
Monday	8x400(72) jog 400	10x400(72) jog 200	8x400(72) jog 100	10x400(72) jog 100
Tuesday	12 miles (alt)			
Wednesday	2(5x300) 54s jog 300/800m	3(4x300) 54s jog 200/800m	4(3x300) 54s jog 100/800m	5(3x300) 54s jog 100/800m
Thursday	50 mt Fartlek			
Friday	10 miles			
Saturday	Competition Cross Country Indoor Time Trial etc			

Monthly Pace 72 sec for 400m. Next month 71 secs

Fig. 124. In Oregon, or complex, trainings the week is very structured, with long runs on Sundays; 12 miles alternating on Tuesdays; fartlek on Thursdays; 10 miles on Fridays and competition/time trials on Saturdays throughout each month. The two key progressed sessions are the 400m and 300m sessions on Mondays and Wednesdays respectively. Each of these two sessions are progressed to a maximum number of repetitions, with the minimum recovery all at the monthly goal pace, which is then changed the following month.

following month. All of the other days remain the same, with a variety of long runs, steady-state runs, alternate-paced runs, *fartlek* and competition.

TIME-MANAGEMENT SKILLS

Neither method, however, will be successful unless the athlete has good time-management skills. This is particularly important for the athlete who has a full working day that involves travel, has a family, as well as a social life, and is also trying to fit possibly two daily training sessions into this already hectic lifestyle. The ideal situ-

ation for the high performance athlete, particularly with family commitments, is to be either a full-time athlete, or to work part time.

Nothing must be left to chance. To help monitor sessions and make feedback more professional, as well as the standard stopwatch, such items as heart rate monitors, lactate probes and GPS watches (global positioning system) can be included in the coach/athlete repertoire. The heart rate monitor helps to give instant feedback and read-outs during the training sessions. The lactate probes give rapid feedback with the lactate response to the training sessions and the GPS watches show the amount of distance covered in each repetition and collectively, or on a training run.

Fig. 125. The Bod Pod – a machine used to test the athlete's body composition and body fat percentages. An elite long-distance runner would be around 5–8 per cent.

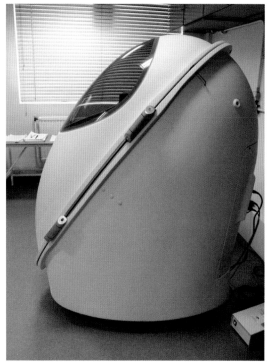

Fig. 126. The Bod Pod, from the other side showing the dimensions of the machine in which the athlete sits.

The GPS watch is particularly useful not just for normal training runs whatever the intensity, but for repetition sessions done on a road or an off-road circuit that is not as accurately measured as a track. With these aids, the feedback can then be reviewed immediately after a training session.

SUPPORT SYSTEMS

Built into the planning and preparation for any athlete, particularly the more successful they become, are the support systems (see Fig. 16). These systems should be proactive, not reactive, and should be in place and utilized effectively and correctly to ensure that there are no injuries and that minor aches and niggles are stopped at source. The list of the support team is large but important, although they may not all need to be utilized. It includes:

doctor – especially for blood tests

- masseur – especially after intense sessions to get the athlete ready for the next session and to pick up any niggles early before they become too major
- sports scientist – to do physiological testing and blood lactate level tests
- biomechanist – to analyse the athlete's running action to ensure that it is efficient
- podiatrist – to provide orthotics, or supports if necessary, working in conjunction with the biomechanist
- nutritionist – to ensure that athlete has the correct food intake, a balanced diet and is taking the correct supplements
- psychologist – if required, to ensure that the athlete is mentally strong and prepared
- physiotherapist – to ensure that the injuries are diagnosed and cured quickly
- strength conditioner – if the coach has no knowledge in this area, he should bring in an expert
- funding/sponsor – crucial if the athlete is to maximize his potential and have a part-time job, or be a full-time athlete.

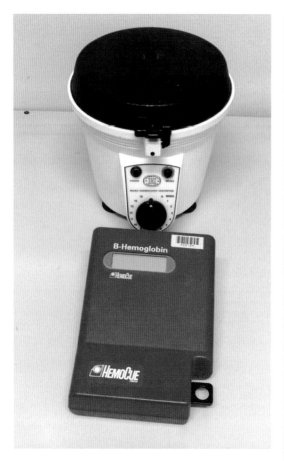

Fig. 127. The machine used for blood analysis. It tests the blood sample to give readings for haematocrit, ferratin and haemoglobin, all important indicators for the long-distance runner.

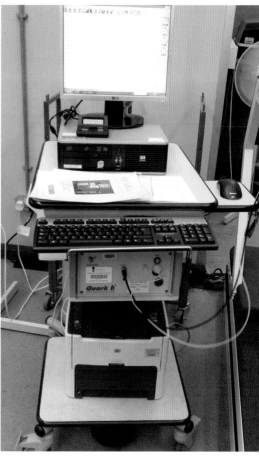

Fig. 128. The machine linked to the treadmill and athlete to give maximum volume uptake readings alongside lactate threshold and lactate turning point.

Testing

Built into the high performance long-distance runner's yearly training plan will be a series of scientific tests that can take place in a laboratory, in the field, or both. These tests will usually be at either the beginning or the end of a block of training or phase. The same tests will be administered to show what progress has been made and how the training programme is progressing and how the athlete is adapting to it.

To ensure that a profile of the athlete is compiled, with which future test results can be compared, the following tests are administered:

* height and weight
* body composition – using a Bod Pod

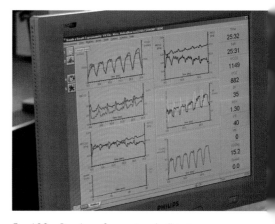

Fig. 128a. Readings from a treadmill test.

Fig. 129. Athlete during a treadmill test. Breathing apparatus taking oxygen level and heart rate readings is attached.

haemoglobin level
haemocrit and blood plasma
lung capacity
VO_2 max
heart rate – resting pulse rate
lactate threshold
lactate turning point.

Fig. 129a. Front view of the test showing the mask and the lactate test equipment ready to take readings every three minutes.

These will then be the indicators upon which future tests will be compiled, assessed and compared against. If conducted in the field, blood samples will be taken at strategic times during an intense training session, then analysed and used as an indicator of the athlete's fitness and training level. Similarly, if conducted on a treadmill in a laboratory, the tests will be taken in the same way at intervals between changes of speed on the treadmill. In a laboratory, the Gunnar Borg exertion chart is used (see Fig. 130) to see what degree of exertion the athlete is putting in.

Once each test is concluded, a report and accompanying graph are compiled, looking at developments in a multitude of areas, including lung function, blood test levels, anthropometry, body composition, heart rate, VO_2 max, running economy, lactate threshold and lactate turning point, all of which are of great significance in a high performance long-distance runner. Improvement in these areas, particularly running economy, lactate threshold, lactate turning point and to a lesser extent VO_2 max, are important to both the development and performance of a high performance

Kilometres per Hour	Exertion Level
6	no exertion
7	
	extremely light
8	
9	very light
10	
	light
11	
12	
13	somewhat hard
14	
	hard to heavy
15	
16	
17	very hard
18	
19	extremely hard
20	maximal exertion

Fig. 130. The Borg Chart, showing the rate of perceived exertion while undertaking the test.

long-distance runner (see Chapter 3). Fig. 131 is an example of a young endurance runner showing the results of two batteries of tests in late November and the beginning of April.

Another test to ensure everything is covered and that he is progressing well is for the athlete to have a blood profile. This will produce a battery of results that is very comprehensive and will show up any abnormalities, deficiencies or problems. The following is a list of what the comprehensive chemistry and CBC blood test metabolic evaluation tests include:

- fasting glucose (blood sugar)
- uric acid
- BUN (blood urea nitrogen): measures liver and kidney function
- creatinine: a test used to measure kidney function
- BUN/creatinine ratio: for diagnosis of impaired renal function
- estimated glomerular filtration rate (eGFR)
- sodium

- potassium
- chloride
- calcium
- phosphorus
- total protein
- albumin
- globulin
- albumin/globulin ratio
- bilirubin: evaluates kidney and liver function
- alkaline phosphatase: Evaluation of liver and bone diseases
- LDH (lactic dehydrogenase)
- AST (SGOT): evaluates liver function
- ALT (SGPT): evaluates liver function
- iron (serum)
- lipid profile: evaluates the risk for developing atherosclerosis (arterial plaque) and
- coronary heart disease:
  − total cholesterol
  − triglycerides
  − HDL cholesterol
  − LDL cholesterol
  − total cholesterol/HDL ratio
- complete blood count:
  − red blood cell count
  − haemoglobin
  − haematocrit
  − red blood cell indices
  − mean corpuscular haemoglobin
  − mean corpuscular haemoglobin concentration
  − red blood cell distribution
  − white blood cell count
  − differential count
  − platelet count.

The Wingate Anaerobic Test (WANT) was developed during the 1970s at the Wingate Institute in Israel. It is a popular anaerobic test, although as a cycle ergometer test it is more specific to cycle-based sports. The most commonly used test length is 30sec, as this is a period for maximal efforts where the major fuel source is anaerobic. It has been adapted to a 'Running-based anaerobic sprint test' (RAST). Both tests are used to determine peak anaerobic power and anaerobic capacity.

The running RAST test comprises a 10min warm-up session, then a 5min recovery. The athlete then completes 6 × 35m runs at maximum pace, with 10sec allowed between each sprint for the turnaround. Power output and fatigue index are then calculated. The coach and athlete must decide in the planning and preparation stage when and which tests − there are others − they are to utilize at strategic points throughout the season.

PHYSIOLOGICAL TESTING:
DISTANCE RUNNING

FITNESS ASSESSMENT RESULTS

Name: D.o.B: Test Dates: 02/12/2009 and 30/04/2010

	NORMATIVE VALUES	RESULTS (Dec 2009)	RESULTS (Test 2)	RESULTS (Test 3)
HEALTH RELATED FITNESS PARAMETERS				
LUNG FUNCTION	**Healthy adult males**			
FVC (l)	3.5 – 4.5	6.2	6.2	
FEV 1.0 (%)	>70%	89	90	
BLOOD TESTS	**Healthy adult males**			
Hematocrit (%)	40 – 45	49	49.5	
Haemoglobin (g/dl)	13.0 – 18.0	16.8	16.9	
PHYSICAL FITNESS RELATED PARAMETERS				
	Well Trained Distance Runners			
ANTHROPOMETRY				
Height (cm)	172.8 – 182.7*	181.0	181.0	
Weight (kg)	58.3 – 71.9*	75.4	70.5	
BODY COMPOSITION				
Body fat (%)	<11.0 (excellent)	16.3	14.7	
Fat mass (kg)	–	12.3	11.4	
Fat free mass (kg)	–	63.1	64.2	
ENDURANCE	**Competitive Male Distance Runners**			
Maximal Test				
Weight adjusted VO$_2$ max (ml/kg/min)	65.0 – 78.0	70.1	72.3	
Absolute VO$_2$ Max (l/min)		5.28	5.28	
Max. Heart Rate (bpm)	187.1 ± 15.2	201	203	
Running speed at VO$_2$ max (km/h)		23.0	24.0	
400m lap time (min:s)		1:03	1:01	
Economy				
13 km/h (ml/kg/km)		180	180	
Lactate Threshold				
% VO$_2$ max.	60 – 75	56.0	59	
Heart rate (bpm)	–	146	144	
Running Speed (km/h)	–	13	13	
400m Lap time (min:s)	–	1:50	1:55	
Lactate turnpoint				
% VO$_2$ max.	80 – 95	64.2	68.1	
Heart rate (bpm)	–	178	175	
Running Speed (km/h)	–	17	18	
400m lap time (min:s)	–	1:25	1:15	

Values taken from Australian Institute for Sport

NOTES

Health related fitness

Lung function is fine with value for FVC (an indicator of lung volume) and FEV 1.0 (an indicator of lung power and resistance to flow) being well over normal values. Hematocrit (percentage or blood made up from cells) and haemoglobin concentration are also fine with both values being towards the upper end of the normal range. Both lung function and haematology values show excellent attributes for endurance running performance.

Body composition

Body composition scores shows that you are reasonably lean compared to the general population with a predicted body fat percentage of 16.3%. Normal values for elite distance runners would be in the region of 5-8%. As mentioned in the lab at the time, it's probably year at an optimal competition weight. The level of body fat exhibited by distance runners during peak periods of the year may not necessarily be the healthiest level of body fat to carry for the remainder of the year. My advice would be to perhaps drop 2-3 kilograms of fat mass by the time you want to be competing at your best.

Fig. 131. Chart showing results of two tests at different stages of the season for a young endurance runner. To be reviewed in conjunction with graph read-out in Fig. 24.

Endurance

Performance on the treadmills shows that oxygen uptake (VO_2 max), when related to body mass, is in line with that of elite distance runners. VO_2 max is the term given for for the amount of oxygen than can be extracted from the atmosphere and delivered to the working muscles. It is related to genetic factors such as the composition of fibre types you have inherited from your parents with the greater relative proportion of type I (or slow-twitch) fibres being a prerequisite for success in endurance sports. The attainment of a high VO_2 max is desirable for success but it is not the only factor that will lead to improvements in performance. Another factor is your lactate response to exercise.

Lactate profile

The chart below illustrates you lactate response to exercise and can now be used to set training zones and monitor improvements in performance over time.

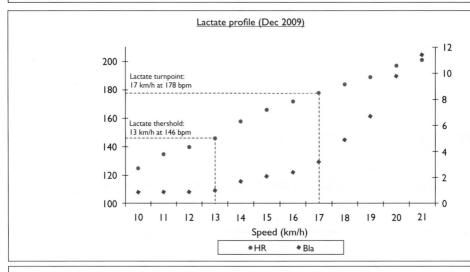

It was possible to determine two significant points that occur during this incremental exercise test; the lactate threshold and the lactate turnpoint. The lactate threshold is the point on the graph just before lactate production begins to rise above resting levels, for you, this was at 13 km/h and a heart rate of 146 b/min. For recovery runs, such as the day after a hard race or training session, you should try to run below this pace to ensure unnecessary further fatigue does not hinder the recovery process. The lactate turnpoint is the running speed, beyond which, lactate production begins to exceed its removal processes with a corresponding accumulation of lactic acid in the muscles and blood. This point for you occurred at 17 km/h and a heart rate of 178 b/min.

It is possible to determine information about your current training status by associating these thresholds with the percentage of VO_2 max at which they occurred. In highly trained individuals, lactate threshold and lactate turnpoint occur at approximately 60 – 75% VO_2 max and 80 – 95% VO_2 max respectively. Your results suggest that lactate threshold occurs at 56% VO_2 max and lactate turnpoint occurs at 64% VO_2 max. It is expected that these values will improve with time spent in training, particularly when the higher quality training begins.

One of the more impressive results from your test, along with the large VO_2 max value, was a high running economy. This value is expressed as millilitres of oxygen consumed per kilometre of running per kilogram of body weight (ml/km/kg). Values of around 200ml/km/kg are suggested to be excellent although your value of 180ml/kg/min are along the lines of elite athletes.

Conclusions:

The bottom line, in laymen's terms, for your results are that body composition is your weakest area but should easily be addressed. On the endurance side, you have a big 'engine' in terms of a large VO_2 max but it simply needs tuning so that you can run it at higher percentages of maximum, and speed work will probably address this as the season progresses. From a running economy point of view, you're one of the most economical runners that has visited the lab, which basically means that for a given speed, you require less oxygen compared to other runners. The flip side of this is that when you utilize your full oxygen uptake you can sustain a higher running speed, which reflects your choice of the faster distance running events. One factor that doesn't support the choice of event is the relatively low lactate values in the final stages of the test compared to other middle distance runners. Those that excel in these events usually have a fibre composition with slightly more relative contribution from fast (type 2) fibres. During lactate tests, these athletes' exhibit very lactate values during the final stages as type 2 fibres preferentially produce energy anaerobically and produce more lactate as a result. Your results indirectly point to muscle fibre make up more akin to classical distance runner, i.e., you possibly have a greater number of pure slow twitch fibres as lactate values towards the end were slightly lower. Together with a high running economy and large VO_2 max this may point to a possibly lucrative move to longer distance events in the future should you wish·

Fig. 131. Continued.

Fig. 132. An altitude tent, showing how it is set up and the size of it in the bedroom. The generator, which controls the flow of hypoxic air into the tent, is shown at the foot of the bed. Because of the noise, this is usually placed in another room.

Another area that needs to be legislated for in the monitoring aspect of the planning and preparation is the triad (see Chapter 5 for full details). In sum, the triad refers to three distinct areas of development, which, if not strictly monitored, can become areas of concern. The three areas are:

eating disorders – including disordered eating – energy availability
osteoporosis – bone mineral density and healthy bones
amenorrhea – menstrual function.

OTHER CONSIDERATIONS

Altitude Acclimatization

a high performance long-distance runner wishes to compete at world level he has to consider whether

Fig. 133. Intermittent hypoxic training apparatus attached to the athlete.

Fig. 134. A different view of the IHT machine.

training at altitude as part of his planning and preparation will be of any benefit. There has been a great deal written about the benefits, or not, of altitude training for sea-level-domiciled athletes. The following is an overview of some of the undoubted merits of this type of training. What the athlete and his coach have to decide is the length of time required to be spent at altitude, and whether the attendant time away is worth the returns that may be achieved. What is without question is the fact that a large percentage of the elite high performance long-distance runners in the world today, both male and female, are altitude-raised athletes. There are, of course, other reasons, such as genetics, diet, socio-economic, culture, limb length, hard work and so on that play important roles in their success and dominance, but it is highly likely also that training at altitude their whole life has been a contributing factor toward their success.

Before looking at the value of altitude training, it is important to note that some centres both in Europe and the USA are unusable at certain times of the year because of the snow and climate (see Fig. 135). Because of this, the athlete and coach may at times have to travel much further afield, which may involve a great deal of travel and an extended period away from home. Some athletes may therefore prefer to experience simulations of altitude conditions. These artificial altitude training conditions, which cause hypoxia – oxygen deficiency – can be achieved by using the following methods:

Hypoxic or altitude chambers   These types of chambers are purpose-built for training at altitude and were first used by prospective astronauts on the space programme. The athlete will cycle or preferably run on a treadmill in a hypoxic decompression chamber, which reduces the air density to simulate altitude. These are useful training facilities in which to replicate altitude conditions and training. However, these chambers are very expensive to hire and there are few of these facilities in the UK to access (Loughborough, Rossendale, St Mary's Twickenham). They can also be very useful for topping-up altitude training if the athlete has already been to altitude, or in preparation before going to an altitude training camp.

Hypoxic or altitude tents   Here, athletes simulate altitude by sleeping or training in an altitude tent. The idea is that a third of the time is spent asleep, during which time the body will adapt to altitude. An altitude tent, also known as an altitude simulation tent or a hypoxic tent, is an enclosed living space that simulates high altitude by maintaining a lower oxygen concentration, in order to stimulate the body's natural adaptations to altitude, including an increase in the number of red blood cells and enzymes. Red blood cells carry oxygen to the body; athletes will therefore benefit from increased delivery of oxygen to the muscles.

Sleeping in a simulated altitude environment allows the body to achieve some of the positive adaptations to altitude while still permitting the athlete to perform workouts at an oxygen-rich lower altitude, where muscles can perform at their normal work level. An altitude tent is one way to enable athletes living at any elevation to sleep in an altitude-like environment. A more expensive option gaining popularity amongst full-time athletes is to convert their entire bedroom to altitude!

Rather than simulate altitude with low air pressure, the altitude tent remains at normal air pressure, substituting low concentration of oxygen for low pressure. While normal air contains 20.9 per cent oxygen independent of altitude, the air in an altitude tent contains as little as 12 per cent oxygen (the remainder being nitrogen). Most altitude tents create the low-oxygen environment with a 'hypoxic air generator' outside the tent pumping the hypoxic (low oxygen) air into the tent. This displaces the more oxygen-rich air inside the tent and with it the excess carbon dioxide exhaled by the occupant(s). Most athletes use altitudes between 8,000–12,000ft (see Fig. 135).

The tents themselves come in several styles and are expensive. Displaced air escapes the tent through small outlets, seams or zippers. Air delivery can be through a hose long enough to allow the generator to be placed in a different room, reducing noise. Some specially designed tents can be placed over normal-sized beds to make sleeping more comfortable. The tent should be neither too well sealed, nor too leaky.

Intermittent Hypoxic Training (IHT)   With intermittent hypoxic training the athlete uses a portable system – see Figures 133 and 134 – which is strapped to the chest and attached to the head and nose. This apparatus simulates being at altitude, which he uses in short breathing bursts, of altitude type air, while at rest. This air is set at predetermined levels of oxygen (15–10 per cent) to simulate conditions found at slowly increasing levels of altitude. It is then alternated with room or ambient air (20.9 per cent) every 3–5min.

This type of training is recommended for an hour for up to fifteen consecutive days. The effects of which should last for three months – if topped up with IHT work every five days. This method naturally enhances the performance and improves the endurance of athlete's and can also be used to pre-acclimatizes people who are going to altitude to train. The portable machines can either be hired or bought.

Nutrition and supplements The Institute of Sport in San Diego believes that the same effect as altitude training can be achieved through nutritional means with a scientific diet involving vitamin pills. This diet of tablets has great emphasis on vitamin C, vitamin B6, folic acid, vitamin B12, iron tablets and zinc tablets.

EPO (erythropoietin) is a peptide hormone produced naturally in the body by the kidneys. The role of EPO is to stimulate the bone marrow to produce and release new red blood cells into the blood stream. Increasing red blood cell levels in the body can result in increases in haematocrit, the percentage of blood volume composed of red blood cells. There are oxygen-sensitive cells in the kidney that are able to determine the concentration of oxygen in the blood. When oxygen levels are low, the kidney releases more EPO into the blood stream. To provide a better picture of how EPO production works, think about going to high altitude, where the amount of oxygen available to the body decreases. The kidney cells detect this decrease in oxygen and release EPO into the bloodstream to stimulate the production of more red blood cells.

Red blood cells contain a protein called haemoglobin, which transports oxygen from the lungs to other parts of the body. With the addition of new red blood cells and haemoglobin, the body now has an increased oxygen carrying capacity. This process is the basic principle used in high altitude training in endurance athletes.

Synthetic EPO is a drug that is manufactured for the treatment of disease and should *not* be used by endurance athletes. The main use of administrating exogenous sources (not produced within the body) of EPO in humans is to treat patients suffering from anaemia, especially those with kidney failure and those undergoing chemotherapy for cancer. Therefore *the use of EPO is illegal* and it is on the WADA banned drugs list. There are supplements available (or example, EPO-BOOST™), which claim legally to simulate the effects of altitude, but these claims have not been scientifically proven.

The use of EPD and blood boosting is banned by the IAAF.

Altitude Training

The basic concept of living or training at altitude is to cause the body to adapt to the lower oxygen content found at altitude by producing more oxygen-carrying red blood cells and haemoglobin. This improves the athlete's ability to perform, because more oxygen is available to the working muscles. This is even more pronounced when the athlete returns to sea level.

The mixture of gases in the air we breathe is the same at both altitude and sea level and is comprised of 20.93 per cent oxygen, 0.03 per cent carbon dioxide and 79.04 per cent of nitrogen. However, the partial pressure of each of the gases is reduced in direct proportion to the increase in altitude. This reduced partial pressure is what causes decreased performance and affects the oxygen transportation system. Similarly, air temperature and water vapour decreases as the altitude increases. The drier air can lead to dehydration. Effects of altitude include:

- increased breathing rate
- increased Heart Rate
- decrease in VO_2 max
- greater arterio-venus O_2 difference
- rapid increase in haemoglobin concentration
- sleeplessness
- nausea
- giddiness and dizziness
- headaches
- dilation of the blood vessels.

All the above lead to a reduction in work capacity. Long-term effects of altitude include:

- increased erythocite volume (more red blood cells)
- increased haemoglobin volume and concentration
- increased blood viscosity
- increased capillarization
- contined lower VO_2 max
- reduced stroke volume
- decreased lactic acid tolerance.

Recommendations for training at altitude

Most scientific studies on altitude training show that in order to increase red blood cell mass, maximum VO_2 and performance, athletes should go to altitude for a minimum of three weeks. Most high performance athletes need to train at an altitude of between 2,000–2,500m to realize this effect. The reason for this chosen height is that for every kilometre of altitude height, an athlete's VO_2 max deteriorates 7.7 per cent per kilometre. At 5,600m, an athlete's breathing rate is double what it would be at sea level. It has also been proven to be the most beneficial for a training effect. From a training persepective, the following heights are classified as altitude training zones:

- 2,000m–3,500m – moderate altitude
- 3,500m–5,500m – high altitude
- 5,500m+ – extreme altitude.

Studies have shown (Bonetti and Hopkins, *Sports Medicine*) that at 2–3,000m and for a stay of a minimum of three weeks, controlled groups on returning to sea level will improve their performance by between 3.7–4 per cent. This will occur assuming the athlete is fit and healthy, is at the correct altitude and has stayed for the minimum recommended time. During this three weeks, there will be an increase in the athlete's red blood mass (total haemoglobin) of 7.4 per cent, and by 12.5 per cent if he stayed for four weeks at altitude to train. Similarly, on returning to sea level, a 17 per cent increase in oxygen-carrying capacity has been recorded and similarly with VO_2 max. There may be other unproven benefits of altitude training, such as running economy, muscle buffering capacity and psychological benefits.

Other opinions surrounding this issue are to live high and train low. This view can be interpreted in two ways. Either, live at high altitude over 3,500m and come down to train at moderate altitude (2,000 –3, 500m), or live at altitude and come down to sea level to train. There are other theories such as live high and train high, live high and intermittently train low, or live low, train high. But these have not proved as beneficial as living high for a period of time, then training low.

When going to altitude, the athlete and his coach have to decide what benefits they want to obtain from their stay. If they want to improve his ability to handle greater volumes in training and improve his recovery on returning to sea level, they should go in the general preparation phase in October/November. If they wish to improve his fitness levels ready for higher intense training and quality work, they should go towards the end of the specific preparation phase in March/May. If, however, it is to improve his competitive performance on returning to sea level from altitude he should go about six weeks before the beginning of the competitive phase in May/June, depending when the pre-chosen competition is taking place. If possible and if finance and other constraints allow, he would go on all three occasions to maximize his training and performance.

Once the athlete gets to altitude during the three-week period he should break his training down as follows:

- days one to three: a period of acclimatization to altitude, facilities and the training environment, with a low training volume that is progressively increased
- days four to seven: volume of mileage increases, as does the intensity of work
- days eight to fourteen: high quality intense training takes place
- days fifteen to seventeen: volume decreases slightly and intensities are mixed
- days nineteen to twenty-one: preparation for returning to sea level; low volumes and intensities.

Some athletes will continue to work at high intensity levels until a few days before returning to sea level. It is important to note that the intensity levels of both the runs and training sessions will be at a lower intensity than at sea level. Similarly, recoveries between repetitions will be longer than at sea level for that phase of the year's training. The following are comparisons for the same sessions at both altitude and sea level for the same female 10,000m runner:

- 20 × 400m at sea level in 71/72sec, with 1min recovery
- 20 × 400m at altitude in 73sec, with 90sec recovery
- 5 × 1,000m at sea level in 3min 9sec, with 2min recovery
- 5 × 1,000m at altitude in 3min 10sec, with 4min recovery.

On returning to sea level, in order to get the optimum benefit during the following three to four weeks, after a few days of reacclimatization, training loads for ten to twelve days will be of high intensity, followed by eight to ten days of developing high performance levels for racing. Similarly, to gain the optimum benefit from a racing perspective, it is realistic to look at the performance being within twenty-one to twenty-eight days after returning to sea level. It is possible to achieve a good training performance within nought to seven days of return if the trips to altitude have been frequent throughout the year. However, the worst time to race and expect an improved performance is within seven to twenty-one days after returning to sea level.

Athletes, being individuals, will respond differently, or even not at all, to altitude. High performance long-distance runners tend to adapt quickly, particularly to high volume training loads. This is because of their low lactate levels (80–85 per cent of their VO_2 max) and their heart rate returning in less than 45sec to well below 140 beats/min after tempo or lactate threshold training.

They usually do not respond particularly well to high intensity anaerobic training, usually due to a higher percentage of slow twitch muscle fibres than other athletes. Medium responders tend to be 3,000–10,000km runners with a reasonable mixture of slow and fast twitch fibres, higher lactate percentage levels of their VO_2 max, a reasonable response to high intensity anaerobic work, a moderate response to a high aerobic volume of training and a pulse that will take double that of quick responders to return to below 140 beats/min after lactate threshold or tempo work.

The slowest responders tend to be the middle-distance runners (800–3,000m). These athletes have

Centre	Country	Approx. Altitude Height
Difficult Access		
Ilfrane	Morocco	1,900m
Atlas Mountains	Algeria	1,700m
Tsaghkadzor	Armenia	1,700m
National Centre	Romania	2,000m
National Centre	Ethiopia	2,200m
Suitable Late April–October		
Albuquerque	USA	1,575m
Boulder	USA	1,500m
Colorado Springs	USA	1,500m
Oregon	USA	1,500m
Flagstaff	USA	1,500m–2,134m
Boise	USA	1,500m
Los Alamos	USA	2,200m
St Moritz	Switzerland	1,800m
Davos	Switzerland	1,750m
Font Romeu	France	1,850m
Mammoth Lakes	USA	2,400m
Corina del Paso	North Africa	1,700m
Sestriere	Italy	1,850m
Belmeken	Bulgaria	2,100m
Sierra Nevada	Grenada, Spain	2,300m
Thredbo Village	NSW, Australia	1,365m
Suitable All Year		
Mexico City	Mexico	2,200m–2,900m
Johannesburg/Secunda	South Africa	1,760m–2,000m
Nairobi	Kenya	1,500m
Thompson Falls	Kenya	3,000m
Iten, Eldoret	Kenya	2,300

Altitude – Days		
Acclimatization to Altitude	**Increased Training Load**	**Recovery**
Three to six days	Twelve to fourteen days	Two to four days
Sea Level – Days		
Reacclimatization to Sea Level	**Normal Training**	**Competition**
Three to four days	Twelve to thirteen days	Ten to fifteen days

a higher percentage of fast twitch fibres and respond well to high intensity anaerobic training. They also have a slow response to high volumes of training, high percentage levels of VO$_2$ max and, when doing lactate threshold or tempo work, their pulse takes a long time to go below 140 beats/min.

Therefore, it is very much down to the individual high performance long-distance runner and his coach whether he goes to altitude or not If they feel there will be benefits, they then need to decide where and when to go, what height, for how long and how often.. The minimum amount of time should be three weeks. The ideal is five weeks up and three weeks down. However, the more often the athlete goes to altitude, the quicker he will readapt and the longer the adaptation will last on his return to sea level. It is wise to have a treadmill fitness test before going to test all his basic levels and then retest a couple of weeks after his return to see how his levels, running speed and economy have adapted and changed.

It is important that the athlete is in good physical shape before he goes, that his iron levels are more than adequate and that he follows the pattern prescribed above for his stay there. When doing high intensity work, he must also realize that his recoveries need to be longer than they would normally be at sea level for the same session at the same time of year. The effects of altitude can be continued on return to sea level by sleeping in a hypoxic/altitude tent, by using an IHT machine or a hypoxic chamber (see above). Finally, the athlete must realize that altitude training is not a panacea that will make him a great athlete on its own, but that it is part of his strategic plan to improve progressively through sustained hard work.

Some of the centres used regularly and recommended by high performance long-distance runners are detailed in Fig. 135.

With all types of training – altitude, training camps, warm weather – that take the athlete out of his normal training environment and regime, judgments have to be made about the benefits and non-benefits of fitting these types of training into the training plan. Similarly, whether to include testing procedures and which ones is also a judgement call that only the athlete and his coach can make. But whatever they include, it must be based on experience and sound judgment, and be to the benefit of the athlete's overall plan.

Acclimatization to Temperature/Humidity

Because of our climate, British athletes on the whole are not equipped to compete in either high temperatures or humid conditions. This can lead to hyperthermia (overheating), which usually occurs when the body temperature reaches 104+°F, or fluid loss reaches 6 per cent of the athlete's body weight. Kit is essential in these types of conditions, with vests being either wide mesh or string, and made of natural fibres to allow the body to breathe and air to circulate. Fresh kit should be used in competition and, where possible, in the cool-down, with the neck and head being protected from the elements. In colder climates, the opposite is the norm.

When performing in high temperatures, the circulatory system cannot supply both nutrients and regulate body temperature. Overheating can lead to deterioration in performance and heatstroke:

- heat-exhaustion signs – fatigue, profuse sweating nausea, dizziness, headaches, slow, shallow breathing
- heat-exhaustion treatment – shade, wet sponges, wet towels, ice, fluids, including salts, sugar and electrolytes
- heatstroke signs – headaches, disorientation, nausea, unconsciousness
- heatstroke treatment – decrease the athlete's temperature rapidly; remove clothes, use ice, tub of cold water, wet towels and keep in the shade
- safeguards – fluid replacement, including water, glucose-electrolyte solutions; the solutions should be cool, palatable and taken as often as required
- also note that even minimal sunburn will affect the ability to thermal-regulate, therefore no sunbathing

Heat acclimatization can be accelerated by using heat chambers in the home environment before departure. Heat acclimatization begins with the first exposure and is developed by four to ten days. It can be introduced by intermittent exercise, 1–4hr at 60–70 per cent effort, which is progressively increased to maximum effort. Inactivity achieves only slight acclimatization. High performance athletes, because of their high fitness levels, will acclimatize much more quickly than sedentary adults. Inadequate water and salt replacement can retard acclimatization, which is maintained for up to two weeks after departure.

With wet heat (humidity), it takes seven to fourteen days to acclimatize. Up to 100min activity initially of wet-heat exposure is required daily to acclimatize (24hr exposure gives no advantage). The rest of the time should be spent in an air-conditioned environment. It is sensible to train in the cool of the day. Competition warm-up should be limited in hot or wet-heat climates.

Athletes should drink constantly, but must realize that thirst is not a reliable guide. The likelihood is that if a runner is thirsty, he is already dehydrated. Even for a sedentary adult in hot climates, fluid consumption doubles, therefore the high performance athlete needs a great deal more daily fluid. Body weight and urine should be checked regularly. In heat – or at any time – athletes should not train post-lunch, but preferably when they are at their optimum peak efficiency, which is in the early evening.

Acclimatization to Time Travel

Everyone is affected by jet lag, which occurs after a 3hr+ flight. Time change affects our circadian rhythms (body clock), for example, our sleeping, eating and toilet patterns, and puts them out of their usual synchronization. The fitter the individual, the quicker he will adapt to and recover from time changes. The following are points to note with any travel involving time change:

- for every 15 degrees of longitude of travel, a time change of 1hr occurs, for example, Moscow 3hr, Canada 8hr, Australia 12hr
- a basic rule is that it takes one day of acclimatization for each hour of time change, therefore the further the travel involved, the athlete should travel out as early as possible
- jet lag is more severe when travelling to the east rather than the west
- to make the change easier on the flight, a lot of non-alcoholic liquid should be drunk and the athlete should eat selectively
- upon arrival (east), caffeine intake should be in the morning and if travelling westwards in the afternoon
- watches should be set to the local time and no daytime naps taken
- initial training should be light and preferably in the morning for the first three days
  adjustments begin to occur after four to five days and training can be progressed.

With any acclimatization, adaptation or jet lag – just as in their individual training programmes – all athletes are individuals and their adaptation and tolerance will vary, as it will with the environment and change they are adapting to. These acclimatization needs should be factored into the overall plan with regard to the training programme. Also, the athlete must be aware of the need to notify the drugs testers of his change of environment and that he is just as likely to be tested when away from home.

RECOVERY STRATEGIES

These are extremely important during a session, after a session and as ongoing strategies. The types of recovery strategies include recovery nutrition, regeneration, hydration, hydrotherapy, hot and cold treatment, massage and rest.

These strategies must be included in a well-devised training programme so that the athlete and coach are always working proactively and not just adapting reactively when problems, fatigue and overtraining occur. These strategies are covered in detail in Chapter 5, but it is important to stress that they must be part of any long-term plan, or during a normal microcycle, whether this be for seven, ten or fourteen days.

EXTERNAL FACTORS

External factors will play an important role in the overall plan of a high performance athlete, particularly if they are hoping to compete at a major championships. Invariably, these championships will be held in hot and/or humid conditions. Other factors that could also affect the athlete are altitude, time change, what time of day the event takes place and whether they will be in a holding camp or an athlete's village.

These factors can affect an athlete greatly, particularly when they are trying to taper their training so that they are in peak condition for their targeted race. The major problems they will encounter if away at a holding camp or in the athlete's village are listed below. However, these must be planned and prepared for in advance. If possible, a pre-camp/village visit would be helpful, or at least experience of similar situations:

Boredom This is a particular problem if an athlete is used to working and training. The problem is exacerbated if he then fills the day by overtraining, rather than easing down for the competition ahead.

Group mentality It is easy to get sucked into inappropriate group training sessions that will not be beneficial, or to go on tiring sightseeing visits instead of resting and recuperating.

Loneliness This becomes a particular issue if the athlete has a family and is away for a long time. Lots of books, music and so on are essential to get through those many hours of down time when not training and before the event.

Food Athletes tend either to overeat or not eat enough when away, particularly in a strange country. They need to be judicious in their choice and take cereals, energy bars and so on with them, or ensure that the team support staff has catered for these needs.

Massage If the athlete is not used to massage, he should not have one prior to the competition as the body will not adjust to it. If, however, he does have them regularly, massage is an excellent way of preparing the body for competition and also ensuring that there are no niggles or strains. It is also a good way of passing away a few hours productively and leaving the athlete with a sense of well-being.

Training It is all too easy, because of the time available, to overtrain, train inappropriately with a group, or come without an individual plan. It is amazing how many athletes during these final few crucial weeks arrive at a training camp or village without a training plan. The athlete should have his own individual training schedule drawn up in conjunction with his coach. This would be part of the overall strategic plan drawn up during the planning review at the commencement of the season. The runner should as assiduously as possible follow this plan – as it is designed specifically for him – during his tapering period.

Time zones If there are time zones to cross and jet lag occurs, the necessary recovery days (see p. 129) should be built into the training programme with easy running. It takes approximately one day to recover from each hour of time change.

Nerves If it's a major championship, an athlete can become very nervous and must ensure that he has enough to occupy himself and take his mind off the race. This must be a constructive use of time and not involve any activities that will be tiring, get the athlete overexcited or make him lose focus on the task at hand. He must also ensure that he can cope with the two call rooms he has to enter before the competition.

Hydration It is key that the athlete always has either a bottle of water or an isotonic drink with him to ensure he completely hydrated. He must be constantly sipping these drinks. The 'P' test should be followed – at most major games the charts are available in the toilets – and urine checked regularly. Basically, the urine should be clear; the darker it becomes, the more dehydrated the athlete is becoming and this situation should be addressed quickly.

TAPERING

Tapering is the art of peaking for the targeted race of the year, whether that is a qualifying race, or the championship race itself. The taper will start two to three weeks prior to the competition date. During this period, the emphasis is on quality throughout. Intense sessions will become less, with more recovery and regeneration. However, some athletes like to work intensely as close to the championships as possible. This shows that in every facet of endurance running, all athletes are individuals in every respect.

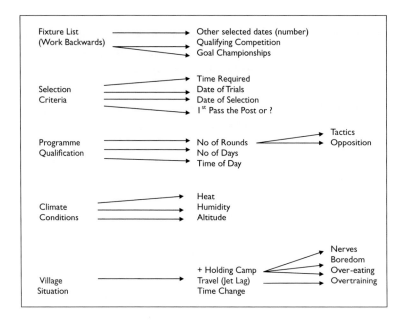

Fig. 137. Planning a peak – this is part of the planning strategy that takes place before the commencement of the season. This takes into account the main competition climax of the year, the selection criteria and what races are needed to get there, when selection is and what is the qualifying time. It also factors in the date of the major competition, any heats and whether there is a holding camp or village. All of these factors have to be planned for so that the athlete arrives at the race in the best condition both physically and mentally.

Competition Day – Track

4:30pm	pre-race meal
5:00pm	rest/check kit packed in bag/mental preparation
6:30pm	leave village and travel to warm-up track
7:00pm	arrive at warm-up track/get bearings
7:30pm	massage
8:00pm	start warm-up
9:10pm	call-up room 1 – plenty of stretching
9:30pm	call-up room 2 – strides
9:45pm	race
10:30pm	cool-down
11:15pm	drugs test – plenty of hydration required
12:00pm	return to village
12:45pm	eat
02.30 am	sleep

Fig. 138. Competition day on the track at a major championships.

The taper has to be built into the athlete's training plan and should not be disrupted by either being at a holding camp or in the athlete's village. To ensure that the taper is effective, the following must happen:

- the number of daily/weekly sessions will decrease, either in number or volume of miles
- strength work will be just to consolidate the work already done
- training will consist of mainly quality sessions and easy running
- the sessions will be light to retain energy and to keep the athlete fresh
- the sessions should also emphasize technique and relaxation
- the sessions will have few repetitions
- the recoveries will be long or complete
- the training sessions will be of high intensity
- the training session will preferably be done at the race time
- these sessions will also keep the athlete mentally as well as physically sharp.

The major difference between the high performance long-distance runner and the high performance middle-distance runner during the tapering phase is that the high performance long-distance runner will still be maintaining a high weekly mileage that will be relevant to their event.

Competition Day

At a major athletics championships, the athlete's whole day is geared to the competition. Therefore everything else has to be worked backward from the competition race time and the day planned accordingly. The athlete has to decide when he wants to start his warm-up, so that it finishes coinciding with the first call-up time. Next, he has to decide at what time he wants to arrive at the warm-up track, prior to commencing his warm-up. This will then determine what time he has to leave the athlete's village, taking into account the time it takes to get from the village to the warm-up track. From this information, he can then decide at what time he should eat and relax prior to starting his journey to the warm-up track.

Many athletes have a check list that they tick off on competition day – and repeat if there are heats and finals – which includes time of getting up, breakfast, packing kit, rest, any other meals prior to competition, further rest, travel to the warm-up track, massage if required, warm-up, call room 1, call room 2, race, cool-down, return to village, meal and bed. Any review of the race is best left to the following day when the athlete is not as emotional and fatigued. Fig. 138 and Fig. 139 below show two different competition days' schedules.

Competition Day – Marathon

2:30am	rise
3:00am	pre-race meal
3:30am	check kit packed in bag
3:45am	leave village and travel to marathon start
4:00am	arrive at warm-up for marathon – find base and relax
4:30am	light massage
5:00pm	start warm-up
5:40pm	call-up room 1 – plenty of stretching
6:00am	race
8:30am	cool-down
9:15am	drugs test – plenty of hydration required
10:00am	return to village
12:00pm	eat
12.45pm	regeneration

Fig. 139. Competition day for the marathon at a major championships.

Fig. 138 is for a normal evening long-distance track final taking place at a major championships. Fig. 139 is for an early competition marathon start, again at a major championships to avoid the heat of the day.

TAPERING FOR THE MARATHON

Tapering for the marathon can be a complex process. It involves knowing when to ease back and by how much, as well as if, or when, to introduce the carbo-loading diet so popular with marathon runners. Each high performance marathon runner will respond differently to tapering and approach it with his own personalized plan. However, certain physiological principles apply and should be considered when selecting a tapering method to suit the individual athlete's needs, such as:

* rebuilding depleted nutrient stores in the body (such as glycogen) to their maximum requires two to three days of lowered training activity
* rebuilding minor injuries in muscle or connective tissue takes a minimum of five days, preferably longer, particularly after a major championships. This is where time-zone travel can have an advantage, in that because of jet lag the high performance

marathon runner will cut back on his normal training loads
* the body's store of oxidative enzymes diminishes in 72hr if not stimulated by aerobic exercise, therefore training at a slightly reduced level is essential.

Any training effect from hard activity during the ten days prior to the race will be minimal. All the hard work has been done before this and training too intensely so close to the competition could even have an adverse effect. Therefore it is wise to ease off training somewhat before a major event. An example of an approach to marathon tapering is given below. It should begin the week before race week. During this week, the final sharpening will be done and the last hard workouts. It is advisable not to do a long run the weekend before the race; instead, an easy run of 10–15 miles would be more advantageous.

Four days before the major race, a normal length steady run is acceptable and could incorporate a few accelerations, to help loosen up the legs. The next two days' steady training runs should be half the norm. The day before the marathon, an easy run of about 15–30min is useful in keeping the legs loose and burning off excess nervous energy. Some athletes may want to rest on this day, while others may differ slightly from the above. To summarize, the last long run is done two weeks before the major competition to allow the

Fig. 140. Marathon race at the Berlin World Championships 2009, showing the proximity of the runners on a tight turn at the Brandenberg Gate.

body complete recovery. The mileage is cut to less than half during the last four days for rest and carbohydrate loading. Some short accelerations can be done in one of the training runs four days before the marathon so as to keep the legs loose. Whatever approach is used, it is important that the athlete comes to the race rested and with his legs feeling fresh.

Carbohydrate loading   This is an important part of the marathon runner's taper, being most essential in the last three days before the marathon. This is the time for the runner to increase his carbohydrate intake, while at the same time avoiding fats and protein.

Systemized training utilizing the energy pathways to the full will help the athlete to run better on fat metabolism, storing more carbohydrates (CHO) or glycogen to be utilized when required. Glycogen metabolism must be happening for fat metabolism to function and so easily occur. It is possible to store even more carbohydrates through a process called carbo-hydrate loading. Normal stores will last for between 90–120min of running, but carbohydrate loading is required for the marathon because of the length of time it takes to complete it. If this sort of diet is not utilized, the marathon runner is likely to hit what is known as 'the wall' after his glycogen stores are com-pletely depleted.

Carbohydrate loading, which was first introduced in the 1960s, has been studied intensely by many exercise physiologists and over the years different plans have been used and subsequently refined. The original plan involved a six-day programme, with many pasta meals and a three-day depletion phase that would trigger over-compensation by the muscles to store glycogen. In many cases, however, this proved exhausting. David Costill, of Ball State Human Performance Lab, has since shown that an intensely trained endurance athlete depletes his muscles to low levels daily and therefore obviously does not need the depletion phase. He normally needs a high carbohydrate diet to replenish his muscles. Costill's studies showed that eating a high carbohydrate diet (70 per cent carbohydrate intake) following a normal 50 per cent carbohydrate diet leads to virtually the same muscle glycogen stores as a 70 per cent carbohydrate diet following the original 15 per cent carbohydrate depletion phase. The high carbohydrate diet must be done in conjunction with a reduction in training. Costill's research has also revealed that for over 48hr of loading, complex carbohydrates produce greater muscle glyco-gen storage than eating simple carbohydrates. The daily requirement for protein and fat should be fulfilled, but the more carbohydrate eaten, the more will be stored. Experts differ on whether storage is best facilitated by two large meals, or a number of smaller ones.

Other researchers (for example, Anita Bean, *The Complete Guide to Sports Nutrition*) have been specific in stating that the aim should be for the athlete to up his carbohydrate intake to 8–10g per kilogram of his body weight. For a 70kg runner, that works out at between 560–700g per day. Each gram of carbohydrate equates approximately to around 4kcal, so that's up to 2,800kcal carbohydrates per day during the carbohydrate loading phase for a 70kg runner. In sum:

- the carbohydrate load for three days before the event should be accompanied by a period of reduced exercise
- no alcohol and limited caffeine should be taken during this period, only water and/or high energy drinks
- the first day of loading is the most important. It should begin with a big carbohydrate breakfast, such as pancakes or French toast. This is the day for the traditional pasta dinner of spaghetti and bread. As many complex carbohydrates as pos-sible should be taken in these two meals
- as the days progress, the switch to more simple carbohydrates should be made, but there should be no loading on large quantities of fruit or other foodstuffs not usually eaten
- high-fibre foods and foods that cause gas (for example, broccoli, beans, bran and so on) should be eliminated. The athlete should eat only low-residue foods and ones he knows will not affect him in any way.

The last major meal should be taken 12–15hr before the race and should not include too much bulk. It is important that it should be easily digestible and will pass through the athlete's system before the race. It is advis-able to experiment with this meal before long training runs so that the athlete knows what and how much of the desired food works best for him. It is important, where possible, that he takes his own pre-race meal so as to avoid having to eat untried foods that may cause a digestive or even worse problem.

If the runner plans to eat on race day morning he should be used to doing so – a light, bland carbohydrate meal such as toast can be consumed 2–3hr before the race. Some high performance marathon runners will not eat, choosing only to drink on race day. If the runner does choose to eat, no carbohydrates, especially simple sugars, should be ingested within 2hr of the race, as this could lead to a blood insulin reaction, resulting in weak-ness and fatigue.

A large glass of water can be drunk 1–2hr before the start of the race, but then nothing more to drink until the starting gun. That will start the runner off well hydrated, but give him enough time to eliminate any extra added by the breakfast carbohydrate loading. He can always replenish his stocks at the feeding/drinking stations en route, where he will have placed at strategic points his own specially prepared high energy drinks that will fit with his expected requirements at each stage of the race.

It is important that these practices have already been tried out in training and/or at minor races prior to the major event. There must be no experimentation or untried practices leading up to or on the day of the major race, as this could cause major problems that would affect his performance and negate all the hard work that has gone before.

In general, an athlete needs around 5–7g of carbohydrate per kilogram of body weight, or 60 per cent of his daily calorific intake from carbohydrates. This usually works out at around 1,500kcal from carbohydrate per day for most women and 1,800kcal for men. Meals high in carbohydrates include:

- wholegrain bread with peanut butter
- a large bowl of porridge or cereal with milk
- a large bowl of spaghetti carbonara (pasta with eggs, parmesan cheese and bacon)
- grilled chicken breast with a large serving of brown rice.

The following are quick ways or snacks to top up carbohydrate stores, each of them crammed with 75g (300kcal) of carbohydrates. They include:

- one large handful of raisins, dried apricots or other dried fruit
- two energy bars
- three slices of bread thinly spread with honey
- four thick slices of bread or toast
- five rice cakes spread with jam.

If the athlete is still concerned about the amount of carbohydrates he is taking on board, he can as an alternative utilize sports drinks, which will, as well as supplementing the carbohydrates, also aid hydration. Adding protein to his meals will give him an extra energy boost. Protein helps to slow down the digestion of carbohydrates, lowering the glycaemic index (GI) of the meal and encouraging the body to release energy slowly and steadily rather than quickly, exactly what is required by all endurance events and in particular the marathon. To achieve this glycaemic effect, beans, lentils and peas, or a chicken breast on a large portion of rice, are ideal for the GI-lowering effect.

The athlete will know if he is loading effectively by keeping a record of his daily weight, which it is advisable to do anyway. He will notice a 2–5lb (1–3kg) or

more weight gain over the three-day period. As the carbohydrates are stored, water is also stored in the muscle, leading to the weight gain. This water storage could make the legs feel sluggish during the last training runs, but it could be useful during the marathon as a source of sweat. The runner may also feel sleepy, edgy or even tired due to the blood sugar and insulin responses to all the extra carbohydrates. However, during the race he should feel supercharged. Carbohydrate loading without the depletion phase should be safe for most healthy individuals who are competing at this level.

Feeding Stations

Another important aspect of marathon racing that needs to be planned for both before and on race day is the feeding stations, which occur at designated intervals during the marathon. The marathon refreshment stations are provided approximately every 5km, where the athlete's own prepared refreshment will be placed. These are handed in the day before the race by him or his representative, stipulating at which refreshment station each should be placed. They will then be kept under strict supervision in refrigerators by the organizing committee until the day of the race. The refreshments need to be well marked and easily accessible at the refreshment station, so that the runner can easily recognize them in the confusion of the race and not waste valuable time searching for them, or even drop or miss them. They can also be placed by authorized personnel into his hands as he passes, so as not to waste time and minimize the possibility of missing them. In hot, humid conditions he could suffer later in the race if he misses his prepared refreshment.

In addition, drinking/sponging stations for water only are placed approximately midway between the refreshment stations, or more frequently if weather conditions warrant such a provision. Any athlete who collects refreshment from a place other than the refreshment stations renders himself liable to disqualification.

Part of the planning process, as well ensuring that the personal bottles are well marked and made up of the correct constituents, is to practise retrieving or receiving the bottles during training and drinking from them on the run so that any chance of making mistakes in the race situation is eradicated. This means that the athlete needs to practise taking the refreshment bottle from a table and from someone placing it his hand while running. The second part to practise is ensuring he can drink the prepared refreshment while continuing to run at race pace, and also how to get rid of the

Fig. 141. Hydration – an illustration of the amount of water used in a championship race as these are being readied for moving to a feeding station.

refreshment bottle while on the run. Similarly, he needs to practise receiving and using a sponge while continuing to run.

The final part of the athlete's refreshment preparation to practise is the type of refreshment he will have at each designated feeding station. These will be high energy foods and drinks that will replenish and sustain him during the race. The high energy foods should be high GI, meaning that they will quickly release energy and give him a fast energy boost. Good high GI foods that are convenient foods on the run are energy bars, energy gels and sports drinks. However, it is wise to have tried out these drinks and foods – particularly on very long training runs – to ensure that they agree with the athlete and will not adversely affect him during the race. Nothing should be left to chance in the planning and preparation for a race and everything should

have been practised and tested many times before the event.

It can be seen that planning and preparation are key to a successful season. Commencing with the reappraisal of the previous season, during the transition period all the way through to the tapering phase, then the competition day itself, everything has to be meticulously and methodically planned. Nothing should be left to chance. Everything necessary should be included at the correct time and in the correct place, to ensure that the aims for the season are met. An overview of what is required to plan the athlete's yearly peak is shown in Fig. 139. The success of the current season and future seasons is determined by the planning and preparation, what goes into the plan, where it goes and how it links with the other requirements. Remember:

If you fail to prepare, you prepare to fail.

CHAPTER 7

TACTICS

No matter what has gone before – even though it may have gone perfectly – whether it is the progressive training system, the adaptation to the training system, planning and preparation, support systems or nutrition, it can all count for nought unless the athlete is tactically aware and astute. He needs to come to every important race in not only great physical and racing condition, but also in great mental shape. His focus, concentration, confidence, mental readiness and strength need to be at their optimum for him to be successful. The execution of any tactical plan is therefore of paramount importance. With the high performance long-distance runner, unlike his high performance middle-distance counterpart, there is the likelihood that if a small mistake is made early or in the middle of a race it can be rectified. However, because of the race distances involved (5,000m to marathon), concentration, focus, awareness and mental strength are perhaps of greater importance.

Once the planned preparation and training have been completed, these must then be realized in the race situation. This means adopting and using tactics, which will enable the athlete to take full advantage of his strengths and perform to his full ability. He has to have confidence in both himself and his preparation if he is to execute his tactics perfectly in the race. He knows that at world level, high performance endurance runners, whether on the track, cross-country or road, are going to be extremely tough to defeat. With the continuing change of African personnel at the highest level, although difficult, it is still important that he tries to gain as much knowledge of the opposition's strengths and weaknesses prior to the competition as possible. This is due to the fact that he will not have raced against this opposition as much as his domestic opponents. Therefore, self-knowledge and self-belief will be the key when preparing tactics for the race. The athlete, in conjunction with his coach, must ask himself the following questions before the final race plan is devised:

How fit am I? The answer to this question will determine the tactics that he is able to employ. The fitter the athlete, the more confidence and the more involvement he will have in the race. If it is early season or he is just coming back from injury, he may find it difficult to

control the race as he may have done had he been fully fit. If the athlete is in the peak of condition, he will be confident in being able to not only devise a race plan, but also being able to execute it and being prepared for any eventuality that may occur in the race.

How important is the race to the athlete? Is it a minor race, a qualifying race, a heat or the target championship race of the season? Whatever the answers are to these questions will determine the athlete's choice of race plan.

What time of day is the event? In a major championships, heats and qualifying rounds can be run in the early morning or late evening, therefore the athlete should have prepared for this in his planning.

Will the climatic conditions have an effect? Is it hot and or humid? If so the warm-up will have to be adjusted accordingly, the correct kit worn and the athlete should ensure that he has a continuous intake of fluids. This is to give him every opportunity to execute his race plan effectively. If every eventuality is not correctly covered, the race plan will fail. Hot and/or humid conditions will mean it is not as easy to be a front runner, so alternatives must be planned.

Has the athlete travelled through one, or more, time zones en route to the event? If he has, the correct amount of time should have been allowed for him to adjust and be back to running normally. A lack of focus and alertness brought about by jet lag could ruin any race plan.

Is the race at altitude or above sea level? If so, the tactics employed should allow for the race to be run at as economical a pace as possible, particularly the longer the race distance.

Is it cold, wet or windy? Any of these factors could affect the plan for the race. If it is windy, it is very energy-sapping to lead into the wind. This is particularly so in the longer distance track and road events. It is far better to shelter behind the opposition until the chosen time to attack.

Once all of these variables have been taken into account the athlete should consider the various permutations in which he could run the race. Either along with his coach or independently, he should now, from the following options, devise a race plan that takes into account his own ability, the opposition, environmental factors and the magnitude of the race. All races are different (see Figs 142 and 143 on marathon championship races), therefore every eventuality has to be covered and catered for in the planning and training preparation phases.

DIFFERENT METHODS OF RUNNING A RACE

Short Sprint

Whether the race is run at a fast or slow pace, the athlete employing a short sprint finish will not attack and take the lead until well into the final 200m of the race, or even closer to the finish. This type of runner is known as a 'kicker', 'waiter' or 'sitter', meaning that he will wait until the last possible moment to attack, thereby conserving his energy and making it very difficult for the opposition to respond to his attack. This type of finish not only requires good basic speed, but also the ability to accelerate quickly, be decisive and have both the leg speed and power to maintain the speed of the attack.

Long Sprint

Here, the athlete who is not as strong or explosive in a short sprint finish will attack from much further out in the race. This attack is likely to occur between 300–600m

from the finish line. The idea of the long sprint is to nullify the effect of the short sprint finisher, making it difficult for the latter to harbour his energy and utilize his normal race tactics as successfully. To utilize the long sprint tactic effectively, the runner has to position himself in the correct place at the correct time, and ensure that there are no other athletes in the way to obstruct his long run for the finish. Once committed, he must keep going at full pace. If he fails to do this, he will allow the short-sprint finishers to remain in contention and in a position to attack and pass him in the finishing straight. More and more elite world-class endurance races, particularly championship races, are being determined by either the long, or particularly the short, sprint finish.

Building Up the Pace

Athletes who have not got either a particularly good short or long sprint finish could adopt this race tactic. In a 10,000m race the athlete employing these tactics would take over the lead with five to six laps of the race remaining. From here, he would ensure that the pace got progressively quicker over each of the successive 100m, or laps. This is taking into account that this increase in pace, particularly in a championship race, would be on top of an already high tempo pace in the race. With this tactic, he hopes to nullify the finish of both the long and short sprint finishers, or at least get rid of most of them before the finish. This tactic requires not only good strength endurance, but also good pace judgment and great self-confidence. Again, once committed the athlete must carry on increasing the pace or his rivals will hang on to him and potentially be able to launch their own short sprint finishes. He must be very strong mentally, for once he hits the front of the race on

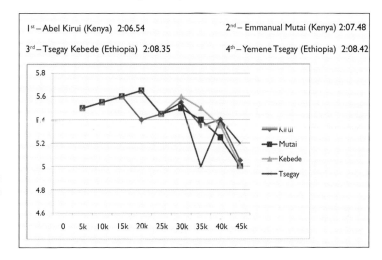

1st – Abel Kirui (Kenya) 2:06.54   2nd – Emmanual Mutai (Kenya) 2:07.48

3rd – Tsegay Kebede (Ethiopia) 2:08.35   4th – Yemene Tsegay (Ethiopia) 2:08.42

Fig. 142. Graph showing the 5km splits for the Men's World Marathon Championships in Berlin 2009. Note how the pace, having been quick earlier in the race, begins to slow towards the finish. (Courtesy of the IAAF)

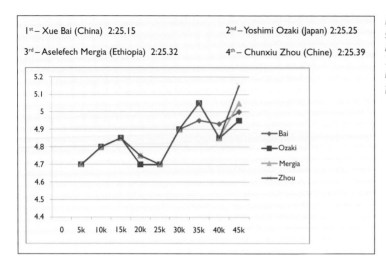

1st – Xue Bai (China) 2:25.15   2nd – Yoshimi Ozaki (Japan) 2:25.25

3rd – Aselefech Mergia (Ethiopia) 2:25.32   4th – Chunxiu Zhou (Chine) 2:25.39

Fig. 143. Graph showing the 5km splits for the Women's World Marathon Championships in Berlin 2009. Note how the pace, unlike the men's, begins to quicken towards the finish. (Courtesy of the IAAF)

his long progressive build-up he is completely isolated, with no help and only his inner strength and belief to assist him.

Lead Throughout the Race

An athlete who has not got a great deal of basic speed, or finds it difficult to accelerate, will make little, or no, impact in a sprint finish. Whether it is a long or a short sprint finish, the runner lacking in basic speed should look for an alternative tactical plan. One of the methods is to lead from the front of the field, making it a hard pace throughout the race, from gun to tape. This tactic is often employed in cross-country and road races of varying distances. It has three main advantages. First, it ensures that the race is not slow and therefore will not play into the hands of the sprint finishers. Second, when it comes to the sprint finish, assuming the runner still has company, it puts everyone on a more level playing field than it would have been in a slow-run race. Finally, because the athlete is in the lead, he can dictate the pace; he has an uncluttered run throughout the race, is running the shortest route and is not caught up in the physical contact of the pack. However, if it is windy, hot or humid, this is a very difficult way to run the race and needs a strong athlete both physically and mentally to be able to execute this tactic successfully.

The athlete employing this tactic must have confidence in his ability to run the race in this way, as it will only become apparent in the closing stages of the race whether the tactical plan has been effective enough and has eroded the sprint of the fast-finishing runners. If the athlete is not at the peak of his fitness he would be wise not to attempt this tactic. As well as his inner strength and belief, his ability to concentrate and focus is also essential, particularly if he gets away from the chasing field and is running in isolation. This requires great

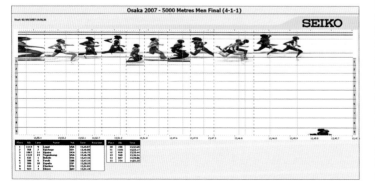

Fig. 144. The short sprint finish is shown graphically on this photo-finish picture of the Men's 5,000m World Championship race in Osaka 2007. It illustrates how competitive elite long-distance running is. The first four are covered by 0.91sec. This is just an example of races at this level – and also at 10,000m – and in many cases they are much closer, with eight athletes and more at times being in with a chance of a medal in the finishing straight. (Courtesy of the IAAF)

Fig. 145. The long sprint for home – athletes come to the line at a major championships with three laps to go. The long, progressive sprint for home begins, not only slowly increasing the pace, but also gradually taking the 'finishing kick' out of the short sprint finishers.

resolve and inner strength to ensure that his lead is not eroded by the chasing pack or individuals. This type of tactic is becoming less and less successful in major track championship races.

Mixing Up the Pace

Another tactical method, particularly for an athlete who has not got a good sprint finish and also does not mind leading throughout the race, is to mix up the pace. This type of method of constantly surging faster to increase the pace, then slowing the pace, only to then increase it yet again, upsets the rhythm of the following athletes. Athletes tend to like to run at a constant pace and not have this pace disrupted. Therefore, not only is the pace of the following athletes disrupted, it also saps their energy and their confidence as they try to conserve energy for a sprint finish. The longer the distance, then the more often this tactic can be used and the more

Fig. 146. Leading from the front – an athlete sets off from the gun running at the front of the field where he can control the race. From this position he can aim to maintain a good economical pace, mix up the pace throughout, attack in the middle of the race, or leave it to mount either long or short attack for the finish.

Fig. 147. An athlete – sometimes with assistance from his team mates – is constantly changing the tempo of the race so that his opposition and main rivals cannot settle into a rhythm and execute their own race plans. It takes the other runners out of their comfort zone.

likely the chasing opposition is to get frustrated, tired and dispirited.

This type of tactic requires great strength endurance and speed endurance, as well as self-belief. It also needs strong concentration throughout the race by both the athlete using the tactic and his pursuers. One of its big advantages is that only the athlete using the tactic knows when the burst or increase in pace will take place, how long the burst or attack will be, and if in fact it will become a sustained burst or attack to the finish. There-fore, the pursuers have the dilemma of not knowing whether it is just one of many bursts or attacks, or the continuous one. They must therefore follow every burst or attack, or they could miss the crucial sustained burst or attack for the finish. This type of tactic – which is similar to *fartlek* training – is more likely to be used by African runners than athletes from the other continents.

Attacking in the Middle of the Race

For someone without a fast finish and who does not like to lead throughout the race, or who knows there are some quicker athletes in the race, this is an ideal tactical method to use. However, it requires a strong athlete both physically and mentally and with a strong inner belief. There is always a point in the race where athletes consciously, or subconsciously, relax and run slower than in other parts of the race in an attempt to save energy for the finish. In a 5,000m race this is usually between the sixth and tenth laps, and in 10,000m race it will invariably be in the middle of the race around

laps twelve to sixteen. Therefore, this is where the athlete employing this method would attack. He will run this part of the race much quicker than expected to ensure that the other athletes suffer physically and are also taken by surprise. This should get rid of most of the opposition, hopefully creating a gap over the chasing athletes, and negate the finishing effect of either the short or long sprint finishers. The athlete then, however, must have the inner strength, both physically and mentally, to ensure that his lead is maintained. His opposition have the dilemma of either upsetting their rhythm by trying to go with him, or sitting off the pace because it is too suicidal at this point in the race, hoping he will slow because of the pace and they will catch him later on.

An example of this type of running in a 5,000m race at the highest level would be to run the three to four laps between laps six and eight or nine at a 60sec, or sub-60sec, pace (World Record pace is 60.6sec per lap). In a female 10,000m race it would mean running four laps between laps fourteen and seventeen at sub-70sec pace (World Record pace is 70.87sec per lap).

Even-Paced Running

This is relevant to all events, but particularly the longer distances such as the marathon, in which an equal distribution of effort is of paramount importance. With this particular tactic therefore, the aim for the athlete is to maintain both his efficiency and economy of effort throughout the race by running each of the

Fig. 147a. Even-paced running is important to the long-distance runner to assist with his running efficiency and economy. In this championship race, the three athletes from the same country share the load of even-paced running until the race enters its final serious stage, which could involve any of the race strategies covered above.

kilometres in as similar a time as possible. The greater the distribution of effort, the less likely is the athlete to suffer in the middle and later stages of the race. This is where the athlete's running economy is vital, because he will be able to perform at the same rate or pace as his competitors, but with less expenditure of effort (see Fig. 147a) and greater utilization of oxygen. Therefore, he will be in good condition come the latter stages of the marathon. He must also know his own capabilities in that he can maintain his set, even pace for the whole race and will not panic and deviate from the plan by allowing himself to run quicker if other athletes are going much more quickly in front of him in the race.

PACE JUDGMENT

It is also essential, if any of the above tactics are to be executed efficiently and effectively, that the athlete has a good understanding and inner sense of pace judgment. Knowing intuitively the pace at which he is operating, and just as importantly what pace he is capable of sustaining, will help the athlete to make any key decisions, or be able to execute his prearranged race plan, as the race unfolds. Good pace judgement also allows him to be more efficient and economical throughout the duration of the race, thus conserving energy for when the chosen tactic can be successfully deployed. Obviously, the greater the duration of the race, the greater the need for running economy and efficiency. All training sessions can be used to improve and develop pace judgment, as well as other tactical methods. However,

two of the better training sessions for pace judgment are 'differentials' and 'split intervals' (see Chapter 3 and Fig. 148).

Fig. 149, showing the world and British records respectively, gives a -good indication of the pace that a high class long-distance runner needs to be operating at throughout a race. It also is a good indicator of how good his pace judgment needs to be and the times he should be aiming to run during his high intensity training sessions.

NB: David Moorcroft's 3,000m and Steve Jones's marathon times were world records when set. Paula Radcliffe's marathon time is the current world record. Her half-marathon UK record was set on a course unacceptable to IAAF rules (it had a 30.5m drop from start to finish).

All of the above tactics can be employed in any long-distance endurance event, from 5,000m through to the marathon, with obvious caveats regarding where in the race, from how far out and for how long or how late attacks are employed during the course of the race. Similarly, with high performance long-distance running encompassing road and cross-country, the aforementioned tactics may well be dictated by the terrain and the type of course. An athlete may therefore use a hill, either the up or down section, a twisty section of the course or flat, straight piece to make his tactical move. Unlike a track race, where the opposition is constantly in view, with the twists and turns of either a road or cross-country course it is sometimes possible for a short section of the race to be out of view of the opposition. This is an ideal place and opportunity to make a tactical and/or decisive move or attack.

Fig. 148. A training session to ensure that the athlete has good pace judgment using 'split intervals' or 'differentials', as well as even-paced running laps.

THE CHOSEN TACTICAL APPROACH

There are certain aspects that have to be taken into account before the athlete decides upon which of the race strategies he is going to adopt. He must consider what his strengths and weaknesses are and adapt both his training and race plan to accommodate them. He must decide how fit he is at this particular part of the season, for the fitter he is, the more flexible his race strategy can be. He must take into account how good his pace judgment is and also his ability to accelerate. These are areas that he should have highlighted as part of his training throughout the build-up phase. In the build-up phase, he should have also worked on his ability to relax, particularly when fatigued, and how to distribute his economy of effort. The weather, too, will play a part in which tactical approach to choose (see Fig. 150).

If a road relay race (see Fig. 152), depending on which leg he may have to run, a lot of the pressure and prior subjective judgments are not as apparent. Depending on the length of the course, the terrain, the known opposition on his leg and the position he takes over in, the athlete will have to make instant value judgments

about how to run his leg of the race. This could involve running hard early on to get into a rhythm and have people to chase, running economically to save energy for later in leg, or whatever other judgment he makes. But, above, all it is a great learning environment, with no pressure in how to react when prearranged race plans are not viable. This is an ideal learning situation for when this happens to the athlete in a proper race situation.

However, before making the decision regarding choice of tactics, there is one more important point to take into account, if this information is known: that is, who are the main opposition and what are their main strengths and weaknesses?

THE OPPOSITION

In a major championship race – whatever the distance – the opposition is going to have a considerable input into the outcome. There will be more than a dozen athletes wanting to make an impression on the race's outcome; all will be determined to seize the initiative and take control of the race. To help prepare for any eventuality, if the opposition is known the coach and athlete will be able to work out the various strengths and weaknesses. It is also likely that the preferred methods of racing will be known.

When considering the opposition's strengths and weaknesses and preferred racing methods, one factor that must be taken into consideration is whether the favoured methods of racing would be sustainable through two or three rounds of a championship 5,000m competition. This does not apply to other long-distance events, which tend to be one-off competitions. It is also wise to consider which runners do not like being in a pack and dislike the physical contact and constant jostling that this involves. Other issues to consider are:

- Who prefers to lead and is easily discouraged if he loses the lead position?
- Who would not relish either a long, hard run, or a long sprint finish?
- Who is good in paced grand prix races, but finds it difficult in slow-run tactical races?
- Who crowds the leader, clips his heels and tries to upset his rhythm and concentration?
- Who is strong, or weak, mentally when the pressure is on?
- Who prefers a slow pace because he has a very strong short sprint finish?
- Who would find the call-room situation at major championships, where the athletes are held for 20min in two different rooms in close proximity to their opposition, a daunting and strength-sapping experience?

Distance	Athlete/Country	Year	Record Time	Pace of Race
3,000m	Daniel Komen, Kenya	1996	7m 20.67sec	58.76sec per lap
	David Moorcroft, UK	1982	7m 32.79sec	60.37sec per lap
	Junixa Wang, China	1993	8m 06.11sec	64.80sec per lap
	Paula Radcliffe, UK	2002	8m 22.20sec	66.96sec per lap
3K Steeplechase	Saif Shaheen, Qatar	2004	7m 53.63sec	63.15sec per lap
	Mark Rowland, UK	1988	8m 07.96sec	65.06sec per lap
	Gulnar Galkina, Russia	2008	8m 58.81sec	71.84sec per lap
	Helen Clitheroe, UK	2008	9m 29.14sec	75.88sec per lap
5,000m	Kenenisa Bekele, Ethiopia	2004	12m 37.35sec	60.60sec per lap
	Mo Farah, UK	2010	12m 57.4sec	62.24sec per lap
	Tirunesh Diaba, Ethiopia	2008	14m 11.15sec	68.10sec per lap
	Paula Radcliffe, UK	2004	14m 29.11sec	69.53sec per lap
10, 000m	Kenenisa Bekele, Ethiopia	2005	26m 17.53sec	63.10sec per lap
	John Brown, UK	1998	27m 18.14sec	65.53sec per lap
	Junixa Wang, China	1993	29m 31.78sec	70.87sec per lap
	Paula Radcliffe, UK	2002	30m 01.09sec	72.04sec per lap
Half-marathon	Samuel Wanjiri, Kenya	2007	58m 33sec	4m 28 per mile
	Steve Jones, UK	1986	60m 59sec	4m 40 per mile
	Lonrah Kipligat, Netherlands	2007	66m 25sec	5m 04 per mile
	Paula Radcliffe, UK	2003	65m 40sec	5m 01 per mile
Marathon (42.5K)	Haile Gebrselassie, Ethiopia	2008	2hr 03m 59sec	4m 43 per mile
	Steve Jones, UK	1985	2hr 07m 13sec	4m 51 per mile
	Paula Radcliffe, UK*	2003	2hr 15m 25sec	5m 09 per mile
	* also world record			

Fig. 149. World/UK record paces.

THE RACE

While these questions are not as important as the questions the athlete has asked about himself, they will have a bearing on the chosen tactical approach to the race. In major championships, taking into account the varying opposition from around the world, it is quite conceivable that in the 5,000m the athlete will have to adopt at least two and possibly three different tactical plans, depending on the number of rounds in the competition.

Once the athlete has taken into consideration his own ability, whether he is racing for a time or racing to win, the ability of the opposition, the weather, the race's importance, the qualifying conditions, if relevant, he must formulate a tactical plan. He must decide where he would ideally like to be positioned in the early stages

Fig. 150. Athletes on a muddy cross-country course not only have to take account of the opposition when planning their tactics, but also the course variants and the underfoot conditions.

Fig. 151. This shows a particular part of a cross-country course with a prominent undulation on a downhill section of the course. This is where, for obvious reasons, some athletes are a little wary and therefore could be vulnerable to an attack.

of the race and where the best position is in relation to the leaders. However, he needs to ensure that he does not get boxed in during the later important stages of the race (see Figs 153 and 154) and is in the correct position for when he has decided he will make his attack. The best position is on the shoulder of the race leader, or about 1m further back (see Fig. 155). In the early part of the race – particularly a long race such as the marathon – it is important to be close to the lead pack in order to cover any eventualities that may occur. This allows the runner to be free from any physical contact, plus in this position he can respond quickly to any sudden changes of pace ahead of him and react to any changes or attacks that may come from behind. He is not wasting energy either by setting or forcing the pace of the race. He is also – in a track race – blocking off the runners behind him, so that they will have to run wide if they wish to overtake him, giving him time

Fig. 152. Road relays are excellent vehicles for learning how fit the athlete is at a particular point of the year. They also give him a good workout in a non-pressurized situation and similarly help him to learn tactics and pace judgment.

Fig. 153. This picture shows a great example of a long-distance indoor race. Athletes are boxed in all the way down the field and are powerless to respond if the pace increases either significantly or dramatically. The narrowness of the indoor track and the large field are also factors that have to be taken into account when planning tactics for this type of race.

to respond to them. He must ensure that he is focused and concentrating at all times and is ready to anticipate any sudden move or attack by the opposition.

If the athlete does get boxed in, he must not panic. He must wait for a slight gap to appear, then quickly fill it and move from his position into the one he wants to be in. It is inadvisable near the end of the race to slow and let other runners pass him, so that he can then move back round the outside of the field. If he tries to slow down and go round the back of the other runners, the pace may have increased and he will be left even further behind.

The athlete must also ensure, particularly if the race is being run at a fast pace, that he does not attack on the crown of the bend (see Fig. 156), thereby wasting valuable time and energy, and must avoid, where possible, undue physical contact, which is also energy-sapping. The 5,000m race, in which at the optimum elite level athletes are running at 94–98 per cent of their VO_2 max throughout the race, there is a finite room for error in both pace judgment and tactical awareness. The athlete must remain calm in this situation and if it comes to a short sprint finish, invariably as athletes turn into the home straight they will drift wide and spread across the first few lanes of the finishing straight. This usually leaves

spaces through which the athlete can take the shortest possible route to the tape (see Fig. 157).

In a tight, tense race, the athlete must be able to maintain his concentration and focus. He must remain relaxed and not become tense or panicked. He must be aware at all times of what is happening around him. He must repeat what he has been doing constantly in training, which is to maintain his technique, stay relaxed, focused and coordinated, and keep driving toward the tape. If he tenses up, his technique and running speed are likely to deteriorate. Once he makes his effort, he should focus on the finishing line, be aware of what is happening around him but never look back. He must run right through the tape to ensure that he is not passed by easing off short of the finishing line. Above all, he must be flexible, have a contingency plan and be able to think on his feet in the middle of the race. This means being proactive, not reactive, to any situations that may occur. This is in case the race does not develop as the athlete expects and he cannot put his tactical plan into operation. This is easier to recover from the longer the race distance. If this does happen, the athlete must remain calm and focused, so that he can react positively to the new situation. He must develop a racing instinct.

Fig. 154. In this cross-country race, as they sweep round a long corner at the foot of the hill, the athletes from the middle to the rear of the group are now in a position to respond to an attack up the hill. Some are not round the corner or only have a partial view of the leader. If an attack is made they have first to recognize it, second react to it and finally to extricate themselves and waste valuable time and energy moving out and around the field up to the front of the field.

Fig. 155. The best position to be in during any race – track, indoor, road, cross-country – in the closing stages is on, or just off, the shoulder of the leader. This ensures that the runner knows what is happening both in front and behind, and can attack when he decides and also respond to anyone from behind who moves to go round him. In this picture, the athlete fourth from the left is in an ideal position to cover what is happening in front of them in a matter of moments, as well as blocking off any attacks on their inside and is also able to respond quickly to any threat from behind.

Fig. 156. If a number of runners are all contesting the finish on the last lap of a race, it is inevitable that one or two of them will have to run very wide around the final bend. The key is not to be in that position, but to be on the pole position at the leader's shoulder. If, however, the athlete has made a tactical mistake and is in a situation where he has to run wide around the bend, he has to make a split decision. Does he run wide round the bend close to the leader and waits to unleash his finishing kick down the home straight, but risk wasting unnecessary energy by running further? Or does he stay in the position he is in and wait for events to unfold in front of him? What athletes forget when the panic in the emotion of competition is that the finishing straight is 100m long and therefore a great deal of ground can be made up in that time and also a great deal of time can be saved by not running wide around the bend and conserving energy for the finishing straight.

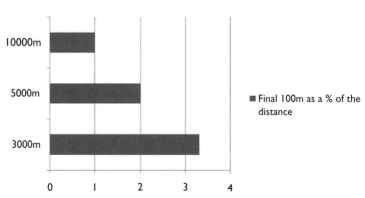

Fig. 157. The finishing straight, as stated in Fig. 156, is 100m metres long. That is 3.3 per cent (3k), 2 per cent (5k) and 1 per cent (10k) still left to complete of the race. The race is not over until 100 per cent of it is complete, so there is still a great deal of time left to make an impression in that last 100m.

PREPARATION FOR VARIABLE RACING SITUATIONS

There are certain types of training that should be included in the athlete's training programme to help him prepare for the many variables he will encounter while racing. He should constantly be working on relaxation and technique, as these are the first areas that deteriorate under pressure and fatigue. He must learn in training how to float, or cruise, when running quickly. This means being able to run quickly in a relaxed way without overexerting himself, while also maintaining his technique. This allows him to utilize a sprint finish at the end of a fast-run race.

Speed is a key element in any endurance race, whether it is utilized from a long way out, throughout the race, or in the finishing straight. Therefore, the speed sessions covered earlier in this book should be an important part of any training programme. These should include acceleration sprints over distances ranging from 50–300m, skills sprinting, drills, downhill sprints, reaction drills, differentials, group running, running with a following wind, over-distance repetitions, speed-endurance sessions and event-specific sessions.

AUTOGENIC TRAINING, IMAGERY AND VISUALIZATION

Another important aspect in planning tactics for the long-distance runner, because of the duration of his event, is mental preparation. Some athletes are naturally mentally tough competitors, while others may train hard but be fragile in a race situation. Autogenic training is similar to meditation and progressive muscle relaxation (PMR), in that it is a self-induced technique by the athlete, in which he focuses on producing sensations in specific muscle groups through warmth to relax the muscles. This then allows him to relax and employ mental imagery and visualization techniques, in which he can visualize the race, how it will progress and all the contingencies he may need to employ during the race. In every scenario that may be visualized or imagined, he will always be successful. Through this mental imagery, the four senses – sight, smell, touch and sound – are employed to create the positive race image he requires. This will give him a feeling of not only comfort and relaxation, but also of well-being, confidence and being greatly positive regarding both his race tactics and preparation.

Deciding which race tactics to employ is not a simple decision, as many variables have to be considered. These include the athlete's own strengths and weaknesses, but above all his self-confidence, in addition to the strengths and weaknesses of the opposition and the tactical methods they prefer. The time of year, the importance of the race and the weather all have a bearing on the final tactical decision. If the athlete is in the peak of condition and believes in himself, he will have the confidence to choose the correct tactical plan for the race and weather, or adapt to the tactics of the opposition. Such a tactical plan will complement his ability, but will also be flexible enough to counter any eventuality that may occur in the race.

APPENDIX

Training Schedules

(1) The following schedule is for a 25-year-old male 10,000m runner with a personal best of 27min 30sec. He has been training for twelve years. The schedule is for the specific preparation phase (late March) and covers 300km per week. The training schedule is excessive and could be a warning as to what can and cannot be achieved with the possibility of breaking down always present.

Day	am	midday	pm
Sunday	8km steady	long run 32km	8km steady
Monday	16km steady	10km steady	19km steady
Tuesday	16km steady	10km steady	8km + 8 × 800m in 2min 12sec
Wednesday	16km steady	10km steady	6km steady
Thursday	16km steady	10km steady run	15km steady + 30 × 200m
Friday	8km steady	10km steady	24km steady
Saturday	8km steady	24km steady	16km *fartlek*

(2) Female: 10,000m/marathon; personal best: 29min 10sec; age: 32; training years: 20; pre-competition phase (early May) for an August championships; 160km per week

Day	am	pm
Sunday	20–32km tempo run	Rest
Monday	10–15km run	steady 10–15km run
Tuesday	steady 10–15km run	track session: 6–8 × 1,000m 1–2min recovery aim: sub-3min each K
Wednesday	steady 10–15km run	rest
Thursday	steady 10–15km run	12–15km *fartlek*
Friday	steady 10–15km run	steady 10–15km run
Saturday	steady 10–15km run	15–20 × 300m

(3) Female: 5,000m; personal best: 14min 55sec; age: 29; training years: 14; pre-competition phase (late June, for a late August competition climax); 120km per week

Day	am	pm
Sunday	long run 20km + core and conditioning in the middle of the day	drills + 35min run
Monday	steady 12km run	6 × 800m (2min 22sec) with 90sec recovery + 1 × 200m quick sub-30sec
Tuesday	40min steady recovery run	lactate threshold run 45min
Wednesday	steady 10km	steady 12km run
Thursday	track session: drills and strides 12 × 500m in 89sec with 45sec for first 8 and 30sec recovery for last 4	reduced weight training session + steady 30min
Friday	steady 15km	rest + massage
Saturday	race or 50min *fartlek* – 15 bursts – 1,200/50m	30min recovery run

(4) Male: 5,000m; personal best 13min; age: 28; training years: 16; tapering phase (late August); 120km per week

Day	am	pm
Sunday	long run 18–20km	drills + acceleration runs
Monday	drills, strides + steady 10km run	track session: at race pace 8 × 400m in sub-60sec 40sec recovery/6min + 4 × 200m with 100m cruising/100m fast acceleration
Tuesday	40min recovery run	reduced weight training session + easy 40min jog
Wednesday	steady 12km run	track session: 500m/400m/300m 200m/100m 30sec recovery faster than race pace, the last 100m of each repetition being the quickest
Thursday	35min recovery run	drills and strides + 30min easy
Friday	steady 12km	massage
Saturday	easy 15min jog + strides	target competition of the year heats

(5) Male: marathon; personal best: 2hr 6min 45sec; age: 28; training years: 17; general preparation phase (early January) at altitude; 240–260km per week

Day	am	pm
Sunday	long run steady run 2hr 30min	
Monday	5 × 3,000m on trails with 3min recovery	1hr continuous run + strides increasing pace
Tuesday	continuous run 75min	continuous run 75min
Wednesday	continuous 90min run – variations in pace	continuous run 75min
Thursday	continuous 90min run	1hr continuous run + strides increasing pace
Friday	continuous run 75min – variations in pace	1hr continuous run + strides increasing pace
Saturday	continuous run 75min	continuous run 60min

(6) Male: marathon; personal best: 2hr 6min 45sec; age: 28; training years: 17; end of specific preparation phase at sea level; 220–240km per week

Day	am	pm
Sunday	half-marathon at marathon pace	
Monday	3 × 7,000m in 21min/20min 50sec/20min 40sec recovery: 1km in 3min 10sec	continuous run 40–50min + core work/stretching
Tuesday	continuous run 75min	continuous run 60min + 10 × strides increasing in speed
Wednesday	continuous run 90min – variations in pace	continuous run 1hr + stretching
Thursday	10 × 90 second repetitions with 90sec recovery + 10 × 60sec repetitions with 1min recovery	continuous run 40–50min + stretching
Friday	continuous run 75min – variations in pace	continuous run 75min + strides increasing in speed
Saturday	60 minute fartlek	continuous 40–50min run + core training

(7) Female: marathon; personal best: 2hr 23min 25sec;
age: 34; training years: 22; competition phase (late June);
170–200km per week

Day	am	pm
Sunday	long run 25–30km at 3min 55sec per km	15km at 3min 20sec per km
Monday	steady 12–15km at 3min 20sec per km	steady 10–15km
Tuesday	steady 10km run with 4 × 5min hard during the run	steady 15–20km
Wednesday	12km threshold run	steady10–15km run
Thursday	10 × 3min hills + steady 10km run	steady 10–15km run
Friday	steady 10–12km	Track: 16 × 1min or 10 × 2min or 16–24 × 45sec
Saturday	steady 10k	rest

(8) Female: 5,000m; personal best: 14min 22sec; age:
26; training years: 14; competition phase (late August);
120km per week

Day	am	pm
Sunday	long run 18km	acceleration sprints: 8 × 200m 3min recovery at a relaxed pace
Monday	steady 10km run	reduced weight training session + steady 10km run
Tuesday	steady 10km run	track session at race pace: 4 × 1,200m in 68–9sec, last 400m of each repetition in 65–66sec; 6-8min recovery; then 4 × 100m acceleration runs
Wednesday	40min recovery run	steady10km threshold run

Thursday	4 × 800m in 2min 16sec recovery: 8min + 4 × 200m 100m cruise/100m fast 200m jog recovery	steady 10km
Friday	steady 12km	rest + hydrotherapy
Saturday	steady 10km	race or 8 × 400m in 66–7sec recovery: 2min + 4 × 150m acceleration sprints 250m jog recovery

(9) Female 10,000m; personal best: 30min 10sec; age:
26; training years: 14; specific preparation phase for an
August championships (early May); 180km per week

Day	am	pm
Sunday	30km long run	rest
Monday	steady 10–15km run	steady 10–15km run
Tuesday	steady 10–15km run	6 × 1 mile with 1min recovery jog 3min 10 × half a mile with 45sec recovery on grass
Wednesday	steady 10–15km run	15–20 × 800m uphill jog back recovery + steady 5km
Thursday	steady 10–15km run	12–15km *fartlek*
Friday	steady 10–15km run	steady 10 –15km tempo run
Saturday	steady 10–15km run	Track: 15 × 600m with 1min recovery; aim:110sec

GLOSSARY

Adenosine diphosphate (ADP)   high-energy phosphate compound from which ATP is formed.
Adenosine triphosphate (ATP)   high-energy phosphate compound from which the body derives energy.
Aerobic   energy pathway involving the oxygen transportation system and the use of oxygen in the mitochondria of the working muscle for the oxidation of glycogen or fatty acids.
Agonist   working a muscle in the movement direction.
Alactate anaerobic system   the energy pathway for the cycle of ATP being broken down into ADP and recycled by phosphates.
Alter G anti-gravity treadmill   this applies a lifting force to the body that reduces the weight on the lower extremities; this allows the athlete to train normally and run with their natural rhythm, minimizing stress on the lower joints, allowing work at the highest intensities and during rehabilitation from injury.
Amenorrhea   absence of a menstrual period in a woman of reproductive age.
Anabolism   the building of body tissue.
Anaemia   lack of red blood corpuscles.
Anaerobic   in the absence of oxygen.
Antagonist   a muscle counteracting the action of another muscle, for example along with agonist muscles working against each other on the opposite sides of a joint.
ATP-PC system   a simple anaerobic energy system that functions to maintain ATP levels; the breakdown of creatine phosphate frees phosphate, which then combines with ADP to form ATP.

Basal metabolism   energy output of the entire body, necessary for the maintenance of life and performance.
Beetroot juice   a drink concentrated produced from organic beetroots that boosts natural nitric oxide (NO), which assists exercise efficiency and oxygen utilization.
Biomechanics   study of the human body and movement in sport.

Catabolism   the tearing down of body tissue.
Compression socks   specialist athletic socks – sometimes referred to as support socks – which are designed to support and increase blood circulation through graduated pressure on the lower leg and foot, thus ensuring there is no pooling of blood in the lower limbs.
Concentric action   muscle shortening.
Core stability   the area bounded by the abdominal wall, the pelvis, the lower back, the diaphragm and its ability to stabilize the body during movement and exercise. The main muscles involved include the transverses abdominus the internal and external oblique muscles, the quadratus lumborumand and the main breathing muscle the diaphragm.
Creatine phosphate (CP)   an energy-rich compound that plays a vital role in providing energy for muscle action by maintaining ATP concentration.

Dehydration   loss of body fluids.

Eccentric action   muscle lengthening.
Erogenic aid   a substance or phenomenon that can improve athletic performance.
Erythropietin   the hormone that stimulates red cell production.

Fast twitch fibres (FT)   a muscle type with low oxidative capacity and a high glycolytic capacity; associated with speed or power activities.

Glucongenisis   the conversion of fat or protein into glucose.
Glucose   a carbohydrate and the principal supplier of energy during muscular work.
Glycogen   the storage form of carbohydrate in the body, found predominantly in the muscles and liver.
Glycogenesis   the conversion of glucose to glycogen.
Glycolytic system   a system that produces energy through glycosis.

Haemoglobin   iron-containing pigment in red blood cells that binds oxygen.

Homostasis   the stability of the life process.
Hormones   chemical substances produced or
released by an endocrine gland and transported by the
blood to a specific target tissue.
Hydration   ensuring that the body's water and fluid
levels are in balance.

Intracellular fluid   the approximate 60–65 per cent
of total body water that is contained in the cells.

Lactate threshold   the point during exercise of
increasing intensity at which blood lactate begins to
accumulate above resting levels, where lactate clearance
is just able to keep up with lactate production.
Lactate turning point   the point during exercise
of increasing intensity at which blood lactate begins to
accumulate above resting levels, where lactate clearance
is no longer able to keep up with lactate production.
Lactic acid   produced in the body during the initial
phase of work and heavy exercise.

Maximum aerobic power   the maximum figure
achieved as measured by the maximum volume uptake
test.
Maximum volume uptake (VO$_2$ max)   the body's
maximum aerobic power that can be attained through
physical work; oxygen uptake is the difference in oxygen
content between the air inspired and the air expired.
Menarche   the first menstrual cycle in females.
Metabolic reserves   called upon in periods of
special need; a decrease in these substances is a sign of
health problems or functional defect.
Muscle fibre   an individual muscle cell.
Myocardium   the muscles of the heart.

Nerve impulse   an electrical signal conducted along
a neuron; it can be transmitted to another neuron or a
group of muscle fibres.
Neuromuscular junction   the site at which a
motor neuron communicates with a muscle fibre.

Orthotic   used in running shoes and spikes to keep
the body's balance when there is a deficiency.

Osteoporosis   a disease of the bones that leads to
an increase risk of fractures; a reduction in mineral bone
density.
Oxidative system   the body's most complex energy
system, which generates energy by disassembling fuels
with the aid of oxygen and has a very high energy yield.
Oxygen debt   the total oxygen uptake after exercise
minus the initial resting oxygen uptake.
Oxygen transport system   the components of the
cardiovascular and respiratory systems involved in the
transporting of oxygen.

Podiatrist   in conjunction with a biomechanical
expert, will provide orthotics for running shoe/spikes to
correct any imbalance in the running technique.
Plyometrics   a series of ballistic type exercises
involving single, alternate and double footed hopping
and skipping to improve power and the strength at
speed of the athlete.
Pronation   an anti-clockwise movement of a limb.

Running economy   the measure of how efficiently
an athlete utilizes his maximum volume oxygen uptake
at a given pace and is expressed as the rate of oxygen
consumption per distance covered (ml/kg/km).

Slow twitch fibre (ST)   a type of muscle fibre that
has a high oxidative and low glycotic capacity; associated
with endurance-type activities.
Sodium loading   drinking fluids with a high sodium
concentration (including sodium citrate); aids fluid
balance and improves tolerance in male athletes when
training and competing in the heat.
Speed endurance   to keep oneself from slowing
down when at maximum speed, particularly when the
energy supply is produced predominantly through anaerobic breakdown of glucose (lactic-energy production).
Supination   the clockwise movement of a limb.

Triad   sometimes referred to as the female triad –
but also relative parts of it are applicable to men – it is
a combination of disordered eating, amenorrhea and
osteoporosis.

BIBLIOGRAPHY

P-O. Astrand & K. Rodahl, *Textbook of Work Physiology* (McGraw-Hill, 1986)

V. Bondarenko, *Interval Training in the Systems of an Olympic Champion* (EACA Congress, 1991)

F. Bosch & R. Klomp, *Running – Biomechanics & Exercise Physiology Applied in Practice* (Elsevier, 2001)

F.W. Dick, *Sports Training Principles* (A & C Black, 2003)

Dr D. Faraggiana, *Evaluation of the State of Efficiency of Marathonists* (EACA, Congress 1991)

AAF Level II Advanced Coaching Theory Textbook, 2003

A.M. Jones, 'The Physiology of the World Record Holder for the Women's Marathon', *International Journal of Sports Science and Coaching*, 2006)

Professor A. Loucks, *An Introduction to the Female Triad* (conference paper, 2009)

D.E. Martin & P.N. Coe, *Better Training for Distance Runners* (Human Kinetics, 1997)

J.H. Wilmore & D.L. Costil, *Physiology of Sports Science and Exercise* (Human Kinetics, 1994)

H. Wilson, *Running My Way* (Sackville Press, 1988)

USEFUL WEBSITES

Association of International Marathons and Distance Races: www.aimsworldrunning.org

Athletics Northern Ireland: www.niathletics.org

Australian Athletics Association: www.athletics.com.au

British Milers Club: www.britishmilersclub.com

Canadian Track & Field: www.athletics.ca

England Athletics: www.englandathletics.org

Ethiopian Athletics Association: www.athleticsethiopia.org.et

European Athletics Federation: www.european-athletics.org

International Athletic Federation: www.iaaf.org

International Olympic Committee: www.olympic.org

Ireland: www.athleticsireland.ie

Kenyan Athletics Association: www.athleticskenya.or.ke

London 2012: www.london2012.org

London Marathon: www.virginlondonmarathon.com

New Zealand Athletics Association: www.athletics.org.nz

Scottish Athletics: www.scottishathletics.org.uk

Shoe Guide: www.shoeguide.co.uk

South African Athletics Association: www.athleticssouthafrica.com

UK Athletics: www.uka.org.uk

USA Track & Field: www.usatf.org

Welsh Athletics: www.welshathletics.org

INDEX